That Lively Railroad Town

THAT
LIVELY
RAILROAD
TOWN

*Waverly, New York, and the Making of
Modern Baseball, 1899–1901*

WILLIAM H. BREWSTER

LUMINARE PRESS
WWW.LUMINAREPRESS.COM

That Lively Railroad Town
Copyright © 2020 William H. Brewster

All rights reserved. This book or any portion thereof may not be reproduced or used in any manner whatsoever without the express written permission of the publisher, except for the use of brief quotations in a book review.

Printed in the United States of America

Cover Design: Gary Joseph Cieradkowski

Luminare Press
442 Charnelton St.
Eugene, OR 97401
www.luminarepress.com

LCCN: 2020923176
ISBN: 978-1-64388-434-9

Dedicated with love and appreciation to
Howard George Brewster, Jr.

Table of Contents

Notes on Sources and Approach ix

Preface 1

CHAPTER 1
The Silversmith 11

CHAPTER 2
Bill Ging with the Wonderful Wing 33

CHAPTER 3
Bergen Lights the Spark 46

CHAPTER 4
Jovial, Pleasant and Good Natured 58

CHAPTER 5
Building a New Team 72

CHAPTER 6
Champions of Western New York 109

CHAPTER 7
Conservative Shrewdness 124

CHAPTER 8
We Believe Baseball Will Take
on a New Life 155

CHAPTER 9
Too Fast for an Independent Club 178

CHAPTER 10
Into Its Proper Class At Last 199

CHAPTER 11
I Done My Duty 223

CHAPTER 12
The Last Out 239

CHAPTER 13
Waverly's Baseball Legacy 247

*Summary of Waverly's Professional
Seasons* 287

Acknowledgements 303

Notes 305

Sources 337

Index 351

Notes on Sources and Approach

- Unless otherwise indicated, all game accounts are based on historical box scores and news stories.

- Team mascots and nicknames are not used unless there is sufficient evidence that they were used by the applicable players/management/town at the time.

- Unless otherwise indicated, team rosters, player statistics, and player career movements are based on Society for American Baseball Research (SABR) records as documented on Baseball-Reference.com.

Preface

"Do as we ask and we believe that base ball will take on a new life."

—Harry L. Taylor, Counsel to the Players' Protective Association, petitioning National League owners for players' rights on December 12, 1900.

Growing up in the village of Waverly, New York, in the 1960s and 1970s, it was easy to assume that certain things were inevitable.

For example, the Western Auto store on Broad Street, across from the old Woolworth's, with the iconic sign that looked like a number nine, inevitably had the most interesting plastic car models. I could smell the glue (in tiny tubes) and the paint (in tiny square glass jars) almost as soon as I opened the door. Across the street, Harper's newsstand (officially Waverly News) inevitably had all the big city dailies, the best selection of monthly sports magazines, and the latest shipment of baseball, basketball, hockey or football cards (depending on the season). Its smell was a combination of newsprint and bubblegum.

All this was reachable from home by bicycle, and within earshot of the town clock. Philly Sales, just a block east of Harper's, had the least expensive baseballs and bats, and, since it was directly across the street from the police station, there was rarely a need to lock our bikes when shopping there. In fact, we rarely locked them anywhere, even when stopping in at the old Jolly Farmer for ice cream, several blocks east, near Spaulding Street.

The village was small and manageable as a kid, and it was well located – straddling two states in a river valley with three other towns (Sayre, Athens and South Waverly), on major railroad lines near the very center of the Twin Tiers of Southern New York and Northern Pennsylvania. This meant that Waverly's on-going viability as a transportation hub also seemed inevitable, even as interstate highways replaced the railroads, canals, indigenous trails, and rivers that preceded them. The sound of rumbling trains and their periodic horns was commonplace day and night, as was waiting for the caboose to pass before the bells stopped and the guardrails lifted at rail crossings. The sight of a workman waving to us from the passing caboose was a bonus.

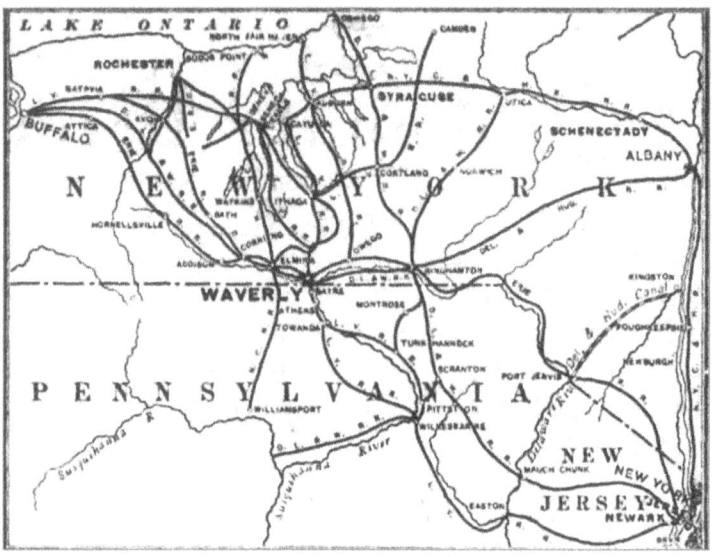

1907 map showing Waverly's central location at the nexus of multiple railroad lines. From a Waverly Chamber of Commerce brochure.

Another inevitability was major league baseball. Since 1901, the National and American Leagues were where the action was. The primacy of their brands and those of their teams was unquestioned, and at least four generations of fans had grown up with them. Sure, there were some changes in the 1950s and 1960s, but none of them (even the Designated Hitter's introduction in 1973), prompted us to think that major league baseball, with stadiums holding tens of thousands of fans, had ever been anything other than inevitable.

I thought the shops, happenings and mores of my childhood would inevitably continue, but economic progress intervened. Trains became longer, more efficient and less frequent. Not long after leaving Waverly, most all of the shops we perused as kids, and even the ubiquitous town clock that towered over Broad and Fulton Streets, were gone.

But, what about major league baseball? Was it always destined to become a huge enterprise? Would it remain so in the future?

For me, my brothers and our friends, major league baseball personified the big city, and Waverly was simply a sleepy little town.

It was a major event for us to travel the 220 or so miles to New York City for a game, and the traffic, crowds and excitement were light years removed from our typical small town lives.

On Opening Day 1978, for example, when I was a High School senior, three friends and I drove to Yankee Stadium to watch the Yankees play the White Sox, and raise their first World Series Championship flag in fifteen years. The Stadium was packed, and Mickey Mantle and Roger Maris were among the dignitaries.

On the way to our seats, we were each given a free Reggie bar, a new chocolate candy bar in an orange wrapper, created as a testament to Reggie Jackson's prediction years earlier that if he ever played for New York, there would inevitably be a candy bar named after him.

In the bottom of the first, with two men on, Reggie hit a Wilbur Wood knuckler for a home run, giving Ron Guidry an early three-run lead. It was Reggie's first at-bat at Yankee Stadium since he hit three home runs in his last three swings of the 1977 World Series.

Four consecutive home swings. Four home runs.

The Stadium erupted in cheers – and in Reggie bars. Suddenly the air and the field were full of the little orange squares. It took several minutes to clean them up. "It was just a shame that something like that has to happen," Wood complained.[1]

"It shows you we have sweet fans," quipped Yankee manager Billy Martin. On- deck batter Lou Piniella, himself a future manager, threw a couple bars into the air during the cleanup and swung at them, missing twice. "I'm in a slump," he laughed.[2]

I do not recall if my friends fired their Reggie bars onto the field, but I can attest that I did not. I had eaten mine not long after receiving it. In my case, that was inevitable.

The Yankees won the game and we drove back to our sleepy hometown, with Top Ten tunes like "Staying Alive," "Night Fever," and "Dust in the Wind" playing repeatedly on the AM radio. The tunes became increasingly mixed with static as distance from the great city grew.

The gulf between Waverly and New York City never seemed wider than on days like that. Years later, I discovered Waverly once had a professional baseball team, in 1901, and so I did additional research. I spent many hours reviewing online records as well as archives at locations such as the Waverly Historical Society, the Waverly Free Library, and the National Baseball Hall of Fame and Library. I also contacted a number of experts and player descendants. I found old local newspapers to be especially helpful. I relayed many results of this research (related to the years prior to 1899) in my first book, *The Workingman's Game*.

As it turned out, 1901 was Waverly's one season in the New York State League, and it was also the American League's first season as a major league competitor to the National League. It was not yet clear whether the American and National Leagues would learn to coexist, or would beat each other's brains out in a protracted salary war. Therefore, at the time, Waverly's future as a professional baseball town was nearly as inevitable as major league baseball's survival as a whole.

Waverly was an underdog fighting for its professional baseball life, and major league players were in a similar boat, fighting for the survival and ultimate success of their sport.

Success in either case was far from inevitable.

THE LATE 1890S HAD NOT BEEN KIND TO PROFESSIONAL BASEball. At the end of the 1898 baseball season, in fact, followers had serious concerns about whether the sport would survive as a commercial enterprise. The average attendance for major league games was less than 3,000, and five teams had average per-game attendance of less than 2,000.

Team owners were looking for ways to reduce expenses. Individual team finances continued to be unstable, and owners had yet to invent ways to earn significant ancillary income from concessions, souvenirs, memorabilia and media. Most, if not all, professional players had to maintain non-baseball careers during the off-season. Pensions and health insurance, even treatment for baseball-related injuries, were rare or virtually non-existent.

Meanwhile, the quality of the game and the players' skill levels had been climbing throughout the 1890s. In fact, a new era of superstars was looming, with future Hall-of-Famers like Napoleon Lajoie, Honus Wagner and Jimmy Collins just starting their major league careers after successful tours in the minors. Moreover, the Baltimore Orioles of the mid-1890s proved that intelligent, hard-working and fast team play could win ballgames and draw big crowds. Several of the Orioles biggest stars (John McGraw, Hughie Jennings, Willie Keeler, Boileryard Clarke, Kid Gleason and Wilbert Robinson) by 1899 were emerging as leaders both on and off the field, translating their success as ball players into even greater success as coaches, managers and labor leaders.

These two emerging developments on behalf of the players – the presence of new superstars and the maturity of unified leadership – formed a powerful counter to the owners. While the owners wanted to shrink the game to control expenses, these player leaders wanted to grow the game to expand their opportunities and earning potential

A clash was inevitable.

Players who haled from and/or played in the Twin Tiers of southern New York and northern Pennsylvania were integral to the circumstances that led to this confrontation. As explored in *The Workingman's Game*, former catcher and manager John Clapp was an Ithaca, New York, native who played for local amateur town teams like Owego in the 1870s, and then played for a variety of major league teams. At the end of his baseball career, he managed the New York Gothams (soon to be Giants) and was a player/coach for the semi-professional team in Waverly, New York.

Early in his career with Philadelphia, Clapp was a teammate and close friend of Cap Anson, one of the most influential baseball leaders of the nineteenth century. They both participated in the first ever world baseball tour (in 1874), led by Albert G. Spalding, another important pioneering Hall-of-Famer. While managing in New York, Clapp's mentees included young John Montgomery Ward, a native of Bellefonte, Pennsylvania, who had played as a teenager in Binghamton, New York.

Ward went on to complete law school in Columbia while with the Giants, and create the first baseball player union, the Brotherhood of Professional Base Ball Players. He also participated in the second big baseball world tour (in 1888), and in 1890 created the Players' League in an unsuccessful effort to counter major league ownership's efforts to restrict player movements (via a contractual reserve clause) and enforce a salary cap.

In addition to Ward, Clapp mentored many others, including a young Harry L. Taylor, who was a Halsey Valley, New York, native, and captain of the baseball team at Cornell. Taylor played second base for Clapp at Waverly in 1887, and for the next two summers played in Elmira, New York, where his teammates included Athens, Pennsylvania, native John Doran, Elmira native Bill Heine, and Truxton, New York, native Bert Kenney.

John Doran, the son of a blacksmith, was a strong left-handed pitcher who went on to play professional baseball for many seasons, including a nationally prominent 1890 season with New Haven in the Atlantic League and a short time in the major leagues in 1891. By the mid-1890s, he settled back in Athens and mentored other pitchers, including a young Fred Talada, who settled in Waverly, changed his last name to Tucker, and became the town's leading baseball organizer.

Bill Heine was a hard-hitting catcher and infielder who played professional baseball for many seasons and was a teammate with (or competitor against) many of the era's budding superstars, including Willie Keeler, Jimmy Collins and Honus Wagner. He eventually joined Tucker in Waverly in 1900 to help build the region's most powerful semi-professional team.

Bert Kenney was a good ballplayer as well, but was best known as mentor to young fellow Truxton native John McGraw. At fifteen, McGraw was too young to play with Kenney in Elmira in 1888, but he worked as a butcher boy on the railroad during that summer, and spent downtimes in Elmira hanging out with the team and learning pointers from the likes of Kenney, Heine, Doran and Taylor. Within two years, he and Heine would be teammates together in Olean, New York, and just a year later McGraw launched his major league career with the Baltimore Orioles.

Harry Taylor's connection with McGraw and the Orioles became even more explicit in 1892, when he and his close friend and mentee Hughie Jennings, were traded to the Orioles from Louisville to join McGraw.

Hughie Jennings, a native of Pittston, Pennsylvania, worked in the coal mines as a boy, and found close allies in Taylor and McGraw. McGraw and Jennings were products of a scrappy, competitive and hard-working Irish-American background, and understood from the example of fellow small-town natives like Ward and Taylor how education could enable them to differentiate themselves. They became students together at Allegany College (soon to become St. Bonaventure) as well as pillars of the Orioles championship teams of the mid-1890s.

Following the trade to Baltimore, Taylor was named captain of the 1893 Orioles team, and retired after the season to commence his career as an attorney in Buffalo. He had earned his law degree at Cornell during the off-seasons and persuaded Jennings to do the same. Jennings started his Cornell law schoolwork following the 1899 season, and shared baseball-coaching duties at Cornell with Taylor.

In addition to coaching at Cornell, Jennings was among the National League's most prominent veteran players in 1899, as were McGraw and Keeler. The National League was the only major league at the time, and began the 1899 season with twelve teams. It would be an understatement to say the teams' ownership situations were convoluted, and it is understandable why many fans were unhappy. The Robison brothers (Frank and Stanley), for example, wound up owning both the Cleveland and St. Louis franchises, and moved so many of the best players from the former to the latter that Cleveland in 1899 wound up with the worst record in major league history (20-134) and drew an average of just 145 fans per game. These so-called syndicate ownership arrangements, whereby the same individual or group could own multiple teams, was symptomatic of monopolistic tendencies in the broader U.S. economy.

True to form, Harry Von der Horst was for a time owner of the both the Brooklyn and Baltimore franchises, and wound up moving the Orioles manger Ned Hanlon and many of the best Orioles players (including Jennings and Keeler) to Brooklyn. Thanks to the help of Hanlon and the former Orioles players, Brooklyn won the 1899 National League championship with a record of 101-47.

Meanwhile, many players and fans continued to agitate for different kinds of changes; ones that they believed would expand rather than contract the game. These included providing players with health insurance, placing limits on owners' abilities to "reserve" players, and preventing owners from requiring players they did not want to play for specific minor league "farm" teams rather than being free to sign with a different major league team. These "evils," according to certain leaders, such as those who would lead the Players' Protective Association, rendered players as "slaves" of the owners, rather than independent craftsmen.

Much of this sentiment for player rights germinated in the bustling minor leagues, in the ball yards of smaller towns like Waverly throughout the U.S., where tomorrow's superstars rubbed elbows with miners, factory workers, farmers and craftsmen while they worked to refine their own craft of baseball. Many in fact honed factory and similar crafts in the mornings before spending their afternoons at the ball yard.

It is in one such working class community, Taunton, Massachusetts, where we continue our story.

CHAPTER 1

The Silversmith

George Washington Grant, born in 1873, was the latest in a long line of Massachusetts craftsman. His grandfather, Simeon, had been a carpenter in the shipbuilding town of Somerset, and Simeon's neighborhood in 1850 was full of ship carpenters, sailors and painters. George's father, George A., meanwhile, settled in the "Silver City" of Taunton, and, throughout George W.'s childhood and youth, was an engraver with a local silver manufacturing company. The largest silver manufacturer in town, Reed and Barton, was throughout this period one of the world's leading makers of silver flatware, candleholders and the like. As an engraver, George A. would have been one of the highest paid workers in the plant.[3]

A versatile fielder, speedy base runner and steady hitter, George Grant was a valuable contributor to multiple New England League teams in the late 1890s. Portrait by Gary Cieradkowski.

Grant likely worked alongside his father at Reed and Barton or at another Taunton silver factory in the 1890s, but during the summer he was also busy playing catcher and outfield for local baseball teams. By 1894, he was a professional New England League player based 175 miles north in Lewiston, Maine. Over the next few seasons he bounced to independent teams a little closer to home in Haverhill, New Hampshire, and Lowell, Massachusetts, before rejoining the New England League in Newport, Rhode Island, in 1897.

Grant had a promising season in 1897, and was earning a reputation as a talented fielder at multiple positions. In an exciting 8-7 loss to the barnstorming Cuban Giants on April 26, for instance, he had two hits, a stolen base and a "great catch" in left field. Playing short stop for the Giants that day was arguably the century's greatest African-American player, Frank Grant, who himself cracked two singles and scored a run.[4] The thirty-one-year-old Frank Grant had been playing for traveling teams (and not in organized baseball) since 1890 when he teamed up with Hughie Jennings in Harrisburg. Despite being prevented from playing on such teams due to his race, he continued to excel to the point where he was typically the most outstanding player on whatever field and against whatever opponent he played.

George Grant's 1897 season was successful enough that in November he married a local lady named Bertha, settled in Taunton, and agreed to terms with the Taunton New England League team for 1898. Silver manufacturing, like many businesses at the time, was undergoing tough economic challenges, but if silver work was available, he likely pursued it at one of the plants during this time, as his baseball season salary (probably no more than $90 per month during the season) would not have been nearly sufficient to last the year.

At Taunton in 1898, George Grant's teammates included twenty-five-year-old John Auchanbolt "Sandy" McDougal, who was blessed with an arsenal of trick pitches and deliveries, and had appeared in one major league game for Brooklyn in 1895. McDougal itched to get back to the majors, if for no other reason than to prove to his displeased Buffalo father that a ball player could earn a respectful living.[5]

Even more importantly, like George Grant, McDougal was married, so for him professional baseball was no lark. In fact, heading into the 1898 season, McDougal and his young wife had a daughter and were expecting a second child. He had pitched well enough in 1897 to earn a brief promotion to Toronto with the Eastern League during the season, but he was still far from the secure major league career he craved.

A crafty right-hander with an arsenal of trick pitches, John "Sandy" McDougal appeared in one major league game in 1895, and itched to prove he belonged back in the majors. Portrait by Gary Cieradkowski.

Given their circumstances, there was tremendous pressure on both players to succeed in 1898, or possibly give up on their baseball dreams and concentrate on more reliable careers.

The 1898 season, however, was inconclusive. The Spanish-American War interfered with the public's focus on the game, and the New England League ended early for financial reasons. Grant and McDougal undoubtedly felt they deserved more time to pursue their baseball dreams. Both players had reason to be encouraged. Grant finished the abridged season with a mediocre .249 batting average, but was considered such a good fielder at multiple positions, that the *Boston Globe* dubbed him one of the league's best utility players.

McDougal, meanwhile, had a similarly mediocre record, winning seven games and losing ten, but continued to keep batters off-balance with his intelligent mix of pitches, and was also a potent hitter, often playing outfield on off-days to keep his bat in the line-up. He even had moments of pure dominance, winning two games on May 30 for instance, by throwing a six-hit shutout in the morning against Newport and pitching nine innings of relief in the afternoon against Pawtucket. Attendance was in the 2,000 range for both games, which was higher than the typical major league crowd that season. According to the *Boston Globe*, the morning 4-0 shutout "was as pretty a game as ever was played here."[6]

When the 1898 New England League season ended early, both players hoped to secure a "trial" with a major league club. One of the big advantages of playing in the New England League was that the League President was Tim Murnane, a former player who was also the *Boston Globe*'s baseball editor. Consequently, any New England League player who did well ran a good chance of receiving a kind word from Murnane in the newspaper and perhaps a nudge or a whisper in the ear of some major league manager or owner.

Unfortunately, neither Grant nor McDougal received a major league trial in 1898. Instead, in August, Boston called up the only Newport player to smack two hits against McDougal on that "pretty" morning of May 30, twenty-four-year-old outfielder David T. Pickett from Brookline.

It was quite a momentous time for Pickett. He had hit .336 with nine home runs for Newport in 1897, and was on pace to exceed .300 again in 1898 before the season ended early. He worked as a "motorman" during the off-season, meaning he operated one of Boston's streetcars. He was also a frequent subject in the *Boston Globe*'s "Baseball Notes," a sign that he had Murnane's attention. The Notes even mentioned his May 1898 marriage to "one of Jamaica Plain's fair daughters."[7]

The newly married Pickett's tenure with Boston went well. He played in fourteen games and batted .279, and was only released when a number of regulars returned to the line-up following injuries. "Pickett did good work for Boston," said the *Globe*, "and would have held his job for the close of the season but for the return of [Billy] Hamilton and [Chick] Stahl."[8]

Thus, Pickett entered the 1899 season in a very similar circumstance to those of McDougal and Grant. All three were in their mid-twenties, married and seeking a secure baseball contract, with the likelihood of alternative careers lurking ever so temptingly within reach. Furthermore, both McDougal and Pickett had tasted the major leagues, and were eager to get back.

THE 1899 NEW ENGLAND LEAGUE SEASON BEGAN WITH MUCH fanfare and promises that there would be no repeat premature finish.

To help ensure secure finances, League leaders set explicit spending limits, agreeing that each team would have a $900 monthly salary cap, with a $100 limit per player excluding managers. Without such a limit, teams had the tendency to inflate salaries to the point where the entire league would topple. The 1899 League would begin in May with eight teams: Taunton, Fitchburg, Portland, Newport, Pawtucket, Brockton, Cambridge and Manchester. In mid-April, Taunton announced it had signed McDougal, Grant, Pickett, and a third baseman named J. W. King. Among the next wave of signees would be New Jersey native William "Bill" Vought, like Grant a fast and versatile infielder/outfielder. Taunton's fans had reason for optimism.

Tim Murnane's *Globe* believed optimism was appropriate for baseball as a whole.

"Last year the [Spanish-American] war made people serious and the fans alone followed the league games," the *Globe* explained. "Other games and pastimes flourish for a time, but the national game, with its fifty years of history, grows stronger with age simply because it is, first of all, a boy's game, and later on only well-trained athletes can play for the entertainment of those who have passed off the diamond as well as those who love the sport for the opportunity it gives for team work and active thinking under trying circumstances."[9]

Taunton's season opener was held May 10 at home, with McDougal the starting pitcher, Grant batting leadoff and playing right field, Vought batting second and playing second base and King batting eighth at third base. McDougal struggled to keep Pawtucket off the bases, giving up fifteen hits and suffering through eight Taunton errors, but the Taunton bats were up for the challenge – pounding twenty five hits of their own and winning 22-14. Grant and McDougal each smacked two doubles, with Vought and King knocking a double each, and the four combining for twelve runs scored. McDougal pitched the complete game to earn the win.

It was an auspicious start to the season, and portended still better things in the season's early going, as Taunton ended the season's first week in second place with a 5-1 record. Portland, the leader, was undefeated at 7-0.

While Grant, McDougal, Vought and King led the Taunton attack, Dave Pickett did not play and was nowhere to be found in the New England League.

"Can it be possible that Dave would rest content with a motorman's position on a Boston street car, when the merry shout of the rooters and the swish of the horsehide was abroad in the land?" asked the *Boston Globe*. But never fear. "Handsome Dave," the *Globe* reported, "is a heavy leading man" in New York.[10]

In fact, Pickett had moved to Binghamton in the New York State League, where he was also reportedly working for the nearby Lestershire Shoe Factory, at the behest of floor manager and baseball fanatic George F. Johnson.

Pickett may have left New England for New York, but the *Globe* continued to keep tabs on him during the season, albeit humorously. In mid-summer, for example, "Baseball Notes" reported "Handsome Dave Pickett has resigned the captaincy of the Binghamton club." In a dig at Pickett's larger-than-average girth, the *Globe* added "He claimed the overwork interfered with his appetite."[11]

By the end of week two, Taunton continued to cling to second place, despite a four-game losing streak that brought its record to 7-5. Portland remained in first at 11-1.

At the end of May, Taunton continued to compete for respectability, opening June in the middle of the pack with a record of 9-9. It was at this point, however, that financial realities mandated that the bottom two teams of the league would have to go. There were simply not enough fans coming to the games. Teams from Lawrence and Lowell briefly replaced those in Cambridge and Fitchburg, but neither was competitive on the field or in the stands, so the league dropped them, leaving just six teams.

On June 6, Taunton hosted first place Portland before a crowd of 450. Grant led the Taunton hitting attack with four singles and five runs scored, as Taunton defeated the league leaders 13-11. The victory brought Taunton's record to 11-12, which, although just a game under .500, was still seven games behind Portland, and in last place.

On June 16, before a home crowd of 400, Taunton scored two runs in the ninth to upend Manchester 6-5. McDougal pitched another strong game in relief, and scored a run to support his victory. Grant and Vought also had good games, combining from the top of the order for five hits, a stolen base and two runs scored. The win propelled Taunton into fifth place by a full game over Newport, and the hope was that the winning would continue and that larger crowds would ensue.

By June 20, however, Taunton had lost two games in a row, and fallen back into last place with a 14-19 record.

Portland continued to lead the League, but much of the season's optimism was fading. Attendance for the League as a whole was running lower than expected, and teams began to unload some of their reserved players in a battle for survival.

To trim expenses, Taunton's management released several of its most expensive players, including McDougal, but held onto

Grant and Vought. "Taunton will release a bunch of the 'never wins' and try for a few hustling young men," the *Globe* explained, in an apparent effort to dress up the move for the local fans.[12]

So far, the 1899 season was not looking much different than 1898 for Grant, McDougal and Pickett.

JUST AS 1899 WAS SHAPING UP AS A CHALLENGING SEASON economically for professional league teams, so it was for barnstorming teams. The Cuban Giants, for example, were prolific and had a roster of many of the best known African-American players in the late 1890s, but other teams were also adopting their barnstorming business model, and this increased both the number of playing jobs available to African-American athletes, and the competition among them.

In fact, it was an era of significant competition among all the big "negro" teams to determine which was the best. In the Northeast, the Cuban Giants, owned by E. B. Lamar, and the Cuban X Giants, owned by John Bright, were well known to have the most competitive and profitable schedules, while in the Midwest, several others vied to be considered the "champion" of "negro" teams, most notably the Chicago Unions and the Chicago Giants, formerly known as the Page Fence Giants.

To help confirm what player Sol White called "the first real championship between East and West" for African-American teams, as well as raise money, the Cuban X Giants in early 1899 agreed to meet the Chicago Unions in a Midwest tour with weekend games in Chicago. They played fourteen games, and the Cuban X Giants won nine.

"The games were hotly contested all through the series," Sol White wrote, "but the superior hitting of the Cuban X Giants won for them the title of Champions."[13]

The Cuban X Giants were loaded with talent for their Championship tour, featuring a line-up of top players like Sol White,

Frank Grant, Clarence Williams, Bill Seldon and Andy Jackson. E. B. Lamar lured many of these X Giants players from John Bright's Cuban Giants, hence the "X Giants" name.

While the Cuban X Giants spent June battling the Chicago Unions, the Cuban Giants were in the midst of their annual tour of Northeast towns, competing with school and town teams in Pennsylvania places like Altoona, Bellefonte and Pottsville. The Giants were no slouches, featuring longtime stars like Pop Watkins, Clem Sampson, William Malone and Kid Carter, but they were noticeably less potent without Frank Grant.

Following a game in Pottsville on June 20, the Giants arrived in Honesdale, Pennsylvania, for a two-game series, eager to pull off a sweep. Although renowned for being "Merry-Makers," the Giants also relied on a reputation for high skill and winning, similar to today's Harlem Globetrotters, in order to maximize local interest and crowd sizes. A long losing streak would not bode well for upcoming games.

Honesdale was similarly geared up for a big series. "Honesdale knows it has a very good nine, able to give a satisfactory account of itself with our neighboring towns," wrote one local newspaper.[14]

The teams faced off in the first game on June 22, and the Giants won a nail biter 5-3. "The coaching of the 'Black Diamonds' was one of the attractive features of the game," wrote *The (Scranton) Tribune*. "Considering the practice and excellence that the Cuban Giants have had Honesdale should feel proud of the close score."[15]

Perhaps unrealistically, Honesdale's town leaders were none too pleased with losing to the Giants, and were desperate to win the second game. A big crowd was expected and a lot of civic pride was on the line. They did not want this to be just another local game against the travelling Giants. They wanted a victory, and, in an effort to improve their chances, they sent notice to one of their former pitchers in nearby Factoryville. Was he available to pitch tomorrow?

Christy Mathewson, eighteen years old and fresh from his first year at Bucknell, was at home with his parents and family when the request arrived. He had received many such requests in the past. Just three years earlier, in fact, he had turned down such an invitation from the team in Waverly, New York. This was different, though. Yes, he was able and willing to help his old Honesdale team.

The next day, June 23, the veteran Giants must have been curious watching the tall, young hurler warm up. He had a unique combination of speed and control, but also probably seemed to them a bit young and nervous. Given his youth, he was likely hittable, especially in the later innings once his fastball slowed down.

As soon as the game started, however, it was clear Honesdale was setting a different more confident tone. Not only was Mathewson an effective pitcher, he was a powerful hitter as well. He pitched the complete game and yielded just a few scattered hits, earning a 4-2 victory.

"Mathewson arrived and materially strengthened the home team in every way," the *Tribune* reported. "Mathewson pitched a grand game, and won the applause of the fans from the moment he stepped into the box till the game was completed. His timely hitting and cool head went a great ways towards winning the game."[16]

Honesdale was ecstatic in victory and the Giants "were shrouded in gloom."[17]

The Giants continued their tour, heading from Honesdale sixty miles south to Bangor, where on June 24, they lost again, this time 9-8.

Meanwhile, the Cuban X Giants were finishing up their Championship tour and returning East, where in early July they played teams in the Philadelphia and New Jersey areas, including Atlantic City, West New York and Chester.

Neither the Cuban nor the Cuban X Giants were comprised of or affiliated with actual Cuban baseball. The teams used the name "Cuban" to give them an exotic yet less racially threatening aspect, ideal for luring as many working and middle class white patrons as possible. This had not been an issue when Cuba was under Spanish rule, as the Spanish authorities were notoriously skeptical about baseball and obstructed its organized play whenever possible.

Now that Cuba was independent in the wake of the Spanish-American War, however, the "Cuban" name became more confusing, especially in July when an actual Cuban All Star barnstorming team, the "All Cubans," arrived in the United States to play American teams. Led by Cuban promoter Abel Lenares and promoted in the U.S. by former ball player and erstwhile organizer Alfred Lawson, the All Cubans featured the best players from Cuba's first professional post-independence baseball season.

Lawson had a history with Cuban baseball tours that extended from his trip to the island in 1891, where, among other things, his team included young John McGraw, a native of tiny Truxton, New York, who had been a teammate of Lawson's in Wellsville, New York. McGraw's energetic play on the tour gained attention and prompted Cuban fans to nickname him the "yellow monkey" after the yellow uniforms Lawson used for his team.[18]

The All Cubans, Cuban Giants and Cuban X Giants competed with local town teams throughout the summer of 1899, confusing not only fans, but also news writers who frequently misnamed the teams in game accounts.

For the All Cubans, although they were disappointed to be playing before relatively small crowds in small towns rather than major league cities, and failed to earn enough money to return to Cuban without extra financial help, the trip represented the first of what would become a long tradition of bi-lateral Cuba-U.S. baseball trips.

Interestingly, while the Cuban and Cuban X Giants were "colored" teams, the All Cubans, at least in their native Cuba, were considered "white." This was particularly confusing to Cuban fans when the Cuban X-Giants visited Cuba in early 1900. Although Cuban baseball followed its own unique racial pattern, the only Cuban players who would join major league rosters in the U.S. prior to Jackie Robinson's integration in 1947 would be considered "white."

Following his victory over the Cuban Giants in Honesdale, Mathewson returned home to Factoryville, where he mulled offers to play summer baseball.

Among the leagues looking for help was the New England League, and no team in the League was more eager for pitching help than Taunton, especially after unloading their ace, McDougal, whom rival Manchester snapped up.

Summer professional baseball was completely legal for college players at the time, and had a long tradition, best demonstrated by John Montgomery Ward of Penn State and Columbia and by Harry Taylor of Cornell. In more recent years, it was also demonstrated by John McGraw and Hughie Jennings at Allegany College, although for them professional baseball came first.

Taunton offered a $90 per month contract to Mathewson, and he accepted, joining the club in mid-July. By the time of his first game, Taunton had fallen far below its early-season promise, sitting in last place with a 24-34 record. It was a poor record, but far from insurmountable.

From its original list of reserved players, Taunton still had George Grant, Bill Vought and J. W. King, who likely welcomed Mathewson and the hope for improvement that he represented. At a minimum, he was likely to attract more attention from fans and possibly from Tim Murnane and the rest of the baseball media. This would make it more likely they would be exposed to potential offers to move up, if not to the majors, then potentially to a higher-level league.

Young, powerful and ambitious Christy Mathewson, fresh from his first year at Bucknell, vowed to give his best effort to turn Taunton's fortunes around. Portrait from the 1901 Bucknell University yearbook.

George Grant was having a good season, all things considered. He continued to be one of the league's top fielders and bat lead-off where his speed helped him earn extra base hits and stolen bases as the opportunities presented themselves. However, with the exception of large crowds on Memorial Day (which many newspapers also called "Decoration Day" due to the practice of spending the day decorating the graves of war dead), most of the season's attendance was meager, at most a few hundred per game, and the level of play was not consistently high enough to attract greater numbers of fans.

It was a tough situation overall for Taunton's team. "The town had one of the worst ball clubs I ever saw," Mathewson recalled years later, and he vowed to give it his best effort to turn things around.[19]

His first game was on July 21 before a crowd of 200 in Manchester, New Hampshire. Manchester was vying with Taunton for a middle place in the league standings. Neither team wanted to fold early, despite financial challenges, so winning was critical.

Grant played center field and Vought left field in support of Mathewson, enjoying premier views of the tall husky right-hander at work. Unfortunately for Taunton, however, Manchester's hitters jumped on Mathewson's pitches early, scoring two in the second inning and three in the third inning to take a 5-0 lead.

Grant and his teammates encouraged the young hurler, who settled down in the middle innings. Heading into the ninth, Manchester held a 6-2 lead. At this point, Grant, Vought, King and the other Taunton hitters rallied, scoring three runs and pulling within one run of tying the score. King's and Grant's doubles, and Vought's triple stoked the Taunton attack.

The pressure was now on twenty-seven-year-old Manchester pitcher Tom Smith, a Boston native. These were the days when starting pitchers were expected to finish, long before "closers" were used to close out games. In this instance the seldom used Smith had to shake off the cobwebs and think like a "closer."

Smith was equal to the task, extinguished the Taunton rally, and held on for a 6-5 win.

Manchester's win brought their record to 29-28, six games ahead of Taunton in the standings. Taunton did not want to fall too much further behind, since the league might drop teams again before the season was out, and neither team wanted to be at the bottom of the standings when that time came.

The two clubs met again two days later on July 23, and Manchester won again, this time 11-3 in a much less interesting contest. The teams' relationship in the standings remained roughly the same a few games later when they met on August 2 in Manchester before a slightly larger crowd of 350. McDougal started in the box for Manchester versus twenty-five-year-old Tom Brady, a native of New Bedford, Massachusetts, for Taunton. Taunton had added Brady to the roster at about the same time as they added Mathewson, following McDougal's release.

The wily McDougal out-foxed Brady, as Manchester jumped to a quick 13-0 lead after three innings. "Brady's arm was in poor condition," the *Globe* wrote, while "McDougal pitched a steady game for the locals."[20]

The Manchester hitting attack was relentless, and even McDougal got into the act, smacking a double, a single and scoring two runs. Taunton finally got to McDougal in the ninth inning, scoring three runs, but it was far from adequate, as Manchester won 19-3. Grant had two singles against McDougal in the losing effort, but failed to score.

The very next day the two teams met again in Manchester for a double-header. With a sweep, Taunton could recover the ground it had lost the previous day and pick up a game on their rivals. A Manchester sweep, on the other hand, would increase the chances for an early end to Taunton's season.

A relatively large crowd of 1,200 was on hand to watch the contest, a good sign for both teams. In the first game, Manchester took a 1-0 lead in the first and held on until the fourth when Taunton scored two runs and added two more in the sixth to take a 4-1 lead. Grant, King and Vought each scored for Taunton, with King and Grant each smacking doubles. Taunton pitcher John Kerin, a native of Townsend, Massachusetts who was added to the roster in mid-July, gave up one more run in the sixth, and then held on for a 4-2 win. Kerin would pitch a few more seasons in the New England and Connecticut State Leagues before serving as an umpire in the American, Eastern and Southern Leagues.

Disappointed in the loss, the crowd looked forward to salvaging the nightcap, and Taunton looked forward to a sweep.

As the teams prepared for game two, Mathewson warmed up for Taunton while twenty-three-year-old Frank Morrissey warmed up for Manchester. The crowd likely noticed the difference in appearance between the two. Morrissey, a Baltimore native whose parents emigrated from Ireland, was just five-foot four, a full nine inches shorter than the strapping Mathewson.

The two were well matched on the field, however, as they each kept the opposing hitters off balance and held the score at 2-2 going into the fifth. Grant reportedly played "excellent" center field in support of Mathewson and Thomas Murphy at shortstop in support of Morrissey.[21]

Mathewson tired some in the fifth, giving up two runs which the Taunton batters were unable to match in their half of the inning. Then, in the sixth, the Manchester bats exploded, scoring four runs off Mathewson to take an 8-2 lead. Grant, Vought, King and Mathewson each had hits, but the diminutive Morrissey effectively kept the hits spread out – in the end allowing just four runs and earning Manchester an 8-4 victory. Mathewson had given up only eight hits to Manchester's hitters, but he had also given up four walks and hit two batters.

At this point, the "dog days" of August took command of the season, and it became a drudgery for the Taunton players, many of whom seemed to be tired, worn out and simply going through the motions. In one example of a typical game during this stretch, Mathewson faced Newport on August 8, and gave up thirteen runs on fifteen hits. Ever-versatile Grant caught for Mathewson and he and Vought smacked yet more doubles, but it was not enough, as Taunton fell 13-11 before a sadly typical home crowd of 250.

The very next day, before a home crowd of 200, Taunton lost again to Manchester and ace McDougal, 8-6. Grant clouted two singles and scored three runs, but it was far from enough. McDougal not only earned the win, but also hit a triple and single in his own support.

As the season moved into the second week of August, the league decided to collapse from six teams to four. This was the moment that Taunton had been dreading, since it continued to sit in last place. Surprisingly, for reasons that were not completely clear, the league selected two other teams, Brockton and Pawtucket, for dismissal. The league also decided to reorganize the schedule, declare Portland the winner of the first "division" of the season, re-set the standings back to zero, and give the remaining four teams a shot at winning the second "division."

It was a gambit that had worked in leagues previously. Binghamton, for example, in 1892 won the second half of the Eastern League season, and then won a playoff with first-half winner Providence to win the overall championship. The idea was that giving all four teams an equal shot at winning the second "division" would increase fan interest and crowd sizes, heading into a big Labor Day showdown. The difference in this case was that the second "division" would only be comprised of roughly two-to-three weeks of games.

On August 14, Taunton traveled to Portland to begin its effort to win the second "division."

Mathewson started the big game for Taunton with Grant in his customary leadoff spot and playing center field and Vought batting third and playing shortstop.

Portland manager John "Phenomenal" Smith led the home team, batting third and playing right field against Mathewson. A crowd of 500 was on hand.

Mathewson, staked to a 2-0 lead in the second inning, held Portland scoreless through four innings and gave up one run in the fifth. Headed into the sixth inning, Mathewson held a slim 2-1 lead.

Up to that point, it had been one of Mathewson's most impressive outings. Even when Portland put two runners on base in the sixth, the young right-hander was in control, having yielded just six hits and one walk.

The crowd murmured as up stepped twenty-six-year-old center fielder George Noblit, a native of Chester, Pennsylvania. Noblit was a .338 hitter on the season and the team leader in extra base hits.

He had had no luck this day against Mathewson, and, with two runners on base, dug eagerly into the box and watched for Mathewson's deliveries.

Phenomenal Smith watched from the on-deck circle as

Mathewson rocked, kicked and dealt a straight pitch that Noblit met with a mighty swing. The sound of the bat alerted Grant and the other outfielders that the ball was on its way, but they could only run back to the wall and watch it sail over their heads for a three-run home run and a 4-2 Portland lead.

Twenty-eight-year-old pitcher Vianello Drinkwater held Taunton scoreless the rest of the way for a 4-2 win. Mathewson, although a loser yet again, caught Smith's attention with his ability and demeanor, even in defeat. Smith kept the college boy in mind as a possible future recruit.

Even in the reorganized four-team league, Taunton could not keep pace with the others, dropping to 1-4 after the first week, and continuing to have financial challenges.

Mathewson, for one, began to ponder if he would ever be paid, noting that at a minimum he would need enough money to return to Bucknell after Labor Day.

"I can't remember getting any money," he wrote years later. "I boarded in town, and when the landlady got too insistent for some of the money I owed her, I could occasionally shake down the manager for $5 to pay her on account. But this was the extent of my fortune, and I seldom or never had any money of my own, not even enough to pay my debts."[22]

On August 17, Taunton faced Manchester again to see if either team could get on a run in the season's final weeks. McDougal was in the box for Manchester, facing Mathewson for Taunton. Before a crowd of 400, Mathewson scattered thirteen hits and McDougal gave up just four, but through the sixth inning, Taunton led 3-2.

Would the all-American college boy finally out-fox the crafty McDougal?

Although Mathewson had an impressive fastball, he did not consider it his best or favorite pitch. He likely did not have the mix of tricky "slow" pitches that McDougal had at the time, but he prided himself nonetheless on his curve, which he said was "always" his favorite pitch.

"The slow ball which I have used so often and termed the 'fade away' was always a part of my natural mechanical gifts," he later explained, "though doubtless I have improved it through years of experience."[23]

Mathewson would eventually build the stamina necessary to consistently hold opponents down through complete games, but such was not the case this day, as he yielded two runs in the seventh and one in the eighth to fall behind 5-3. Grant walked and scored and Vought scorched McDougal for a triple, but McDougal smartly held on for the win.

"The season dragged on in a rather monotonous way," Mathewson lamented.[24]

The two pitchers dueled one another again on a rainy September 1 before 200 fans in Manchester. Mathewson gave up just five hits, but McDougal "pitched a fine game," giving up only one lone single to Vought, and earning a 3-0 victory in five rain-shortened innings.

Grant, on August 23, had moved to the Connecticut State League in the hopes of securing greater attention and a potential major league trial, so, with the exception of Vought, Taunton entered the season's Labor Day contests with a totally revamped line-up from opening day.

Labor Day, on September 4, would prove to be very eventful in New England League history. Manchester and Newport each began the day with 14-9 records. Newport felt it had the better chance of securing the "second division" championship, as it had a Labor Day triple-header scheduled with Taunton.

Mathewson started game one for Taunton in Newport on that brisk morning before a crowd of 250, and shut the Newports down for five innings before giving up two in the sixth and two more in the ninth for a 4-0 loss. Taunton managed only three hits in the contest. Taunton went on to lose the next two games in the afternoon before a crowd of 1,200, 12-4 and 11-1. This brought Newport's record to 17-9.

Not to be outdone, Manchester scheduled not just three

games with Portland on Labor Day, but six! The plan was to begin early enough to play all six games before sundown.

Manchester won the first two games in the morning 14-7 and 12-8 before a crowd of 800. McDougal then pitched games 3 and 4 in the early afternoon, winning them for Manchester 12-2 and 8-4. Controversy ensued in games 5 and 6, however, and, instead of being played, the games were each awarded to Manchester by forfeit, 9-0 and 9-0. This brought Manchester's record to 20-9, and appeared to win the league's "second division" championship.

Wise to the chicanery, league officials ruled that the six games between Manchester and Portland were a "farce" that "will do the game no good," and awarded the championship to Newport.[25]

"It wasn't so much the games you won as the games you didn't lose," Mathewson wrote of the season, "which landed you the pennant in that league."

Despite the promise of being Taunton's savior, Mathewson failed to live up to expectations, and returned home to Factoryville. "I felt rather discouraged," he explained. "My summer had been a financial failure and baseball prospects were none too bright."[26]

Once his sophomore Bucknell semester began, instead of dwelling on baseball, Mathewson focused on football, where he was the team's star.

He did not stay far from baseball for long, however, as prior to a football game against the University of Pennsylvania, former Portland manager Smith, attending the game, contacted Mathewson, reminded him of his baseball potential and asked the teenager to join him for the following season (1900) in Norfolk. The offer and encouragement resuscitated the young hurler's baseball hopes, and he wound up joining Smith in Norfolk when Bucknell's season was over. He had so much early-season success in 1900 that Smith sold his contract in July to the New York Giants, promoting the hurler to the major leagues. From that point, Mathewson became one of the greatest pitchers in baseball history.

McDougal clearly out-pitched Mathewson in 1899, and had a strong enough season that he hoped for a major league trial, but no offers came his way. The same was true for Grant in the Connecticut League.

After the season, Grant likely returned to work as a solderer in the silver works, while McDougal returned home to Buffalo.

Perhaps hoping a change of scenery would change their luck, both players would join Pickett in New York State in 1900. Although he had not received a formal trial in 1899, as he had in 1898, Pickett told a *Boston Globe* reporter that his "good work" made him a "mark for the big league," and "some of the magnates have him booked for draft."[27]

Major league trials may not have been in the cards for Grant, McDougal, Mathewson or Pickett at the end of 1899, but there were others who were more fortunate, including a young wiry right-hander from Elmira who had been impressing Connecticut State League fans in New London for the past two seasons, and seemed destined for bigger and better things.

CHAPTER 2

Bill Ging with the Wonderful Wing

William Joseph "Bill" Ging was born in Elmira on November 7, 1872, the second son of Lawrence and Mary Ging. According to the 1900 census, Larry Ging was born in Ireland in 1838, came to the U.S. in 1860, and married Mary, a Canadian, in 1870. By 1878, he was a blacksmith living at 603 South Main Street in Elmira, a residence he would maintain at least through 1901. Like fellow Elmira ball players Jack Barnett and Bill Heine, Ging's immigrant Catholic family was active in local Democratic politics. Ging's older brother John was a fifth ward election inspector alongside Barnett. Like John Doran roughly twenty miles to the east in Athens, the young Gings grew up working with their father "at the anvil," which likely contributed to their strength and stamina.

Doran unfortunately continued to have behavioral problems, as he had during his baseball career, ending up in an incident that was the nineteenth-century equivalent of drunk driving. On March 4, 1899, he was arrested in Waverly for intoxication after he and a man named Maxcy drove a one-horse carriage in such a reckless manner that the horse "ran away and demolished the carriage, throwing the men out on upper Broad Street."[28]

Also like Doran, Billy Ging was a celebrated pitcher, but whereas Doran was a stocky left-hander often described as a hard-throwing strikeout pitcher, Ging was a lean 5'10" right-hander known for his cool finesse.

In 1897, Ging pitched for a semi-pro team in New London, Connecticut, alongside fellow Elmiran Ralph Hutchinson, who later went on to play baseball and football for Princeton before embarking on a successful college football coaching career. Ging and Hutchinson were both known for being smart players. According to the *Elmira Daily Gazette and Free Press*, "Either is capable of the best kind of work with head as well as arm."[29]

During the war-dominated 1898 season, Ging pitched for New London in the Connecticut State League and finished with a promising 22-10 record. "In Ging and [Ike] Van Zant, New London has without a doubt two of the best twirlers in the League," *Sporting Life* reported on July 2. "They are cool and calculating, never 'go up in the air,' as the saying is."[30]

At the time, New London had a population of about 17,500, a 27-percent increase over its 1890 population of 13,757. The town possessed the best deep-water port on Long Island Sound and was an important base of naval operations during the Revolution. Following the Revolution, New London became the second busiest whaling port in the world behind New Bedford, Massachusetts. Income from the whaling industry set a prosperous economic foundation upon which, by 1900, a shipping-related manufacturing industry had developed and flourished.

The Connecticut League was particularly interesting at the end of the century, because two of its stars were prominent old-time veterans from the majors—forty-one-year-old Roger Connor with Waterbury and forty-eight-year-old Jim O'Rourke with Bridgeport—playing out the ends of their careers in their hometowns. They also happened to be former John Clapp teammates.

In addition to Connor and O'Rourke, the Connecticut League included yet another old-timer: Jack Chapman, managing first at Meriden and then at Norwich. Chapman's former ace with the champion 1890 Louisville Cyclones, Scott Stratton, was also in the Connecticut League, pitching for Bristol.

Ging had mixed experiences against Connor and O'Rourke. On July 20, 1898, for example, Ging lost to Bridgeport 7-3, with cleanup hitter and catcher Jim O'Rourke going two for three with two runs scored.[31] On August 13, on the other hand, Ging beat Bridgeport 2-1 and held O'Rourke to one hit in four at bats.[32]

In 1899, the major league scene was vastly different from what it had been a decade earlier. Stability remained elusive, making major league jobs increasingly scarce. In 1890, there had been three major leagues and twenty-five major league teams. By 1899, there was just one major league and twelve major league teams. Moreover, whereas there seemed to be no end to the number of cranks that could be lured to games at all levels in 1890, by 1899, after years of economic recession, labor unrest, and war, attendance at all levels of organized baseball was down. The average attendance for major league games in both 1898 and 1899 was less than three thousand per game. In some cities, like Cleveland–the seventh largest in the U.S.–average per-game attendance in 1898 was below two thousand and in 1899 was below two hundred.[33]

Although hopes remained high for Ging and other 1899 prospects, there was far less opportunity for them than there had been for John McGraw, John Doran, Hughie Jennings, Charlie Hamburg, Harry Taylor, and their peers a decade earlier. For minor league players of that generation, like Bill Heine and Bill Setley, who already had families but had not yet reached the major league level, the window of opportunity was quickly closing.

Even winning did not guarantee financial success. Canandaigua's champion New York State League (NYSL) team, for example, folded after the 1898 season, so its stars had to look elsewhere for work. Charlie Hamburg opted to sign with Oswego in the NYSL and was named team captain. "'Old Ham' has scores of friends among the Utica enthusiasts and will be warmly welcomed," the *Rochester Democrat* reported. Andy Roth also joined Oswego.

Heine finished the 1898 season with Auburn in the NYSL and started 1899 with Wheeling, West Virginia, in the Interstate League. Wheeling was far from his young family at home in Elmira, however, and by mid-May Heine was back in the NYSL, in Oswego with Hamburg and Roth.

Bill Ging had no such family limitations as yet. His older brother, John, was working as a railroad machinist, and Bill was proud to declare himself a "Ball player" in the 1900 census. The major leagues remained a distinct possibility for him.

Ging started the 1899 season with Montreal in the Eastern League, but was back with New London by May 20.[34] That year, New London featured "Colonel" Gil Hatfield, Snapper Kennedy, Mike Lynch, Frank Murphy, Bobby Wheelock, Leo Fishel, Jake Livingstone, and powerful Pete Woodruff. Also on the team was 1896 Waverly star Dennis Ryan.

On August 16, Ging traveled to Boston to watch the Brooklyn-Boston National League contest, where current Brooklyn and former Baltimore manager Ned Hanlon greeted him and asked him to join the Brooklyn team following the Connecticut League season.[35] It is not clear from newspaper accounts if this was a formal offer, or if Ging was unable to on his own entertain formal offers, given his contract with New London. Either way, the attention bode extremely well for Ging's chances to earn a major league trial.

Ging pitched well through the end of 1899, leading New London in wins for the second straight year, but his 1899 record was not quite as stellar as his 1898 one had been. His final win-loss record that year was 16-17. Nevertheless, as September rolled around, he joined numerous other minor league and college prospects in hoping for late-season call-ups to the major leagues, including the possibility of joining Brooklyn.

For whatever reason, the Brooklyn transaction did not materialize. Nevertheless, when the Connecticut League season was over in mid-September, Ging and teammate Woodruff, the league home run leader, were among the fortunate few to receive major-league call-ups or "trials"–Woodruff going to New York and Ging, instead of Brooklyn, going to Frank Selee's defending champion Boston club.[36]

Boston manager Selee was born in New Hampshire in 1859 and left a factory job in Waltham, Massachusetts, in 1884 to form and manage a minor league team in Lawrence, Massachusetts. His success there and in subsequent manager spots in other minor league towns led him to Boston, where he began managing in 1890. He was a "master of putting together a team better than the sum of its parts," and would wind up winning five pennants for the Boston Beaneaters in twelve seasons—three straight from 1891 through 1893 and one each in 1897 and 1898.

Boston's 1899 line-up included multiple future Hall-of-Famers, in addition to Selee himself. At third base was Jimmy Collins, who had teamed up with Bill Heine and John Doran in Buffalo in 1894. Just a few years later, he was a bona fide star, leading the major league in home runs and total bases in 1898. In left field was Hugh Duffy, who led the major leagues in home runs in 1897 and would end up with a .326 batting average across his seventeen-year major league career. Among Boston's star pitchers were former Harrisburg farmhand Vic Willis and Charles "Kid" Nichols. One of the team's most prominent young stars, however—catcher Marty Bergen—was having a difficult season.

Born in North Brookfield, Massachusetts, in 1871, Bergen was tall and thin for a catcher at 5'10" and 170 pounds. He was a solid hitter, posting a .280 average in 1898, and had a powerful throwing arm. No one doubted his talent and potential, but he was also temperamental, and his teammates reported frequent confrontations with him as the 1898 and 1899 seasons progressed. He distanced himself from his teammates and argued with management. He expressed a need to spend more time with his wife and three children, living at their farm in North Brookfield.

The incidents with his teammates came to a head in 1898, when on July 29, at the posh Southern Hotel in St. Louis, Vic Willis sat down next to Bergen at breakfast. The twenty-two-year-old Willis, a former Harrisburg teammate of John Doran and Fred Talada, was a surprisingly effective rookie pitcher, eventually winning twenty-five games for the National League champions. Willis greeted the catcher, and historian William Nack, relying on extensive research of the incident, explained what happened next:

> "If you don't get away from me," Bergen said, "I'll smash you sure!"
> Willis refused to move, and Bergen reached over and slapped him on the face. Smarting from the blow, Willis appeared ready to fight, but he checked himself. Several players urged him to another table, then out of the room.
> Selee warned him not to retaliate. "I'll make a sacrifice of my personal feelings and swallow the insult in the interests of the club," vowed Willis, "but if Bergen makes another break at me, we'll settle the question of which is the better man." Bergen refused to apologize, claiming he was made the butt of jokes on that train, and Selee warned him against any future trouble, telling Bergen, "If you say the word, I'll begin negotiations at once to trade you." Bergen said that he wanted to stay but that nobody would make a fool of him. The other players, trying for a fifth pennant in eight years, admired Bergen as a hustling, hardworking player but were livid over the slapping incident.[37]

Now, in 1899, Boston was not the powerhouse it had been in prior years, and Bergen was more moody than ever. He was experiencing increasing stress and paranoia both on and off the field. To make matters worse, his son Willie died of diphtheria in April while Bergen was out of town on a road trip, and Bergen thought his teammates were making light of it. It was at that point, historian Brian McKenna notes, "the ballplayer's mind started to stray from reality."[38]

On July 20, 1899, just a little less than a year after Bergen struck Willis, the Boston team's train stopped briefly in Washington, DC, on its way to Cincinnati. As his teammates played cards, Bergen hopped off the train, and returned by a different train to North Brookfield. "It would be the longest and most spectacular walkout of Bergen's career, and it infuriated the Bostons because it left them, as they contended for their third pennant in a row, with only their backup to catch game after game in the midsummer heat."[39]

Boston's backup catcher at the time was the former Oriole catcher Bill "Boileryard" Clarke, who, according to *Sporting Life*, "suspected something radically wrong, mentally" with Bergen.[40] Nichols, the Boston pitcher closest to Bergen, noted that Bergen often sat by himself while his teammates were playing cards or other games on trips. Nichols explained:

> His leaving the team as he did left us with only one catcher on our Western trip. Clarke did great work, but if he had been taken ill we would have been in a bad box. Bergen told me afterward that he had got to thinking of his folks while on the train, and when we stopped at Washington he couldn't resist the temptation of taking the first train homeward. It seems to me that the fact that he was all the time thinking that everybody was working against him, was trying to injure him, showed that his mind was unbalanced.[41]

Tim Murnane, in his capacity as a *Boston Globe* reporter, visited Bergen at his farm to assess the situation and was convinced Bergen was not simply being lazy or petulant, but had legitimate health-related reasons for leaving the team. He further believed Bergen was seeking help for his afflictions. "I made up my mind that Bergen was telling me the truth, or was slightly demented," Murnane wrote. "In either case, he was entitled to the undivided sympathy of the baseball public, as well as players and directors." Bergen rejoined the team soon afterward, but by the second week of September, twenty-two-year-old rookie Billy Sullivan was promoted from Grand Rapids as a third catcher, giving Boston more options.

Heading into the final week of September, Boston was in third place, trailing both Brooklyn and Philadelphia. They were still ahead of John McGraw's hated Baltimore Orioles and were well ahead of New York, but a third consecutive pennant seemed unlikely. Many Boston players blamed Bergen. "In their eyes it was as much his fault that the championship had been lost or, at least, as good as lost, as it was of any player in the organization," *Sporting Life* reported.[42]

It was onto this scene that Bill Ging entered.

Ging's major-league debut with Boston was scheduled for Monday September 25 at the Polo Grounds in New York. He would be making his major league start in the nation's largest media market. In 1899, greater New York City boasted a total population of over 3.4 million–nearly a million more people than its five boroughs held just nine years earlier. Joining Ging in his major league debut would be nineteen-year-old catcher John George Eby from Woodward, Pennsylvania, a small town not far from Lock Haven and Bellefonte.

That week, New York City was agog over the coming weekend's giant welcome home celebration and parade for Admiral George Dewey, the hero of the Spanish-American War's Battle of Manila Bay. Just a year removed from consolidating its five boroughs[43] in an effort to fend off Chicago's bid to overtake it as the economic and cultural center of the nation, greater New York City was taking the celebration very seriously. "Seeing that the reception of Admiral Dewey will be by far the greatest municipal pageant that New York has had," the *New York Times* reported on September 10. "Everything that is likely to affect it, favorably or unfavorably, is a matter of intimate concern."

Colorful patriotic decorations covered the city, especially at City Hall and along the parade route. At Madison Square, an elaborate arch, similar to the arch at Washington Square, was constructed in Dewey's honor. It was composed of the same temporary "staff" material—a blend of plaster and wood shavings—that facilitated the speedy construction of large temporary buildings at the Chicago World's Fair and similar events. City officials intended to reconstruct the arch with more permanent materials once sufficient funding was available after the celebration.

The city had planned a naval parade on Friday the 29th and a huge land parade on Saturday the 30th. Nearly fifty thousand men were expected to march, representing at least fifteen state militias, as well as Civil War and Spanish-American War veterans. Among the marchers would be the world-famous Sousa Band, in just the fourth parade of its history, playing "Stars and Stripes Forever" and immediately preceding Admiral Dewey in the parade order. The route would head up Broadway from Battery Park and would be the first "ticker-tape" parade in the city's history to celebrate an individual.

Amidst all the preparations, the weather was only partially cooperative. Although the temperatures were seasonably warm–Monday's high, for instance, was seventy-five degrees–the wind made decorating trickier than usual. "High winds prevailing for the last two days played havoc with the incandescent lights used to form 'Welcome Dewey' on the Brooklyn Bridge," the *New York Times* reported on September 26. "Numbers of globes were smashed by being blown against each other and the south roadway is littered with fragments of the shattered bulbs."[44]

The Boston club observed the preparations as they headed to the Polo Grounds for their afternoon game on Monday, September 25. In fact, second baseman Bobby Lowe was said to have been "a very busy man all the morning, taking snapshots of the Dewey decorations."[45]

The Polo Grounds was the sport's biggest stage, which meant tremendous pressure, especially for Ging.

"Trials" like these were notoriously unfair to the players: you get one chance, twelve teams and the national media would get a look at you, and if they liked what they saw, you might get a contract from someone. If not, it was back to the minors, or perhaps even out of baseball altogether.

The New York team Ging was scheduled to face that day was not yet the Giants that would be the toast of baseball within a decade. John McGraw was still in Baltimore, and Christy Mathewson would not appear in New York until his own trial the next season. However, the Giants of 1899 still had its share of stars eager to feast on a rookie pitcher.

Shortstop George Davis, from Cohoes, New York, led the team in hitting with a .337 average and was widely recognized as one of the game's top stars. "Many ball players regard him as the best shortstop in the business; batting, base running and fielding considered," the *Sporting News* reported in 1899 of the future Hall-of-Famer.[46]

Other New York stars were former Oriole second baseman Kid Gleason from Camden, New Jersey, outfielder Rip Van Halteren from St. Louis, Missouri, and Dirty Jack Doyle from Killorgin, Ireland.

The game began slowly on that warm and windy afternoon. Selee called on the rookie Sullivan to be Ging's catcher, rather than the moody Bergen or the veteran Clarke. The young catcher Eby, also available, sat on the bench in full uniform as Ging completed his preparations and took the mound. Despite being a rookie like Ging, Sullivan's catching style appeared to suit Ging, as both he and New York starting pitcher Ed Doheny traded shutouts for the first two innings. "A few jokes were cracked about his name when he went into the box," *Sporting* Life reported of Ging, "but he clearly showed there was nothing in a name by the work he did."[47] There was no record of what jokes were told, but they were likely not favorable.

Ging started the game by successfully retiring left fielder Van Halteren and third baseman Frank Martin from the field and quickly found his rhythm. Next in the order was shortstop Davis, followed by first baseman Doyle, second baseman Gleason, catcher Jack Warner, center fielder Tom Fleming, right fielder Woodruff, and pitcher Ed Doheny. Although he gave up five hits, five walks, and five stolen bases, Ging kept the New Yorkers scoreless until the seventh inning, when Gleason scored, tying the game at 1-1. Boston recovered the lead in the eighth inning, up 2-1.

Called to the majors following a successful minor league season, Elmira native Bill Ging started on the mound for Boston on September 25, 1899, against the New York Giants at the Polo Grounds, and was "as cool and collected as a veteran." Portrait by Gary Cieradkowski.

Gleason had been a tough workhorse pitcher in his early years– winning 138 major league games from 1888 through 1895—but since his '95 season with the Orioles, he had focused on being an aggressive second baseman. "He was, without doubt, the gamest and most spirited ball player I ever saw, recalled McGraw of Gleason. "He could lick his weight in wildcats and would prove it at the drop of a hat."[48] Years later, as the manager of the White Sox, Gleason's reputation for honesty helped him remain in the game after several of his players accepted bribes and allegedly threw the 1919 World Series.[49]

Throughout the game, Ging remained "as cool and collected as a veteran, and mixed his balls up in a commendable style," *Sporting Life* reported. "The hardest hitters of the New Yorks could not do anything with him."[50]

In the eighth inning, Ging continued to match wits with the New York hitters, but got into a jam, with Davis on second, another runner on first, no outs, and Gleason back at bat.

Gleason already had one hit and a run against Ging that afternoon, and the fierce veteran eagerly eyed the stoic rookie. A switch hitter, Gleason dug into the left-side batter's box and prepared for Ging's pitches. Davis, the team's leading hitter and base stealer, led off second and looked forward to scoring the tying run.

Ging delivered the pitch. Gleason swung and ripped the ball into windy right field. It seemed to the New Yorkers that at least one run would score on the hit, possibly two. "Gleason hit a low line drive toward right field," noted the *New York Times*. "It seemed almost impossible for a fielder to get near the ball." The *New York Sun* added, "Gleason whacked the ball to right field apparently out of [Chick] Stahl's reach."[51]

As Ging watched helplessly and Gleason raced to first, the crowd rose expectantly. Seemingly out of nowhere, right fielder Stahl got a jump on the ball, made a grand run, reached far forward, and caught the ball with his gloved hand at full speed.

The "remarkable one-hand catch by Stahl saved the game for Boston," noted *Sporting Life*.[52]

In the end, Ging shut the New York Giants down for a 2-1 win. His major league trial was wildly successful. *Sporting Life* noted, "New York could not do anything with Ging, a new try from the New London Club, of the Connecticut League. Few newcomers ever made a better debut than Pitcher Ging."[53]

Speculation as to Ging's next step began in earnest in the sports media, and on October 7, *Sporting Life* reported, "Boston had an option on this man but failed to avail itself of it, and it looks like as if Brooklyn would get him. There are few opportunities offered nowadays to get such men as Ging for the modest price of $200. If he enters fast company and does not do well it will be a great surprise to many."[54]

It was not clear from news accounts why there was such a back-and-forth between Brooklyn and Boston for Ging, but it is very possible Ging was simply a victim of the National League's overall financial challenges.

On December 9, for example, *Sporting Life* reported that "Pitcher Ging, who was dropped by Boston after winning one game for the Beaneaters, has been secured by Brooklyn." *Sporting Life* went on to explain that Ging "wanted more than a Class Z salary from the Boston Club, and so they allowed him to go."[55] So, ultimately, Ned Hanlon wound up signing Ging for Brooklyn after all, even though Ging made his debut for Boston.

Catcher Eby did not get into the game, and there is no record of his getting another major league opportunity. According to census records, he eventually became a banker in Centre and Cambria counties in Pennsylvania, not far from his hometown.

As for catcher Marty Bergen, *Sporting Life* reported that it was "an open secret that he will not be with the team next season. In a matter like this the management of the club is powerless. They cannot compel the men to act in a friendly manner to a brother-player if the players are not inclined, and good results cannot be expected if he remains."[56]

Heading into the 1900 season, the National League planned to contract from twelve teams to eight, and a second major league did not appear to be imminent. Such a huge reduction in major league opportunities was a big blow to this generation of ball players. The reduction in teams would cost at least sixty major league player jobs in addition to the jobs of all those who supported each team, which did not sit well with players. They still smarted over the failure of their 1890 Players' League gambit. This was particularly brutal for young players like Ging. All that was needed to fully galvanize the players into yet another unionizing effort was a spark.

CHAPTER 3

Bergen Lights the Spark

As the year 1900 began, *Sporting Life*, *The Sporting News*, and other sports media conducted their regular pre-season discussions of leagues, players, teams, and prospects. Among those who figured in these discussions was Boston's troubled young star catcher, rumored to be a hot trading commodity, if he could only get his head right. "Several parties have tried to get an expression from him as to how he stands with the baseball world, but Martin refuses to let go," reported *Sporting Life* on January 6."[57]

Two weeks later, Bergen snapped. In the early morning hours of January 19, Bergen killed his young wife and two remaining children by striking each of them in the head with an axe. He then killed himself, slitting his throat with a razor. Bergen's elderly father, who lived in a cabin behind the main farmhouse, found the bodies later that morning. The scurrilous headlines spanned the nation: "Bergen's Awful Deed," "Bergen Slays Family and Self," "An Awful Tragedy," "Wholesale Murder," "Family Butchered."

No one specific incident was identified as having prompted the slaughter, but many of those who knew him were quick to say that they feared something terrible like this had been long in coming. "His fellow players feared him," reported the *New*

York Herald. "Captain Duffy more than once said he was afraid Bergen would attack him with a bat."[58]

"I somehow felt that Bergen was of a temperament to do some atrocious act some day," pitcher Edward Lewis told the *Herald*. "I noticed more peculiarities about him last year than ever before, and remarked to my wife that some day he would do something dreadful."[59]

Boston owner Arthur H. Soden characterized Bergen as "despondent," and said he feared for the team's safety in Bergen's proximity. "While the team was playing last summer the thought flitted through my mind several times that something fearful would happen. In fact, I thought something would happen during the time he stayed away last summer. I am very sorry that his insanity should have resulted in this murder of his family. It is too terrible to imagine."[60]

This near-universal reaction prompted some media and players to question whether the team was in part responsible for Bergen's condition. If the team and owner had known Bergen was in such bad shape, why had they done nothing to help? Why, for instance, was he fined for leaving the team, rather than given medical attention?

Articles representing both Bergen's and Soden's sides of the issue ran in newspapers across the country. According to the *New York World*, the pro-player side could be summarized as follows: "The statement that Marty Bergen was paid a salary of $2,400 by the Boston Club is given as evidence that he was well treated by the management. But three fines of $500 each and other little fines imposed on him during the season may have cut into his income and placed himself and family on the verge of starvation. When the bodies of Bergen and his wife and little children were found their cupboard was bare and all things pointed to the fact that just before the tragedy they were lacking the necessities of life."[61]

In response, Tim Murnane, representing the owner's point of view, explained that Bergen's earnings over the previous few years had given him sufficient means to live well: "There was no reason to believe that he was not leading a pleasant life. In fact, he had decided to give up base ball and take things easy on the farm. The Boston magnates did everything for him that they did for the other men, and, in fact, a great deal more, and are in no way responsible for any misfortune that overtook the player."[62]

Days after the murder, in the midst of this debate, Bergen's back-up catcher in Boston, Boileryard Clarke, who was also then the manager of the Princeton baseball team, decided to publicly throw down the gauntlet with respect to player rights–specifically regarding medical care:

> I do not fear being either suspended, blacklisted or fined by the league, and I think the other players should feel the same way. I am fully convinced that the reserve rule is all wrong, and that we players would welcome an organization that would treat us like men, and not sell us around as thought we were so many slaves.
>
> At present if a young player or one without a great reputation gets hurt in a game through no fault of his own he is often laid off, without pay and not even his doctor's bill is paid for him. To remedy some of the present evils I would suggest that each team select one or two of its members as a committee and that the various committees then meet and form a protective union. Our demands would not be unreasonable. Our principal object would be to fight the reserve rule and help a man who had been laid off without pay for being injured while during his duty to the owners.[63]

Clarke's outspokenness in the wake of his teammate's tragedy spurred several other players to pledge their support to this plan, not the least of whom were two of his old Orioles teammates, Hughie Jennings and Harry Taylor. The fact that all three also had extensive experience coaching and mentoring college baseball players was reflective of their interest in players as humans with needs and not simply as cogs in the organized baseball machine.

Yet another old Oriole, Willie Keeler, "rebutted the argument that the ballplayers should be grateful for earning seven-and-one-half times as much as a coal miner, six times as much as a factory worker, four times as much as a street railwayman, twice as much as a federal clerk. Once a ballplayer's brief career was over, Willie asked, 'how do we find ourselves? Why, we have spent the best years of our lives on the diamond, those years usually employed by young men in acquiring commercial or professional knowledge that will prove lucrative to them for many times the period usually allotted to a ballplayer. At the end of our baseball career we then find ourselves unfitted otherwise to earn any considerable money. This makes plain that we must make all the money we can during the short period we may be said to be star players.'"[64]

The stability of organized baseball–and especially the desire for a realistic balance among the interests of players, owners, and the public–became a significant topic of discussion at the national level as the 1900 season began. The fact that baseball players often made more money than their working-class counterparts did not mean they believed their rights were fairly represented, especially given the fact that some owners owned multiple teams and manipulated the rosters to suit their commercial interests. Their relative privilege was evident frequently, as labor strife and tragic accidents were practically daily news. On July 19, 1900, alone, for example, the *Elmira Star Gazette* reported a miners' strike in Arnot, Pennsylvania, and a railroad accident in Watkins where an eighteen-year-old bootblack's left arm "was mangled in a frightful manner."[65] These risks were a daily part of life for the working class at the time. However, if the player was sufficiently injured that he could not play, he could be released without pay, and, as Keeler attested, be in an even less favorable economic position than his working class peers.

Concerns over player safety were exacerbated by the owners' decision to cut the National League down from twelve teams to eight going into the 1900 season. This decision was said to be in response to reduced attendance and the owners' belief that the law of supply and demand would bring attendance back up, but many players, fans and writers objected to this notion, believing that the ownership magnates' "mismanagement" was chiefly to blame for reduced attendance.

To the media, and to many players, a reduction in teams simply resulted in a surplus of good players, driving down their price. "There are enough players of high class outside of those of the best caliber in the 'king' league," wrote J. Pollywog Smith, to form another major league.[66]

In order to bid for more financial security from organized baseball ownership, in June, the players organized for just the second time in their history, creating the Players' Protective Association (PPA). *Sporting Life* was unequivocal in its support for the union:

> Slowly but surely the League magnates who have been for some years industriously sowing the wind are beginning to reap the whirlwind. One manifestation of that is the organization of a players' union, in order to counteract the despotic policies and grasping methods of the little coterie of ancient fossils who are gradually running the League and even the national game to death. The players have at last learned that the only way to meet the League Trust is with counter organization, as in these piping times of trusts the individual cuts no more figure in base ball than in any other line of business.[67]

As officers, the PPA elected veteran catcher Charles "Chief" Zimmer as President, former mine worker Hughie Jennings as Secretary, and Boileryard Clarke as Treasurer. Another highly respected veteran, Clark Griffith, who, with players like Jess Tannehill and Elmira-native Danny Richardson, was known as an advocate of unionization "around whom the players could rally,"[68] was eventually elected PPA Vice President, and Jennings' fellow Cornell coach, Harry Taylor, was announced as one of three candidates to serve as the union's first counsel. The PPA leaders met with Daniel Harris, a representative of Samuel Gompers of the American Federation of Labor, but decided not to join the larger union so as not to unnecessarily "antagonize" the National League owners.[69]

"Justice and fair dealing are what we want," said Jennings. "The organization takes in about all the League players. A League player does not have to join now, however. Nor would a player be tabooed if he did not join. If he has a grievance, however, it would be his alone and not ours. Later minor league players will be taken in."[70]

National League star, Cornell coach, law school student and Secretary of the new Players' Protective Association, Hughie Jennings was arguably baseball's busiest man in 1900. Portrait from the Library of Congress.

The PPA wanted to avoid any inference that it was a "radical" labor organization, downplaying confrontation in favor of a firm but conciliatory tone. This, the officers felt, would help keep the players in favor with the public. It was a lesson they learned from John Ward's Players' League failure in 1890. By being professional and courteous but firm, the new union positioned itself as an attractive advocate for all players and as an ideal partner with all owners, but especially with Byron Bancroft "Ban" Johnson, leader of the still-minor American League, who, taking advantage of the National League's decision to reduce its number of teams, was laying plans to move his American League from the minors to the majors.

Johnson was known for his no-nonsense approach to league management. Since taking control of the Western League in 1892, he sought to attract the "respectable class," and abhorred profanity on the playing field, arguing with umpires and all the other shenanigans that kept women and families from attending games. He was now ready to take his minor league success to the majors. Once the American League was competing directly with the National League in the same cities and for the same players, Johnson expected the worst symptoms of monopoly ownership (a lack of competition, gambling and other reckless player behavior, small ambivalent crowds, and a reduction in the broad public appeal necessary to grow the game) would be reversed.

In short, Johnson confidently believed that more fans would attend games once they were cleaned up, and he believed his minor league experience proved it.

Byron Bancroft "Ban" Johnson was the no-nonsense President of the fledgling American League, who promoted clean baseball and aimed to compete directly with the National League for players and fans. Portrait courtesy of the National Baseball Hall of Fame.

Attendance figures for the National League during this time period bear out the seriousness of these problems. According to Baseball-Reference.com, the average attendance per game in the National League in 1900 ranged from 2,507 in Brooklyn to 4,313 in Philadelphia. For many games in many major league cities, the crowds were less than one thousand, which was comparable to the baseball crowds in Taunton, New London, Waverly and other minor league towns. And this was at a time when there were only eight teams. In 1899, when there were twelve teams, the average ranged from just 145 in Cleveland to 4,686 in Philadelphia. In 1899, the New York Giants averaged crowds of just 1,597 per game. In 1900, they went up to 2,676, but just six years earlier, in 1894, the Giants had led the National League with an average attendance of 5,451. Clearly, this was not a favorable trend.[71]

The notion of major league attendance being so low makes it easier to understand why some excellent players did not think twice about playing in smaller, semi-pro towns where the crowds could be just as big and they would not be under major league control.

By July 14, 1900, the new PPA organization was becoming clearer. Jennings continued to be the spokesman, and Taylor, the former Waverly star, was officially announced as the new counsel.[72] That Taylor, a law school graduate, and his friend Jennings, a law school student, were leaders of the newest player's union was not surprising, given that John Ward, another ballplayer with law school credentials, had led the first player's union. Clearly, legal skills and an acute sense of justice for their fellow players was a heavy motivator.

"It is not the intention of the players to antagonize the magnates," Jennings reiterated in a statement. "Our first step will be for recognition, which, I am assured, we will have no trouble getting. Then we will meet the magnates half way. We want to work hand in hand with them for the benefit of the game."[73]

Support for the new players' union was far from universal, however. To many who were loyal to baseball's owners, the PPA was tantamount to treason, and participants risked ruining their baseball careers. *Sporting Life* columnist J. Pollywog Smith wrote:

> The magnates will not stand dictation by the players, and if the latter persist in making unreasonable demands, they will kill the "goose that lays the golden egg." The ones who own National League clubs can make good

money at other occupations and do not depend upon base ball for a livelihood. But how is it with the players? How few of them could earn a decent living outside of the National game? As far as my memory serves me the majority of them go into the saloon business after their baseball careers are over, and most of them never save a cent of their earnings.[74]

Confine yourselves to the playing end exclusively, for the legislative division is entirely out of your sphere.[75]

Fortunately for the players, their new counsel, Harry Taylor, had experience in both the playing and "legislative" divisions, and did not intend to be "unreasonable."

As counsel to the new Players' Protective Association, Waverly's former second baseman Harry L. Taylor devised a legal strategy that sought to earn players important concessions from owners as well as renewed popularity with fans.

As the summer of 1900 wore on, the National League continued to be in a "deplorable state" in terms of attendance, while the still-minor American League, "with about one-tenth of the population to draw from," was "prosperous."[76] Clearly, the reduction from twelve teams to eight was not the panacea the owners had hoped it would be.

Under these circumstances, the PPA and Ban Johnson's American League increasingly saw their interests merging in opposition to the National League's monopoly. By early September, the handwriting was on the wall. "The players of the National League, or the leaders among the players, are anxious to help form a rival league," wrote Hugh S. Fullerton. "From here, it seems certain that Johnson and his magnates will join forces with the revolting players and that all interests antagonistic to the National League will combine to form a new [major] American League."[77]

The question was how the players would ensure that their rights would be protected and their opportunities maximized under a system of two healthy major leagues, rather than just one. Building a successful strategy to bring this about was where the experience of Harry Taylor, a student of the best minds in both academia and baseball, became indispensable.

CHAPTER 4

Jovial, Pleasant and Good Natured

In the winter of 1897-98, following his semi-pro pitching debut with Waverly in 1896, Fred Talada, embarked on a Waverly-based cigar-making partnership with Dr. John Tucker, and continued to refine it in the intervening years. According to a January 1899 report from the New York State Factory Inspector, Talada & Tucker's firm, consisting of both a factory and a store, employed five men and was one of eighteen firms in Waverly deemed sufficiently large to warrant inspection. Moreover, a June 3, 1899, story pointed out that Talada continued to make improvements to the factory and store, noting that "the interior of Talada's and Tucker's cigar store is being painted today."

Talada and Tucker's partnership was so comprehensive and mutually beneficial that in January of 1900, the 26-year-old Talada petitioned the county court to change his name from Fred Fremont Talada to Fred Fremont Tucker.

The exact rationale is unknown, but it had nothing to do with being ostracized by his family or with any hard feelings concerning his father, Guy Talada, since all three–Dr. Tucker, Fred Tucker, and Guy Talada–reportedly continued to take fishing and hunting trips together following the name change. Obviously, they got along well.

Was Fred Tucker attempting to distance himself from his baseball past–or from some past indiscretions? It's possible, but no such reference appears in the local news. In fact, the *Waverly Free Press* was expressly complementary of the change: "The necessary legal processes in the matter have been gone through and beginning with Jan. 28, 1900, Fred F. Talada will be no longer be Fred F. Talada, but Fred F. Tucker. Mr. Talada is one of the most popular men in Waverly and we congratulate him on deciding to acquire the name of one of our best citizens. The name of the firm with which he has been associated in the manufacture of cigars will be Tucker & Tucker. It will probably be some time before his many friends will cease calling him 'Tal.'"

The Owego Record, on the other hand, was less complementary, but had no alternative explanation. "What Was the Matter With Fred Talada?" the headline read. "Fred F. Talada of Waverly, has been granted permission by Judge Howard J. Mead to change his name to Fred F. Tucker, commencing with Jan. 28, 1900. Mr. Talada was for a season the pitcher for the Waverly base ball team and has played in league games. The firm name will change to Tucker & Tucker."

Just four years after moving to Waverly as a starting pitcher, Fred Tucker established a successful cigar-making business and built a network of regional contacts, making him a natural choice for building, managing and promoting a new local baseball team. Portrait by Gary Cieradkowski.

The most likely explanation lies in the fact that while Dr. Tucker and his wife were perhaps Waverly's most prestigious couple, they lacked an heir. Fred Tucker's grandson, Bill O'Shaughnessy, described Dr. Tucker as having been so prominent in town that his phone number was literally "the number one." Nonetheless, Dr. and Mrs. Tucker were childless, and Fred was an ambitious and talented young man with tremendous enthusiasm and potential. Their business partnership was thus far successful, and Fred Tucker was happily ensconced at the Tucker residence on the west side of Waverly Street, just a couple houses up from Elizabeth Street. He would eventually start his own family there, much to Dr. and Mrs. Tucker's pleasure. Fred's natural father, Guy, meanwhile, continued to reside on Providence Street less than a mile away.

As would be expected of a talented and ambitious young man, Fred Tucker's circle of friends and acquaintances included many of the town's most ambitious young men and women–men and women who were part of his generation and shared many of his interests. His networking skills made him a natural leader.

Among his network of acquaintances were 30-year-old Fred Krist, a band sawyer at furniture-maker Hall and Lyon, the village's largest employer, and 20-year-old Katie Tobin. Krist and Tobin were both attractive and well liked by their peers. Katie was very popular with "hosts of friends all through the valley," and Tucker described Krist as "jovial, pleasant and good-natured."[78]

Longtime Waverly factory employee Fred Krist was the son of German immigrants, and an acquaintance of local ball players, who thought of him as an easy-going, clean-living sort who did not frequent the local bars and similar hangouts like others in their circle.

The Tobin family of Waverly and the Krist family of Ithaca were both examples of hard-working, resourceful Catholic immigrant families in the late nineteenth century. Katie's father, James Tobin, came to the United States from Ireland as a young man in 1872. He settled, likely with his parents, Richard and Mary, in Waverly, and soon married Mary Roach, a long-time resident of Waverly who was born in New York State of parents who had emigrated from Ireland in the 1840s. James and Mary had four children: Mary, born in 1873; Elizabeth, "Lizzie," born in 1875; Katie, born in 1879; and Harold, born in 1893. They lived on Erie Street, near the Erie Railroad tracks where the local Catholic church, St. James, was originally located. James initially worked as a laborer and by 1900, had moved up to be a Railroad Section Foreman.

Fred Krist's father Ambrose married Magdalena in 1862 in Baden, one of the German coalition states before the Empire was formed. The next year, at the height of the American Civil War, they immigrated to New York State. After a stop in Oswego County, the Krists settled in Ithaca, where, by 1880, Ambrose was a pot maker at the local glass works. They had five children: Joseph, born in 1862 in Baden before the family arrived in the U.S.; Henry, born in the U.S. in 1864; Julius, born in 1866; Josephine, born in 1869; and Fred, born in 1870. By 1900, at age seventy-one, Ambrose was working in Ithaca as a street sweeper and living next door to his son Henry, who was a painter and thus likely familiar with another Ithaca painter, John Clapp.

The Tobin family, including Katie, was acquainted with Fred Krist due to the fact that they were co-congregants at St. James Parish in Waverly. Sometime in 1898, however, the friendly relations between Katie and Krist turned into something more intimate. Krist had been married since 1891 to the former Josephine Ganther, a popular lady who ran a millenary store in town, and the two separated when Krist refused to end his infatuation with Katie. By April 1900, Krist and his wife had been living separately for over six months. Despite the estrangement, the Tobin family still viewed the Krists as "married," and was steadfastly opposed to Katie and Krist seeing each other.

Krist came up with various schemes to see Katie. If he knew she had an appointment in town, for example, he would figure out a way to intercept her. On one occasion, Katie and her mother had appointments with Dr. Tucker. While her mother was inside with the doctor, Katie was outside, talking with Fred Krist in front of the Tucker house. On another occasion, in January 1900, Krist and Katie ran off to Wilkes-Barre and took on assumed identities (Mr. and Mrs. Fred Hyland). After several weeks, the Tobins discovered the whereabouts of the "really handsome" Krist and the "bright and pretty" Katie, and brought Katie back to Waverly by train, where confrontations between Krist and the Tobin family became more heated.[79]

As the Krist-Tobin affair heated up, Tucker's baseball mentor, John Doran, was back in the local news. He continued to have significant troubles and was earning far less generous media attention that he had just a decade earlier. "John Doran, a former Elmira base ball player, was arraigned in a police court this morning on the charge of intoxication," the *Elmira Gazette* reported. "He pleaded guilty and was sentenced to five days in jail. He gave himself up Wednesday." Just thirty-eight years old, Doran was already far from the world he expected when he was New Haven's young pitching star.

Also fighting a serious drinking problem was former Waverly and Cuban Giants infielder Bud Waller, who in 1900 worked as a day laborer and lived at 450 Broad Street, across the street from the Hall and Lyon factory. Just two weeks after Doran was jailed in Elmira, Waller suffered a similar fate in Waverly–except that Waller was sent to county jail in Owego for sixty days, the sort of sentence that indicated a repeat offender.[80] He was only twenty-five.

Early Saturday morning, April 7th, just a few days after Waller was thrown in jail for intoxication, Fred Krist went to Mixer's Hardware store on 317 Broad Street, a few doors down from the Tucker and Tucker cigar shop, to purchase a revolver.

As Krist was purchasing his revolver, many of his fellow Waverly citizens were waking up to that morning's *Waverly Free Press*. Page one was primarily dedicated to obituaries, official reports (such as legal notices), and large advertisements. Political news headed page two: Admiral Dewey was lauded as a possible presidential candidate, Grover Cleveland denied endorsing William Jennings Bryan, and New York governor Theodore Roosevelt denied any interest in being McKinley's running mate.[81]

Broad Street in Waverly looking east. The Warford House is to the right on the southwest corner of Broad and Fulton. The Town Clock is on the Northeast corner of Broad and Fulton. The railroad tracks and Erie Railroad Station are south of (behind) the Warford House. The police station and jail are in the tall building visible roughly two blocks in the distance on the south side of the street.

Also on page two were more local advertisements, the lifeblood of local papers then as now. The Saturday, April 7 paper included three ads for the April 11 Guy Brothers Minstrels show at the Waverly Opera House and one for "Krist and Ganther's grand millenary opening April 10th and 11th." Two more ads for Fred Krist's estranged wife's store were on page five, including a nice endorsement: "Mrs. Josephine Krist, who has been in New York for the last three months, returned Sunday with all the latest styles of spring and summer millenary."[82]

As usual, the newspaper also included its share of lurid tales of accidents and crime. As a growing town on booming railroad lines, Waverly had to contend with a steady population of travelers, as well as roving bands of tramps, hobos, thieves, and young men simply down on their luck. On page six, a young man from Elmira, Percy Chase, was reported to have had both of his feet "cut off" while trying to board a moving train. Page six also lauded Police Chief Charles E. Brooks for arresting two young out-of-town men who were "suspicious." What was their suspicious activity? They "were spending money very freely without being able to give satisfactory reasons for having so much money." Upon their arrest, Chief Brooks "ascertained that they were from Ithaca where they broke into a store ... and took $55 in money." They were already on their way back to Ithaca and would likely be sent to the Elmira Reformatory.[83] "The capture is of no mean importance and is due directly to the eternal vigilance of our efficient chief," the reporter noted.

On the more positive side of the news, in addition to train schedules with special excursion fares and numerous advertisements for shops, medicinal cures, and the upcoming minstrel show at the Opera House, there was the notice for an upcoming Polyhymnia Club music concert and a traveling exhibit of London-based French artist James Tissot's paintings at the Baptist Church.

All told, the morning's newspaper suggested a vibrant village with many diverse activities.

Following his revolver purchase, Krist secured room 22 at the Warford House, a hotel and boarding house located at the southwest corner of Fulton and Broad Streets, where he could stake out the Tobin house on Erie Street. The day before, he had applied to the Waverly police for a warrant against Katie, falsely alleging she stole money from him. He expected the police to summon her to formally answer the charges, and walked to the station at least twice during the day to demand that they do so. He also visited his estranged wife's millinery shop, and plied himself with "immoderate" quantities of gin and whiskey at the Warford's ground-floor bar.[84]

Waverly's Erie Railroad Station in the foreground and the Warford House behind it on the southwest corner of Fulton and Broad Streets. The saloon's doors are visible on the ground floor, facing the station.

Shortly after five in the afternoon, Katie and her sister Lizzie began to walk from their house to the police station. They turned north on Fulton Street and were about to cross the tracks when Krist spotted them, exited the saloon through the back door, and headed south on a diagonal path toward the railroad tracks to intercept them.

He held the new revolver in his pocket.

It was a typical Saturday afternoon at the busy intersection. There were no trains at the depot, but several people were walking along Fulton, Broad, and Erie Streets, and at least one wagon, driven by twenty-four-year-old Edward Beardsley and sixteen-year-old Howard Miller, was heading south on Fulton, down the small hill and across the tracks at roughly the same pace as Krist.

George Coyle from nearby Tompkins County was standing just south of the tracks with a group of friends and saw Katie and her sister turn onto Fulton Street. "There's Fred Krist," one of the friends noted, as Krist walked down Fulton from the Warford House to meet the women.

Several others noticed Krist and the sisters as well. Charles Gore of Brooklyn was standing by the first track on the north side of the crossing. Mary Mack had just passed the women on the Erie Street sidewalk. George McDuffee from Athens was also just walking by. Dr. Rufus Harnden was walking down Fulton to the Erie Station to buy a train ticket for that night's sleeper service to Washington, DC.

Krist met the sisters on the east side of Fulton Street near one of the south-side tracks. He took hold of Katie's arm and said, "Katie, you won't go."

"Don't you touch my sister!" Lizzie yelled.[85]

Krist pulled out his revolver, aimed it at Katie's head, and fired.

The sudden loud noise shocked everyone in the vicinity. Katie instantly fell into the coal dust amidst the train tracks.

Lizzie screamed and caught Krist by the arm that held the pistol, but when she saw Katie fall to the ground, she became dazed and loosened her grip. Krist shook his arm free and shot Katie three more times.

After shooting Katie, Krist turned away from the scene and walked a few steps north on Fulton. Police Chief Brooks, having heard the shots, was racing to the scene from the Warford House. Krist noticed Brooks, tossed the gun on the ground, and gave himself up. "Krist looked up and saw me and when he got within four feet he threw the gun and I grabbed him and pulled him back a little and reached down, picked up the gun and put it in my pocket," Brooks explained. He immediately took Krist to a jail cell at the village hall on Broad Street.[86]

Others at the scene also took quick action.

Ed VanNorstrand, a restaurant keeper in the basement of the Exchange Building, on the southeast corner of Broad and Fulton, facing the tracks, was washing dishes when the shots were fired. "I saw three people, a man and two women, talking together on the Lehigh switch," he said. "As I watched them I heard a shot fired and saw one of the girls drop. Then the man fired another shot at the girl as she lay there. The other jumped at him and tried to hold him and he fired two more shots at her, it seemed to me, threw the gun away."[87]

"I jumped out of the wagon," Beardsley recalled, "and went to the girl and picked up her head and put it on the sidewalk. Her face was full of coal ashes and I pushed the coal ashes out of her face. I was directly opposite where the shooting occurred."

Fred Tucker, likely at either his cigar store or one of the local bars, was close enough to have heard the shots, and he raced to the scene right away. Along with Beardsley and Dr. Harnden, Tucker was among the very first on scene to see to Katie's care and help Lizzie. Tucker and the others brought Katie's body to the Carmody house on the southwest corner of the Fulton-Erie intersection.

Katie died about thirty minutes later in the Carmody house, just down the street from her own house.

Within the hour, there was a large gathering at the Waverly jail, as police officers, friends, acquaintances, and reporters congregated, all curious about how and why this had happened. Among them were Fred Tucker and fellow ball player Owen Dunham.

The incident was so shocking that the police did not initially consider the fact that they should lock good old Fred Krist up and keep him away from the public. Instead, he was in a simple jail cell where his friends, the media and the general public could all drop by to see and converse with him. Much of the conversation was reported verbatim in the newspapers.

"My God, Fred," Krist said to Tucker, for instance, "would you ever think of my being here as a murderer?"

"No, I wouldn't, Fred," Tucker replied.

"I did it; yes, I did it," Krist told Tucker, the police justice, news reporters and anyone else who would listen. "They drove me to it–the Tobins. They have tried to keep me away from her, and they have done everything they could to keep me away from her, and I have shot her and it is all right and I expect to suffer for it."

In addition to repeating his lament that the Tobins kept Katie away from him, Krist also implied that they abused her physically. "Katie had begged me to take her away," he explained in one press account, "because her people pounded her and treated her badly."[88]

Later that evening, Krist was finally taken by train to a more secure location, the county jail in Owego, joining Bud Waller and at least one other Waverly convict, Martin Liddy, who had been arrested for "causing a disturbance" on Friday.

"Now I have killed her, the girl I love," he said to J. J. Murphy, a police officer in Owego, "and what will my poor old father and mother say when they hear their son is in a murderer's cell–and my poor sister–she in a convent and I in a murderer's cell."

From the start, many questioned Fred Krist's sanity. Was he innocent of the murder by reason of insanity? The County Sheriff in Owego, for example, reportedly considered Krist so insane that he placed a guard in the jail specifically to prevent Krist from attempting suicide.[89]

News of the murder quickly spread throughout the region and nation, and many lurid headlines drew unwanted attention to the village. "Young Girl Murdered," wrote the *Wilkes-Barre Record*; "Kills Woman He Loved," said the *Brooklyn Daily Eagle*; "Girl Murdered in the Street," declared the *New York Times*; "Shot by Her Lover," wrote the *Topeka Daily Capital*; "Kills a Young Girl," said the *Atlanta Constitution*; "Killed by Her Lover," said the *Daily Review* in Decatur, Illinois; "Woman Shot by Lover," echoed the *Bemidji Pioneer*; "Kills His Lady," stated the *Nebraska State Journal*; "Love Caused a Tragedy," declared the *St. Louis Republic*.

The following Tuesday morning, the ground was white with fresh spring snow[90] as a large number of mourners accompanied Katie Tobin's funeral cortege from the Tobin house to St. James Church. Requiem high mass was said at the church, followed by burial at St. James Cemetery. Six young men served as pallbearers.[91]

St. James Church, at the corner of Chemung and Clark Streets.

"A very large number of friends of the murdered girl were present and the floral offerings were numerous and elaborate," the *Waverly Free Press* reported of the funeral. "The sympathy of the community is with the parents and sisters."[92]

The *Owego Daily Record* reported:

> The church edifice was filled to its utmost capacity by those desirous of expressing their sympathy for the bereaved family and paying a last token of respect to the memory of the deceased. Interment was made at St. James cemetery. At the grave the manifestations of grief were sadly pathetic. Mrs. Donahue, the frail, but heroic little woman who tried to shield her from the assassin's bullet, with tearful eyes gazed intently for a moment into the open grave and then, in agonizing tones, exclaimed "Oh, Katie, I tried to save you, but I couldn't do it." She was led gently away and the earth closed forever over the form she loved so well.[93]

In the wake of the tragedy, local activities went on with an air of dignity and commemoration. The Polyhymnia program on Thursday, for instance, featured several local young ladies on piano and voice and included a especially timely piano solo by hostess Miss Chaffee entitled "The Maiden's Wish."[94] The news reports did not mention if the hostess added the solo at the last minute as a tribute, or if it was a coincidence.

The shock of the scandal and the terrible notoriety threatened to bury Waverly's hopes of becoming a big boomtown. Would the town instead become infamous for violence and vice, or, perhaps even worse, a laughing stock?

CHAPTER 5

Building a New Team

The Tobin murder shocked and then galvanized Fred Tucker and other young businessmen and women in Waverly to come up with activities and programs that would lift the village's spirits. There was an urgent need to have a good, uplifting story to tell. Efforts to lure new businesses and employers with hardy stories of hard-working sober citizens were more important now than ever. Being notorious for a murder involving an illicit love affair and a prospective insanity trial were not good for the village's morale or for business.

This led Fred Tucker and other Waverly "enthusiasts" to canvass the town for interest in creating a new professional baseball team. To avoid the mistakes of 1896, they wanted to be sure they had a large enough subscription from local businessmen to pay for the full season.

Tucker and his fellow enthusiasts had reason to be optimistic. Unlike in 1887 and 1896, there were now two professional leagues with local teams. Elmira started 1900 as part of the Atlantic League, with competitors in Allentown, Jersey City, Newark, Philadelphia, Reading, Scranton, and Wilkes-Barre. Binghamton was part of the New York State League, with competitors in Cortland, Oswego, Troy, Albany, Schenectady, Utica, and Rome. The largest regional cities, Syracuse and Rochester, also had professional teams in the Eastern League that year. The presence of professional teams in nearby cities led to more routine media coverage, better promotion of the sport among likely spectators, and a better talent pool from which to choose to build a club.

Just a few miles north of Waverly, in Ithaca, the Cornell baseball team was gearing up for the season. Hughie Jennings, like former teammate and Waverly star Harry Taylor before him, had made a deal with the university to coach their baseball team in exchange for law school tuition. He worked with the college players from February until mid-April, when he left to join Willie Keeler, Wilbert Robinson and Ned Hanlon on the Brooklyn team. Right from the start, Jennings preached the Orioles brand of inside baseball to the Cornell players, devoting much of his February practices in the Armory to bunting, sliding and throwing.[95] Taylor took time off from his Buffalo law practice to substitute for Jennings at Cornell after his departure. The two would continue to be involved in important baseball business together throughout the season.

Cornell University baseball team. Coach Hughie Jennings top row second from the left.

Before the formal league seasons started, the Elmira and Binghamton squads decided to play each other in a series of exhibition games, which would also serve as a way to see which players were most likely to hang on through the season.

Elmira had done a good job in the off-season attracting players from around the region. Sandy McDougal and George Grant, fresh from their 1899 seasons in the New England League, were among those who traveled to Elmira to join the team at the beginning of the season. McDougal boarded at John Bertram's Palace Hotel at 117 Lake Street with several other ball players, and listed his occupation in the 1900 census as "Baseball player." Grant, on the other hand, brought his wife Bertha with him, and, rather than hang with the rowdy teammates at the hotel, boarded at a quiet family home at 123 Madison Avenue. Grant listed his occupation in the 1900 census as "solderer," but it's not clear from any other sources whether he had soldering work in Elmira, or he simply listed his off-season occupation back home in Taunton. Perhaps Bertha supplied the information on his behalf.

Both McDougal and Grant hoped to capitalize on the same sort of success that Dave Pickett had had in New York. Pickett was back with Binghamton for the 1900 season. Meanwhile, their Taunton teammate William Vought also came to New York for the season, opting for Rome in the New York State League.

On April 24, Pickett's Binghamton club traveled to Elmira and the two squads met at the Maple Avenue Park before eight hundred spectators in the "cold air" for their first game of the exhibition series.

Twenty-one-year-old six-footer Mal Eason started on the mound for Elmira and his catcher was one of McDougal's hotel mates, a twenty-one-year-old from Lynchburg, Virginia, Victor Accorsini. Not only was Accorsini a talented hitter and fielder, he was also one of the very first Italian-Americans active in professional baseball at the time.

Both Grant and McDougal started the game in what for them were slightly unusual positions. Grant was in his familiar center field, but was all the way down to sixth in the batting order. McDougal, meanwhile, was on the bench, waiting for his chance to pitch.

The game began slowly, with each team failing to score until Binghamton scored two in the third inning. Gradually, going into the bottom of the seventh inning, Binghamton built a 12-1 lead. Harry Croft, Eddie Hill and Jim Collopy led the Binghamton hitting attack. Pickett thus far was held hitless, although he scored one run of the runs.

By this time, McDougal had entered the game as relief pitcher, and he quieted the Binghamton bats. He also smacked a double to lead Elmira's ten-run rally in the seventh inning, bringing them to within one run of the lead. Grant and Accorsini each scored, and "the crowd was yelling itself hoarse trying to help Elmira to win," but after the teams traded runs in the ninth, Binghamton prevailed in the contest 13-12.[96]

"At different stages of the game Elmira played fast ball and gave evidence of being able to put up a good game later in the season," the *Daily Gazette* reported, noting that Grant "played a fine game at center field," and that "Accorsini caught a steady game."[97]

In the second game of the series the next day, Elmira traveled to Binghamton. The cold weather kept the crowd down to just 200, but, according to the *Daily Gazette*, "although the wind blew hard and cold, the rooters were a happy lot and cheered the men often."[98]

Grant was back in his familiar lead-off position, and began the game by lacing a "hot liner" to shortstop Harry Croft, who made a strong play to throw Grant out at first. Such was the afternoon for Elmira. Even though Elmira took a 10-3 lead in the top of the fifth against pitcher John Kimble, Binghamton battled back with two runs in the fifth and eleven in the sixth to take a 15-10 lead on the way to a 17-11 victory. Andy Thompson started at pitcher for Elmira, and McDougal did not play. Binghamton center fielder Carlton Molesworth punched three hits and Pickett two to lead Binghamton's attack. Accorsini had three hits for Elmira and Grant had one.[99]

The next day, the two teams met again in Binghamton, with McDougal starting on the mound for Elmira and Farnum for Binghamton. This time, Elmira built a lead and finally held it, winning 9-5. Pickett continued his hot hitting, getting two doubles and a single in a losing cause. Grant had a single and run scored from his leadoff spot for the victors, while Accorsini had a single and three runs scored. Again, the weather was a concern. "The wind made the pitchers wild, but when they located the plate they were effective," the *Daily Gazette* reported. "Elmira out-lucked the Binghamtons in the game."[100]

The weather throughout the region was very poor for baseball that spring. "It was a raw cold day and the wind blew across the diamond with almost the force of a gale at times carrying clouds of dust," the *Daily Gazette* reported on April 27, noting an attendance of just 425 for the fourth game of the series against Binghamton. Accorsini played shortstop in that game and Grant had four hits, including two doubles, but Elmira lost 22-20 in a game that took three hours, a rarity at a time when games had to be completed before dusk.[101]

The next day was no better weather-wise, and Elmira defeated Binghamton 16-10. "The weather is so cold and disagreeable for ball playing that the management refuses to allow the pitchers to let themselves out," the *Daily Gazette* reported. "They are told to simply pitch the ball over the base and depend upon the fielders."[102]

At the conclusion of the exhibition series, cold weather or not, the teams were set for their respective regular season schedules.

Meanwhile, not far from Elmira, Bill Ging was determined to do his best. Although he had signed with Brooklyn, Brooklyn farmed him to Syracuse in the Eastern League in early March,[103] which was the National League's way of reserving Brooklyn's right to retain him. Although he was not on a major league roster, he was unable to sign with another National League club. He remained under contract. This was an example of one of the injustices the Players' Protective Association (PPA) was fighting against, and Ging's only recourse in the meantime was to earn his way back to the major leagues through hard work. The reduction in major league teams from twelve to eight was not deterring him.

On April 26, Ging pitched in relief for Syracuse against Worcester and made a "good showing" despite losing 8-6. He gave up none of the runs, but walked five and only struck out two. Lefty Nick Altrock, who started and gave up the majority of the runs for Syracuse, took the loss.[104] Altrock, then 23 years old, would go on to win 15 and lose 28 for Syracuse in 1900, before embarking on a sixteen-year major league career in Boston, Chicago and Washington. Altrock then became a coach for Washington, and remained for 42 years, the longest consecutive-year tenure for a coach with the same franchise in baseball history. He and Al Schacht, another Washington coach, became widely known in the 1920s and 1930s for their coaching antics and comedy routines.

Ging made his first start for Syracuse just a few days later on May 1, while on the road against Providence. Former Waverly star Ed Dunkle would wind up being Providence's ace in 1900–going 27-13–but Ging did not face him this game. Instead, he went up against twenty-seven-year-old major league veteran Danny Friend.

Friend had no problem with the Syracuse hitters at first, shutting them down for the first four innings. The same could not be said for Ging, unfortunately, as he gave up two runs in the first and three more in the second. His control was better than in his previous appearance on the pitcher's mound, but those five runs were enough for him to earn the loss.

It was an adequate performance that should have earned Ging another start, especially given his successful trial with Boston and two strong campaigns with New London. However, what happened after Ging was relieved set the tone for what followed. Willie Brandt came in to relieve Ging and promptly gave up fifteen runs. In the end, Syracuse lost 20-4. It was an ugly loss.

"Providence hammered both Ging and Brandt all over the lot and piled up twenty runs on Syracuse," said *Sporting Life*. Following the loss, both Ging and Brandt were released and "sent home by Manager [Arthur] Irwin." Had it been a simple 5-4 loss, the story might have been different.

Ging still had options, but his odds of getting back to the majors in 1900 had worsened considerably. "Oswego [in the New York State League] is after Ging," the *Daily Gazette* reported on May 10. "The Oswego team has wired Ging for terms, but as yet has heard nothing from him."[105]

Back in Ging's old Connecticut League, fifty-seven-year-old Jack Chapman made efforts throughout the early spring to improve the Norwich franchise. "Manager Chapman is going ahead in his efforts to organize a team to represent the city, and already signed contacts have been received from [Tommy] Manning, [William] Vought and [Larry] Quinlan," *Sporting Life* reported on March 24. Just one month later, however, Chapman transferred the franchise to Henry Davenport, and by mid-June, he was "out of the game." He had obtained a full-time sales position with H.B. Kirk and Company in New York, a prominent wine and liquor bottler, and decided to focus on that instead of on baseball.

"Manager John C. Chapman, the oldest player, umpire and manager now connected with the national game, except Billy Barnie, has retired to go into other business," *Sporting Life* reported on June 16.[106] By August, the publication's Boston correspondent periodically reported that Chapman was attending games, making comments, and "looking debonair as of yore," but his active day-to-day engagement with baseball appeared to be over.

Chapman's pedigree connected players and teams of many levels and eras, from witnessing legendary pitcher James Creighton's fateful last game on October 14, 1862; to breaking the

Cincinnati Red Stockings 89-game winning streak on June 14, 1870, as a member of the Brooklyn Atlantics; to managing more recent stars like Harry Taylor, John Doran, Charlie Hamburg, Hughie Jennings and Frank Grant. Chapman's baseball network was wide and deep.

Chapman first gained fame as a ball player during the Civil War era, when the organized game was in an early phase, and was far from a mature professional enterprise. Nevertheless, one challenge the eras had in common was finding enough time for working men, women and children to participate in the game. Weekday afternoons were less than ideal for drawing large crowds, especially in poor weather. The best opportunities for finding such game times were on Sundays, when the fewest were expected to work.

Unfortunately for baseball promoters, scheduled Sunday baseball was very controversial. So called "blue laws" that prohibited among other things "gaming and other public sports, exercises or shows" on Sundays had been on the books in New York State since its constitution was created in 1777, and they descended from Puritan laws a century before that. Nevertheless, enforcement was inconsistent, and while many other states had similar laws, they differed in material ways. Sports were permitted in Illinois and Missouri, for example, while they were not in Kansas or Minnesota. Meanwhile, a judge in Ohio in 1897 declared its baseball prohibition unconstitutional.[107]

Support for blue laws was especially prominent in the South (with the exception of some coastal and Texas cities with a heavy Mexican and/or German influence) and in the Northeast, where small-town Protestants "controlled state legislatures" and used that power to impose restrictive laws, even as local machine politicians, more sensitive to the needs of their constituents, could choose to selectively enforce the laws. Sunday baseball was more common in the West and Midwest, where "German communities used their clout to prevent enforcement of the blue laws."[108]

The leaders of Elmira's baseball team wanted to schedule games on Sundays, but did not want to experience the embarrassment of putting themselves, their players and their fans at risk of arrest. There was no question that it was technically illegal under State law, but many other upstate cities, such as Utica, Schenectady, Binghamton and Troy, were not consistently enforcing the laws, so it put Elmira's baseball proponents at a distinct disadvantage.

The battle in Elmira was a microcosm of the larger war, and it was just one of many such battles being waged in towns and courthouses across the country.

The differences in enforcement highlighted the precariousness of the ban, but also enflamed the stubbornness of its supporters, such as the powerful American Sabbath Union, which saw Sunday baseball as a test of whether American culture would successfully withstand foreign influence. While it had been common for decades in America that Sundays were a time for rest and little if any activity, the late-nineteenth-century increases in urbanization, industrialization and immigration brought tolerance for many more diverse ideas of how to best spend the Sabbath, and this included the notion for some that sports were a relatively healthy way to spend the day. Leaders of organizations like the American Sabbath Union, however, characterized these notions as belonging to "Continental Sundays," which they considered to be akin to how Sundays were treated in Catholic and Jewish Europe, in other words, a dangerous foreign anti-American, and anti-English influence.

"Two-thirds of the world's mail is in the English language," Wilbur F. Craft of the Sabbath Reform Bureau sermonized in 1899, "which indicates a corresponding pre-eminence in intelligence and wealth. On the other hand, the Sabbathless and Sabbath breaking nations are poor [in] every way; poor physically—Italy once and France twice in ten years have cut down their standard for soldiers; poor mentally—they have the most vice; poor financially—their workingmen, despite longer hours per day and more days in the week, get the lowest wages; and they are also the worst off politically, vibrating between the extremes of despotism and anarchy, while Sabbath keeping peoples enjoy the golden mien of liberty under law."[109]

Within this broader context, in Elmira and other cities and towns, there raged a continuous debate over Sunday baseball between local Protestant ministers and their followers on the one hand, and baseball promoters, labor unions and businessmen on the other. Due to the issue's complicated relationships to commerce, ethnicity and religion, the political parties were not clearly on one side or the other in 1900, although Democrats tended to be linked to Catholic causes and Republicans to Protestant ones.

Progressive "reform" agitators pursued legislation in New York State to allow Sunday baseball prior to the 1900 season, but the effort failed. Given that widespread night baseball was still an impossibility and that the opportunities to draw large crowds on workdays were meager, baseball proponents continued to agitate for Sunday baseball, and, in many cases, willfully challenged law enforcement to test boundaries.

Local politicians had to steer a careful course, as they did not want to alienate either the ministers or the businesspeople. Responding to rumors of Sunday baseball in Elmira, leading politicians encouraged voluntary compliance. "There will be no Sunday baseball in Elmira," physician and mayor Frank Flood, a Republican, declared at the start of the 1900 season, "if I can prohibit it."[110] Local Elmira self-styled "lovers of baseball," meanwhile, pledged to boycott any Sunday baseball, noting that it is "contrary to law and good morals and the best traditions of our people," and local churchgoers thanked the mayor for his "noble and patriotic stand" in protecting the "American Sabbath."[111]

When voluntary compliance failed, Sabbath protectors demanded enforcement. This put local police forces under unique pressure, as they wanted to do their duty and enforce the law fairly, but many of them were also baseball fans. In addition, police officers were frequently the most competent umpires.

Therefore, when challenged with Sunday baseball enforcement, they would typically announce at the start of the game what they would do in order to avoid on-field confrontations–for instance, stopping the game and arresting just the starting pitchers or the starting battery. That way, they could execute their duties without alienating their ballplayer allies.

One notable illustration of this occurred in Oswego in June of 1900. Just as Andy Roth was about to go to bat at the top of the first on a Sunday afternoon, the local sheriff appeared and stopped the game. "Aw, wait till I get a bat, will you?" Roth asked, familiar with the rule, but frustrated that the sheriff was picking his game and at-bat to enforce it. "The sheriff, who is a fan himself, allowed Roth to hit a high one to the shortstop. The players were then called in from the field and the game was at an end."[112]

Given the mayor's opposition, the Elmira team did not formally challenge the Sunday baseball prohibition in 1900, so scheduled games only Monday through Saturday, thus significantly reducing its potential fan base. This sort of limitation would remain true in most towns throughout the country until Chicago, St. Louis and Cincinnati allowed Sunday baseball in 1902, and the trend spread gradually from there. New York State did not hold its first legal Sunday baseball game until May 4, 1919.[113]

Sunday baseball or not, Elmira's season opened optimistically, as on Thursday, May 3, Elmira defeated Wilkes-Barre 15-6, with McDougal not only demonstrating "masterful pitching," but clouting a triple. Behind McDougal were veteran Billy Bottenus at first base, Jimmy Dean at second, George Smith at shortstop, Peter Haggerty at third, James Grove in left field, George Grant in center field, and Bill Johnston in right field. Former Cortland outfielder Fred Ketchum started in left field for Wilkes-Barre, and former Louisville pitching ace Scott Stratton, now thirty years old, started in right field.[114]

It had been a decade since Louisville won its American Association championship in 1890, and while several of the old

Cyclones—such as Stratton—were still playing professional ball, most, like attorney Harry Taylor, were busy with post-baseball careers. Those who were still playing were in the high minors, but none were left in the majors. In the American League, catcher Jack Ryan was playing for Detroit, pitcher Red Ehret was in Minneapolis, and outfielder Farmer Weaver was with Cleveland. At that point, the American League was still technically considered a minor league.

In the New York State League, Charlie Hamburg and Tim Shinnick started the 1900 season in Oswego. Hamburg had a solid season with Oswego in '99, batting .283, playing first base, and earning the respect and admiration of the hometown fans. He and his roommate, Andy Roth, developed a good rapport both on and off the field, and his comfort in the town led him to find off-season work in a local factory.

Still, back in 1890, there had been twenty-four major league teams. Now there were only eight. It was an ongoing point of contention for the players, especially since a few owners owned multiple professional teams, and they carried the larger economy's monopolistic tendencies into baseball. The political establishment, symbolized by President McKinley, supported the monopolistic status quo, and despite some hot rhetoric, it did not seem likely that William Jennings Bryan or any other Democrat would unseat him in the 1900 general election. Given the low likelihood of a major policy shift in Washington, only a truly strong union–and perhaps some true competition for the National League—would be able to balance the baseball establishment's monopolistic powers.

The movement toward unionizing baseball players was part of similar efforts with the rest of the nation's labor. Manual workers continued to work in treacherous conditions–quarry worker Maurice Powers of New Milford, Pennsylvania, for example, was killed at the Everett Stone Quarry while moving a loaded car of refuse stone in mid-May, 1900, when a chain broke and a large stone fell on him.[115] Meanwhile, farm workers organized to protest what they believed to be unfair pricing by commodities trusts, holding back milk deliveries until they received advances at two cents a gallon, instead of the 1.75 cents they had been receiving.[116]

Closer to home, sixty boilermakers and their apprentices working for the Lehigh Valley Railroad (LVRR) across the border from Waverly in Sayre, Pennsylvania, demanded higher wages, and formally went on strike on May 23. LVRR mechanics in Sayre threatened to join them if replacement boilermakers were brought in.[117] The action threatened to grind Sayre's busy shops to a halt, depress the local economy and put at risk the well-being of the area's working families, not to mention entertainment pursuits like professional baseball.

The cold, wet weather early in the season also contributed to a difficult sports environment, making simple survival challenging for both the Atlantic and the New York State Leagues, as attendance was down across the region. By May 15, teams were losing money and rumors were widespread that the Atlantic League would fold. Between talk of unionizing and financial troubles, players were jumpy.

BY MID-MAY, FRED TUCKER AND HIS FELLOW WAVERLY "enthusiasts" were finally prepared to announce their new independent semi-pro baseball team. According to the May 19 *Waverly Free Press*, Tucker had already collected five hundred dollars for the team, with promises of more, and was planning to open the team's season on Memorial Day. He was already busy putting together the players and the schedule.

"The old circus grounds on Howard Street have been rented and a fence will be put up next week and the diamond prepared," the *Waverly Free Press* reported.[118] The Howard Street Grounds was the same area where the 1896 team played, and was directly across Providence Street from St. James Cemetery where Katie Tobin's graveside ceremony was held. "Two entrances will be made, one on Howard Street and the other on Providence Street," explained the *Waverly Advocate*. "The field will be made into a professional 'skinned' diamond and in view of its central location will prove an ideal place for the National sport to be enjoyed."[119]

"The uniforms of the club will be light gray with red stockings, caps and a large red W on the shirts," the Advocate added, noting that, although the roster was still in development, the players would be comprised of "a fine team of hired men, who are ball players in every sense of the word."[120] Waverly was demonstrating that it had moved past the Tobin murder, and was eager to welcome its new baseball team. Memorial Day would feature a double-header against the semi-pro team from nearby Athens, Pennsylvania, with a morning game in Waverly and an afternoon game in Athens.

Tucker's efforts at attracting excellent players bore fruit before the season even started, when he not only persuaded his pal Owen Dunham and other locals to join, but signed veteran professional Bill Heine to be the team's captain and second baseman.

Bill Heine did not want to play too far from his Elmira home, as his wife, Ellen, was pregnant with their third child. As he had done throughout the late 1890s, Heine sorted through his baseball options, seeking to be either a player or a manager. Although the major leagues were now further away for him than ever, at age thirty-two, he knew he still had plenty of valuable skills and experience to offer. Tucker's desire to have a strong family-friendly team was the perfect fit for him.

BILL HEINE

A teammate and/or opponent of some of baseball's greatest 1890s superstars, Elmira native Bill Heine was exactly the sort of smart, well-traveled, hard-hitting veteran Waverly needed to establish its credibility as a baseball destination. Portrait by Gary Cieradkowski.

Heine and Tucker had a lot in common. They were both enterprising young men with business interests beyond baseball. Heine's skill and experience also brought immediate credibility to the Waverly roster. Having competed with and against some of the biggest stars of the game during the course of his decade-plus career in professional baseball–including John McGraw, Larry Lajoie, Willie Keeler, Jimmy Collins, and Honus Wagner–the thirty-two-year-old Heine would provide much of the maturity and veteran know-how an otherwise young semi-pro team would need.

Waverly's Memorial Day ceremonies "were in every way fitting and appropriate. The day dawned somewhat threateningly, but the slight showers which fell during the morning only tended to cool the air and the afternoon was as beautiful as could be desired."

The festivities were typical for small towns at the time and hardly distinguishable from such events today, starting at the city park with patriotic music from the Waverly City Band, general orders to the Grand Army of the Republic, the singing of "The Star Spangled Banner," a prayer, a reading of the Gettysburg Address, a boys' choir singing "The Battle Hymn of the Republic," a patriotic speech from John R. Murray of Sayre, a chorus of "America" and another selection from the band, directed by Layton Sickler.[121] A large number of schoolchildren clutching flowers then paraded down Providence Street with the band from the park to the cemetery, "where the graves of the deceased were decorated," accompanied by more band music. "Many private residences in town were handsomely decorated and some of the business blocks were adorned with the national colors," the *Free Press* noted.

From there, the band proceeded across Providence Street to lead the Athens and Waverly players onto the Howard Street Grounds for the first baseball game of the season. "A goodly attendance of enthusiastic spectators" greeted the entourage as they made their way onto the field and warmed up. Tucker started on the mound for Waverly, with Tim Connelly at catcher, Tom Dwyer at first base, Bill Heine at second, Hamilton at shortstop, "Reddy" Callahan at third, and an outfield of "Dell" Hughes, Frank LeBaron and Owen Dunham.

Tucker's pitching was highly effective, and he completely shut down the Athens hitters, "pitching with a vim that was invincible," the *Advocate* reported. "He showed terrific speed, excellent control and had the Athenians 'shooting ducks' throughout the game."[122]

Opposing Waverly on the mound that day for Athens, however, was no slouch either. Elmiran Bill Ging, fresh from his stint with Syracuse, was keeping his arm in shape with Athens while awaiting a call from Jersey City in the Central League.

Ging and Tucker battled throughout the morning, but Waverly's timely hitting and some shaky Athens fielding led to six Waverly runs, and a 6-0 Waverly win.

That afternoon, the teams played their second game of the day, this time in Athens. Tucker started Polhamus at pitcher, and Ging started on the mound again for Athens. This time, Ging had better fortune, shutting Waverly out and securing a 2-0 victory that ended after just five-and-one-half innings, due to a ground rule dispute.

It was a strong start to the baseball season, and Tucker was encouraged. The team's first Saturday game was coming up, and Tucker looked forward to another large crowd. The whole town was excited about the season, and Tucker was on Park Avenue in town with friends the day after the double-header, likely talking about the team, when they heard a commotion.

Just up the street, the horse pulling the Wells Fargo express delivery wagon was running away without its driver, and barreling toward the bustling stores, wagons, streetcars and pedestrians on Broad Street.

Envisioning disaster, the group raced into the street to calm the horse and slow the runaway wagon, but this only prompted the horse to panic more and the wagon to careen more recklessly out of control. As the horse and wagon increased speed down the street, Tucker took an angle and raced ahead, jumping into the wagon and hitting the brakes just as it neared the streetcar tracks. "F.F. Tucker jumped in the wagon and stopped it on Broad Street" the *Free Press* noted.[123]

Undoubtedly relieved to have avoided another local tragedy, Tucker was confident his baseball team would be easier to manage than the express wagon. Taking a page from Ban Johnson's book, he wanted the team to be fast and skillful on the field and gentlemanly off so that it could appeal to both the area's sportsmen and to the respectable class. That way he could avoid the pitfalls of 1896 and summon enough of the right sort of success that would draw the attention of local supporters, and produce large crowds for the games.

For the season's first Saturday game on June 2, Waverly hosted Corning, with Garey pitching for Waverly and Hunt for

Corning. Heine, Tucker, and U. S. Grant "Stoney" McGlynn[124] each spent time as Waverly's catcher. There was relatively little additional detail in local newspapers about the game, and first names were not available in this or subsequent news reports for Garey or Hunt. Unfortunately, the home team lost 9-5.[125]

Meanwhile, the Atlantic League was reorganizing itself in an effort to stay afloat. Elmira, Scranton, Wilkes-Barre, Allentown, and Reading would remain in the league, while Jersey City and Newark were out. "The [general financial] trouble in the two Jersey towns combined with the heavy loss of money caused by the bad weather made the players feel somewhat uneasy about the future," the *Elmira Gazette* explained. League organizers also added Harrisburg.

Given the turmoil in the Atlantic League, Elmira had a gap in its schedule, so they traveled to John McGraw and Hughie Jennings' old school–St. Bonaventure[126]–and defeated the Bonnies 9-5. "McDougal pitched a great game, being especially effective at critical stages," noted the *Elmira Gazette*.

Waverly also took advantage of the schedule gap to coax Elmira into a game, and Elmira accepted, meeting Waverly on the Howard Street Grounds on Monday, June 4. It would be the first meeting between the two teams, and the public fully expected Elmira to dominate their opponents. In the end, Elmira did win 11-7, but Waverly, with a crowd of six hundred spectators, showed itself very well. In addition to Heine, Tucker had added several more critical players, including big-league pitching prospect Bill Ging.[127]

Ging had made the mistake of accepting an offer from Jersey City in the Atlantic League just before the team folded. His experience with Athens and his friendship with Heine led Ging to accept Tucker's offer. With Waverly, he would be able to keep himself in shape and make some money while waiting for another offer. He would also be free to pitch with other teams on occasion. Tucker was certainly glad to have him.

In addition to fine pitching, Ging also helped at the bat that day, pounding a home run over the right field fence. Heine also hit a homer in that direction during the contest. "The right field fence seemed to be the objective point Monday," the *Free Press* said, "and Ging and Heine found the ball hard enough to send it away out of sight over it." Bottenus similarly hit a home run for Elmira.[128]

For Ging, just months after his major league victory over New York for Boston, the Howard Street Grounds were a world away from what he had likely expected–but it was still professional baseball, and, at the age of twenty seven, he was still on the ladder going up. The Waverly crowd size was not yet wholly different from many major league crowds.

Hometown hero Owen Spaulding Dunham, a twenty-three-year-old sign painter who lived with his parents James (a wagon maker) and Mary at 409 Broad Street, played with Tucker on the 1896 team, but perhaps felt a bit intimidated in the midst of the new out-of-town talent. Fortunately, he received encouraging kudos from his friends at the *Free Press*: "Dunham won the applause of all by his fine playing Monday. With the exception of one play in holding the ball too long in right field, he played without error."[129]

It's likely that banker Percy Lang and other veterans from Waverly's old 1887 and 1896 teams were on hand. Lang, born in 1861 in Waverly, graduated from Yale in 1885, where he played both baseball and football. He played shortstop for the 1887 Waverly team and was President of the Waverly Athletic Club for the 1896 season. In addition to his involvement in baseball, Lang often served as a referee at local college football games.[130] Others on the 1887 team included former major leaguer John Clapp, from Ithaca, and future major leaguer Harry Taylor, from Halsey Valley.

The Warford House's African-American porter, Charles Boggs, also likely made it, given that he was a notoriously vocal supporter of the team. Born in New York State in 1867 of Maryland-born parents, Boggs was well known for his regular attendance at game and his deep bass voice shouting encouragement to the players. He had been associated with local baseball for years, even occasionally umpiring games for Waverly's high school team. On one such occasion in 1893, Boggs "had the misfortune to have a ball thrown through the crown of his derby hat." To compensate Boggs, "the boys bought him a new 'dicer.'"[131]

THERE WERE MANY ADVANTAGES TO RUNNING A NON-LEAGUE-affiliated semi-pro baseball team. For one thing, the organizers had complete freedom to build whatever schedule they wanted to maximize competitive interest and bring in revenue. For another, players could be paid on a per-game, non-contract basis and could theoretically be pulled from anywhere each game.

There were also many disadvantages. Most notably, scheduling for a non-affiliated team required expert organizational skills. For example, John Bright of the Cuban Giants, worked out an elaborate system for scheduling games and coordinating travel schedules. In addition, independent teams had to continuously compete with the affiliated league teams—where seasonal contracts provided players with more security—for the best available players.

In light of the turmoil in the minor leagues, the National League's monopoly on the major leagues, and the decrease in the number of major league teams, 1900 was an ideal time to put together a top-notch semi-pro team, provided enough good players could be attracted and enough competitive games scheduled.

This was what Tucker set out to do as Waverly's season got underway. The Howard Street Grounds baseball diamond was close enough to the railroad station to be convenient for visiting teams and was reportedly "one of the finest in this section." The diamond's new grandstand was similarly said to be "first-class in every respect,"[132] so Waverly had a home field that could attract good competition. Tucker had Heine, Ging and several other top players on board—at least until they were lured back to league teams. Now he needed to see what other talent might spring loose. In the meantime, he needed the team to build a winning reputation–and quickly.

Securing the field from fence-hoppers to maximize revenue was also a concern. The *Free Press* suggested, "A couple of strands of barbed wire should be strung along the top of the fence and then connected with an electric machine. People who would be very angry if accused of stealing a quarter seem to have no scruples against stealing the price of admission from the management."[133]

Within a few days of Waverly's loss to Elmira, Tucker found more available talent – as the Elmira team disbanded, along with the rest of the Atlantic League. The break-up resulted in legal wrangling, as George Grant and several other players took Manager Smith and the Elmira club ownership to court in order to collect back pay. They won a judgment of $386.26 on June 19, and by that time had scattered to several ball clubs.[134] Several went to the New York State League: Tom Murphy to Binghamton; Carlton Molesworth to Schenectady; Billy Bottenus to Oswego; and Jimmy Dean and Mal Eason to Cortland.

Several others stayed in the immediate local area, as Waverly's success to date was sufficient to attract the services of three of Elmira's best players: catcher Victor Accorsini, pitcher Jack Barnett, and outfielder George Grant.

VIC ACCORSINI

One of professional baseball's earliest Italian-American players, Vic Accorsini was a highly regarded young catcher with tremendous potential and a reputation for toughness. Portrait by Gary Cieradkowski.

Victor Joseph "Vic" Accorsini was born in Atlanta, Georgia, in 1878. His father was born in Italy and his mother, in England. Vic's younger brother Leo also played professional baseball. In the summer of 1900, in addition to McDougal, Accorsini was rooming with fellow players Dean, Bottenus, Molesworth, Al Rosenbach and Haggerty at the Palace Hotel in Elmira. Former Elmira manager Harry C. Smith also roomed there.

Accorsini was a contemporary of the first Italian-American major leaguer, Ed Abbaticchio, a native of Latrobe, Pennsylvania. Accorsini and Abbaticchio would later be minor league teammates in Nashville.

John Francis "Jack" Barnett was born in 1872 in Elmira to Irish immigrant parents Jeremiah and Ellen. Barnett pitched for several years in both the Western and Eastern Leagues, including for the 1892 champion Binghamton club. He was very good long-term friends with fellow Elmiran and new teammate Bill Heine.

Given Grant's many years of success in the New England League, attracting him, even if for a brief time, was particularly beneficial to Waverly's team-building efforts. With such a roster of experienced professional players, Waverly was shaping into an unusually strong semi-pro team.

Grant, and Accorsini were in the line-up for Waverly's game against Reading on June 12, which turned out to be a 10-7 Waverly victory in front of a crowd of five hundred. Barnett started in the box for Waverly and secured the win. Also on the team for the game were William "Dell" Hughes, James O'Neil, and Frank LeBaron. The umpire, listed in the papers as "Waller," was likely Bud Waller, a veteran of the 1896 team, fresh out of jail.[135]

William "Dell" Hughes was born in 1877 and grew up in the Elmira area. His father, Patrick, a day laborer, was born in Ireland in 1849, and his mother, Margaret, was born in New York. Unlike McDougal, Accorsini, Heine, Barnett, and many of the other Waverly players, who, in the 1900 census listed their occupation as some variation of "baseball player," Hughes listed his as "tobacco sizer."

James O'Neil has a very similar background as Hughes. He was born in New York in 1877 and grew up in Syracuse. His father, Thomas, a dealer of coal and wood, was born in Ireland in 1848 and came to the U.S. in 1870. His mother, Emma, was born in 1858 in New York. According to the 1900 census, James resided with his family at 209 Milton Avenue and had three sisters: Mary, Margaret, and Emma. He listed his occupation as "Baseball Player."

After playing infield for several seasons with the Syracuse Shamrocks, James O'Neil played exceptional shortstop for Waverly and contributed many clutch hits. Portrait by Gary Cieradkowski.

Frank J. LeBaron (also sometimes spelled "LeBarron") was born in 1876 and grew up the son of a stonemason in Binghamton. In the 1900 census, he lived with his parents and his sister's family at 26 Cedar Street, and listed himself as a "shoemaker," even though he had played for Auburn and Troy in the New York State League in 1899. He would in later years become an Attendant at the Binghamton State Hospital, and play outfield on its baseball team.

Reading and Waverly met again on the Howard Street Grounds the next day, June 13, and Waverly won again, 7-2. "Tucker was in the box, and played a fine game, there being eleven strike-outs to his credit and his support was almost errorless," according to the *Free Press*.[136]

Waverly traveled to Canisteo on Thursday and won 11-4; it was reportedly Canisteo's first loss of the season. Meanwhile, boxing champion James J. "Gentleman Jim" Corbett arrived in

Waverly on Friday to play first base in its Friday rematch against Canisteo.[137] The thirty-three-year-old Corbett, world-famous for knocking out John L. Sullivan to win the World Heavyweight Championship in 1892, had been dethroned in 1897 by Bob Fitzsimmons. On May 11, he had valiantly attempted to regain his crown in a bruising battle with James J. Jeffries, but was knocked out in the twenty-third round. Now, just over a month later, managed by his younger brother, Joe, an ex-big-league pitcher who had spent time with John McGraw on the Orioles, Corbett was traveling the baseball circuit as a celebrity guest star earning money, promoting the sport and enjoying the adulation of his fans.

Waverly was just 5-5 at this point, but the arrival of so many former Atlantic League stars—plus Corbett—pumped up Waverly's baseball enthusiasts. Their regular starting line-up was set now: Accorsini at catcher; Dwyer, Heine, O'Neil and Grant in the infield; and LeBaron, Hughes and Tucker, Dunham or a resting pitcher in the outfield.

The excitement even drowned out Fred Krist's latest statement from his Owego jail cell, printed in part in the *Free Press* on Saturday morning: "Friends tell me that the people of Waverly think the reason I killed Katie Tobin was that she gave me up and would not keep company with me any longer… Katie did not give me up nor did she do the least act against me, neither did we quarrel or dispute. We parted happy as everything was going to suit both… Why did I kill Katie? Because my sorrow and disappointment at being frustrated made me uncontrollable…. She told me she would rather die than be separated from me."[138] Speculation ran the gamut as to whether Krist's attorneys would pursue an insanity defense at his upcoming trial, which could drag his case out for months.

Notwithstanding the Tobin tragedy and upcoming trial, Waverly's rematch against Canisteo on Friday, June 15 was a huge success. Gatekeepers reported an attendance of 1,800, in large part due to Corbett's celebrity presence, and Waverly scored fourteen runs in the first two innings to coast to a 16-8 victory behind Tucker's pitching and hitting—a triple and a home run. Corbett chipped in with a double and played an errorless first base. "The kodak fiend was there in all his glory and snapshots of the famous fighter are now in many a collection of photos," the *Free Press* said.[139]

The next day, Waverly traveled to Hammondsport and won 17-7. The Waverly City Band, accompanied by fireworks, met the team when it returned to town in the evening.

On Wednesday, June 20, Waverly hosted Lestershire and won 13-5 before a crowd of 250. By this time, ex-major leaguer Sandy McDougal, likely persuaded by his old teammate Grant, had also joined Tucker's team. Lestershire, meanwhile, was led by fellow New England League veteran Dave Pickett, now being retained by the Lestershire team in exchange for a regular job at the local shoe factory.[140] McDougal pitched against Pickett's team and earned the win, bringing Waverly's season record to 9-5.

On Monday, June 25, Waverly defeated Lestershire again, 18-17, with Tucker victorious. Around this time, eighteen-year-old future big leaguer Frank "Wildfire" Schulte, a native of Cochecton—with Lestershire connections—joined the Waverly squad.[141] Schulte and Pickett each played primarily for Lestershire during the season, but also periodically filled in for Waverly and other teams.

Waverly's winning ways continued: on Wednesday, Waverly hosted Hammondsport and won 14-0 thanks to Barnett's shutout pitching, and the next day, they traveled to Hammondsport to win 7-4.

In the midst of the winning streak, the Waverly players looked to promote civic good will and help their fellow working-men, most notably the striking boilermakers and their families in Sayre who had been off the job since May 23, and were in need of groceries and other basics. Although there had as yet been no reported violence associated with the strike, tensions were high. Two weeks earlier, the Lehigh Valley Railroad (LVRR) attempted to hire replacements, "but when they learned that they were expected to be 'scabs' they refused to go to work and are reported to have left town." In the meantime, the LVRR reduced the weekly shops' overall workload to just eighteen hours, putting financial pressure on even more workers and their families.[142] To support the strikers and their families in this environment, Waverly scheduled and promoted a Saturday benefit game on June 30, hosting Moravia. The promotion helped pump up the Saturday crowd, and raised money for the strikers despite challenging weather conditions. Waverly defeated Moravia in the game 13-0, as Tom Dwyer hit a double and Heine and LeBaron hit home runs to support Tucker's shutout. "There was a large crowd present, and both spectators and players suffered from the clouds of dust which swept across the field" due to the wind, the *Free Press* reported.

Fortunately for all parties involved, that same day while the Saturday game was underway, "the last details of the final settlement" of the strike "on amicable and satisfactory" terms were reached between the LVRR and the boilermakers, allowing the latter to return to work starting Monday.[143]

First baseman Dwyer was playing particularly well in this stretch. Against Moravia on Saturday, for instance, he ripped three hits and participated in three double plays, including a difficult 3-4-3 where he had to be both fleet-footed and sure-handed enough to make and retrieve timely throws. He was born in 1870 in Ireland and immigrated to the U.S. as a child in 1877. In the 1900 census, he and his wife, Lillie, were rooming with a family at 62 Lewis Street in Binghamton, and he listed his occupation as "Ballplaying Professional."

TOM DWYER

Born in Ireland and brought to the U.S. as a child, Tom Dwyer was a heavy hitting first baseman, who, like James O'Neil, had prior experience with the Syracuse Shamrocks. Portrait by Gary Cieradkowski.

On July 4, Waverly played Athens in a much anticipated holiday double-header. The first game was at Athens, and Waverly won 4-2 thanks to Barnett's pitching. Hughes, Accorsini, O'Neil, and Tim Hanna helped Waverly's cause, each hitting doubles. In the second game, 1,500 spectators showed up at the Waverly diamond to watch the hometown team win, again with a score of 4-2. Sandy McDougal pitched for Waverly, and, in an odd favor to the visitors–not altogether unusual in semi-pro ball–Ging pitched for Athens. Heine, Dwyer, LeBaron, and Hughes each hit doubles for Waverly.[144] The holiday sweep of Athens brought Waverly's season record to an impressive 15-5.

An additional game—against Binghamton—scheduled for that week was called off on account of rain. Due to the storms, "much damage was done in Chemung and vicinity."[145] The storms were severe enough to spook local animals, as on July 6, a local newspaper reported, that a "horse belonging to Dr. J. T. Tucker ran away yesterday resulting in a badly smashed buggy."[146]

Athens and Waverly met again at Athens on July 7, with Waverly again victorious, this time 5-3. Barnett started for Waverly and earned the victory.[147]

On July 10, Waverly hosted a crowd of about five hundred at the Howard Street Grounds against "the crack Weedsport team" and won 9-3. "Barnett's splendid work in the box was a feature of the game, and the batting by the locals was first-class, as usual," the *Free Press* reported. Grant homered for Waverly, while McDougal and Dwyer slugged doubles.[148] The next day, Waverly defeated Weedsport again, 10-7, bringing the team's record against a combination of league and semi-pro teams to 18-5.

That evening, Waverly welcomed its first "locomobile" when the president of the Syracuse Automobile Company drove the vehicle 110 miles from Syracuse to Waverly in eight hours and presented it to Dr. E. Gamble. "It is of the Stanhope pattern, using steam as a motive power and is very handsome," the *Free Press* said. "Its steering gear is much better than any seen in Waverly before and it is strictly up-to-date in every particular."[149]

The winning ways continued.

On Saturday July 14, Waverly again hosted Athens, though this time before a much smaller crowd of just fifty spectators, and won handily, 5-2. Ging pitched for Athens again and took the loss. Waverly's line-up featured O'Neil at shortstop, Heine at second base, Grant at third base, Dwyer at first base, Accorsini at catcher, LeBaron in center field, Barnett in right field, Tucker in left field, and McDougal pitching.[150] Unfortunately, substitute player Owen Dunham was knocked out of action for a bit after accidentally cutting two fingers of his right hand in an electric fan during an animated baseball discussion at Tucker's cigar store,[151] but the starting line-up was powerful, especially for a semi-pro team, and boasted an unusual depth of experienced professional pitching.

According to the *Elmira Daily Gazette*, the left fielder for Athens was named "Setley," likely the same "Wild Bill" Setley who played in the region in the mid-1890s and starred for Canandaigua in 1898. Like Schulte and Pickett, Setley's main team in 1900 was Lestershire, but this did not prevent him from periodically playing elsewhere when the money and scheduling were right.

On July 20, Waverly defeated Hammondsport 9-5 in Bath, and "betting on the game was lively with the Waverly team the favorite."[152]

On July 24, Waverly defeated Lestershire on the Howard Street Grounds 7-4, with Barnett pitching for Waverly and Ging for Lestershire. In addition to Ging, the Lestershire line-up was stacked with players with major league connections: Frank Schulte played center field, Harry Lumley played shortstop, and Pickett played left field. Lestershire's line-up that day also featured Wild Bill Setley at second base and a right fielder named "Johnson,"[153] most likely George F. Johnson's son, George W. Johnson, who at that time had been "put to work" in his father's shoe factory.[154]

1900 Lestershire team. Front row (L-R): Setley, Schulte and Pierce. Second row (L-R): E. M. Kain, George F. Johnson, W. G. Faatz and John Schulte. Third row (L-R): Manning, Lumley, J. L. Derby, Foster and D. Scudder. Fourth row (L-R): Quinn, George W. Johnson, W. Scudder, Pickett, Hayes and Castleman.

Although they did eventually lose a game to Athens and to several other teams along the way, Waverly's season continued to be extremely successful. Their star players were being kept busy and were adequately paid–even more importantly, the game schedule was exciting enough to keep the crowds coming and the team profitable. Even a 5-4 loss on July 26 to the barnstorming Cuban Giants, playing without Sol White, who was touring with the Chicago Columbia Giants, and without Frank Grant, who may have been injured, failed to dampen their enthusiasm. A crowd of 1,000 saw what the *Advocate* described as an exciting close game, as Waverly gave up the late go-ahead run on Heine's throwing error and made the last out with the tying run in scoring position. Tucker took the loss for Waverly and the Giants' Joe Green earned the victory.

At the very end of July, however, Waverly received a surprise when Oswego moved its New York State League franchise to Elmira. Although the Atlantic League had folded, the New York State League was still going strong in Binghamton, Cortland, and other nearby towns. Now there would be a new professional team in Elmira.

The return of professional baseball in Elmira meant some of Waverly's veteran players might prefer to play there, which would mean Waverly's stable line-up might turn over, disappointing fans who had become accustomed to the players. The Elmira media sounded confident of such, and on July 31, Grant and Accorsini joined Charlie Hamburg and the rest of the new Elmira team in defeating Binghamton 9-8.[155] *The Waverly Free Press* explained that Grant and Accorsini only "assisted" Elmira: "The Elmira papers had them all engaged for Elmira, but they are loyal to Waverly and are still connected with our crack team."[156]

In this atmosphere, many wondered: would Waverly be able to hold onto its star players? The *Gazette* only added fuel to the fire, speculating: "It is expected that McDougal will be signed to twirl for Elmira."[157]

Elmira and Binghamton met again in a double-header before a crowd of six hundred on August 2; Binghamton won the first game, 13-2, and Elmira, the second, 10-4. Ernest Crabill defeated Frank Carriveau and twenty-four-year-old George Lee in the first game, and Lee came back to defeat Viau in the second. Bottenus and Hamburg were both hitless for Elmira in the first game, but they came back in the second game to get four hits between them.[158]

That same afternoon, also before a crowd of six hundred, Waverly defeated Athens again on its semi-pro schedule, this time 11-2. Ging pitched for Athens and Barnett for Waverly.[159] "Barnett had elegant control of the ball," the *Free Press* said, "no one getting a pass to first. Heine's running one-hand capture of a grounder in the last inning was the star feature of the game, he recovered himself in time to throw the runner out at first."[160]

This time, none of the Waverly players appeared with the Elmira team, as they were busy in the game against Athens; the integrity of the Waverly team appeared to be safe for the moment. Tucker was holding them together. Since the crowd sizes were identical, there was no apparent economic difference between the towns, despite the fact that Waverly's population was much smaller and its team was only semi-pro.

Nevertheless, it remained to be seen if these crowds were sustainable during the humid days of August. Fortunately, the Waverly civic community continued to be very supportive of the team, and on Saturday, August 4, following a 16-6 win over Athens, the Waverly City Band put on a benefit concert at the park that "was thoroughly appreciated by a very large crowd of people." The City Band furnished the music, while members of the Waverly baseball team dispensed the ice cream. "The music was fine and so was the cream. The players will receive about $20 as the result of the generous patronage accorded the tables."[161]

On August 8, Waverly hosted Athens once again and won 5-2. McDougal started for Waverly, and Ging, for Athens. McDougal's "superb control of the ball brought him out of a deep hole in the fourth inning in which his two passes to first and Schenck's hard-driven hit had placed him," the *Free Press* explained. "McDougal pitched good ball, Schenck making all but one of the visitors' hits," the *Gazette* reported. "Heine and Hanna, at second for each team, played great ball." Unfortunately, attendance was merely 350.

On Thursday, August 9, Waverly traveled to Hammondsport for its seventh contest of the season with the local crack team. Waverly had won five games in a row against Hammondsport, but local fans thought they had a secret weapon: newly appointed player-union lawyer Harry Taylor. Taylor was a regular summer vacationer in Hammondsport, the home of his mother's sister. The previous summer while on vacation, Taylor had played first base in a game against Rochester. Would the former star first-baseman be persuaded to compete against his old Waverly team?

The Waverly newspapers carried no stories about such speculation, but the *Hammondsport Herald*, doubtless rooting for its hometown team, was hopeful.

Taylor was in town at the time and was asked if he would play. As the teams warmed up that afternoon, many fans eagerly awaited the lanky ex-major leaguer, seeking his presence on the field. It was a great opportunity for Taylor to relive his diamond exploits, particularly given it was against his old team. In the end, however, he did not play. He may have attended the game, but, according to the *Herald*, he "could not be prevailed upon to lend a helping hand to our local team in trying to defeat Waverly." Waverly went on to win 10-4.[162]

Despite the winning record, Waverly's recent home attendance was not sufficient to meet expenses, and, unlike in 1896 when the team ran a significant deficit, Tucker was committed to keeping the team in the black. On August 11, the *Free Press* announced that Tucker was planning to end the season and release the players at the end of the week to avoid losing any money. He did not have to "fold" the team like he would if it were a fully professional league team, and he could resume play any time he could get the players back together. That day, Waverly played against Athens at Elmira's Maple Avenue diamond and won 17-10, with Barnett getting the win, and Ging, once again putting in innings for Athens, the loss. Waverly players Hanna and Schulte also played for Athens in the "uninteresting contest," at which the *Gazette* and *Free Press* reported an attendance of just two hundred.[163]

The *Free Press* stated:

> The attendance has perceptibly fallen off at the past few games, and as it is evident that the Waverly people have about gone the limit in patronage, probably the wisest course is to discontinue. The team has been an expensive one, costing about $225 per week. It is not a dollar behind, however, and every debt is paid–a striking difference from the ending of the baseball venture four years ago.
>
> The team has been composed of players who were gentlemen in every sense of the word. No rowdyism or boisterous manners, but quiet gentlemanly behavior has marked every one of them and they have put up a first-class article of ball. Their many friends in Waverly will regret to see them leave.[164]

The *Free Press* noted that the team's record was 34-6 and the *Gazette* cited it as 29-9.[165] Tucker "is deserving of much credit. The team has been a good advertisement for Waverly as its fame has gone abroad from Buffalo to Albany, and from Rochester to Philadelphia."[166] This was a significant improvement over the town's situation right after the Tobin murder, but it was cause for concern if the season did not continue long into the fall. Fred Krist's trial, originally scheduled for the first week of September, was being postponed to November, which gave the town a reprieve, but better baseball news would be a more positive counter to the trial's impact.[167]

"The season closed in a blaze of glory," the *Gazette* reported. "Fans would like to see the team remain, but the team will disband rather than run in debt."[168]

Despite the financial concerns and the public announcement, Tucker changed his mind within a few days and kept the team going. His primary concern had been that there might not be enough other semi-pro teams to play profitable late-summer games, but he was finding there were enough teams after all. In fact, the team's success brought new scheduling opportunities, with both local and barnstorming opponents. Unfortunately, however, several of the players left in the midst of the confusion, with Grant heading to Elmira and McDougal to Hammondsport.

Tucker cranked the team back up on August 16, with an 11-2 home victory over Moravia. Two days later, on Saturday, August 18, Waverly hosted the team from Susquehanna and won 6-4 before a healthy crowd of eight hundred. "The Susquehanna baseball team came to Waverly accompanied by a large delegation of rooters," the *Free Press* reported. "The most of the latter were on the Susquehanna shop excursion to Elmira," meaning presumably that they originally intended to go all the way to Elmira for shopping, "but the train slacked speed enough at this station to allow them to get off," perhaps at the urging of the players. "The game was called shortly after three o'clock and it was lively enough so far as enthusiasm was concerned." Barnett pitched for Waverly, and Duffy, for Susquehanna.[169]

On August 20, Waverly traveled to Bath for two more games against Hammondsport–a 14-4 victory in the first game, and a 5-4 loss in the second game on August 21.[170] After seven straight defeats, Hammondsport had finally defeated Waverly.

Hammondsport's winning streak reached two on Saturday, August 25, when they defeated Waverly again, this time 14-7. Hammondsport had found a more effective secret weapon than Taylor: pitcher Sandy McDougal. "Just whether McDougal was worth having or not was proved to the local management," the *Free Press* said. "McDougal kept the hits against him very well scattered and proved conclusively that he is a valuable man."[171] Afterwards, Tucker reportedly made arrangements for McDougal to return to Waverly for the balance of the season.[172]

The Season's Greatest Game.

Lestershire vs. Waverly.

On the Fair Grounds, Owego,

FRIDAY, Aug. 31, 1900, at 3 p. m.

ADMISSION 25 CENTS; LADIES 10 CTS.
Grand stand 10 cents to all.

Game advertisement from The Owego Daily Gazette.

Lestershire's strong team was an excellent match-up for Waverly during the late summer, and the teams took advantage of their strong reputations by meeting at a variety of venues in an effort to attract larger-than-usual crowds. On Wednesday, August 29, for instance, the two teams met in a tournament at the Newark Valley Fair, with the winner slated to play Moravia on Thursday. Unfortunately, Waverly lost to Lestershire in the contest, 6-4.[173] In an effort to quickly right the ship at this point, Tucker released Frank LeBaron, Waverly's center fielder, in order to make room for McDougal, who was also pitching that week for Osceola.

Following the contest at Newark Valley, on August 31, Waverly and Lestershire met in another special showcase game, this one at the Tioga County Fair in Owego. The game was heavily advertised and attracted a packed Friday crowd at the Owego Fair Grounds. Ging started on the mound for Waverly and George W. Johnson for Lestershire. Ging had no problem handling the Lestershire line-up, giving up just two runs, but Johnson was "knocked off the slab" early by Waverly's hitters, and left in the fifth inning trailing 7-2. Lumley relieved him, but "proved very wild, especially in throwing to bases," and Waverly earned a big 9-2 victory.[174]

The next day, the teams traveled to Lestershire for a rematch, and Waverly lost 10-9 in extra innings.

It was a tough split, but spirits in Waverly remained high, and Tucker remained eager to take on new and stronger competition before the summer was over.

CHAPTER 6

Champions of Western New York

Following the split with Lestershire, Waverly welcomed one of the era's legendary barnstorming teams–the "much heralded" Nebraska Indians–to a morning-afternoon double-header on Labor Day Monday, September 3, at the Howard Street Grounds.

The double-header's publicity, in addition to the expected large crowds, would go a long ways toward burnishing Waverly's reputation as a successful baseball town, especially in competition with neighboring Elmira and Binghamton. A sweep would be even better.

The Indians, led by lawyer and promoter Guy Wilder Green, had been touring the Upper Midwest each year since Green received his law degree from the University of Nebraska in 1897, and in the past two years expanded the trip East to include Pennsylvania and New York. The team was primarily comprised of Native Americans from Nebraska and Kansas tribes, with a few non-Natives sprinkled through their line-up. In addition to playing excellent baseball—their reported 1899 record was 108-35[175]—the Indians were known to entertain spectators with baseball gags, as well as Native and clown costumes, "Indian village" encampments, mock war chants, and the like. Traveling by train, Green's goal was for the Indians to be a baseball team that was akin to the big Wild West Shows that toured the country, like those of Buffalo Bill Cody, the Miller Brothers, Pawnee Bill, and Gordon Lillie. In fact, they often played in tandem with such shows' performances.

Guy Green's Nebraska Indians

Among the Native American players joining Green on the visit to Waverly was the Indians' best player, Jacob Buckheart, a full-blooded Shawnee who stood over six feet tall, had caught for the Carlisle Indian School in 1897, and "had the strength of an ox." [176]

The 1900 Indians were expected to be a big challenge for Waverly. They began their trek from Nebraska to New York in the spring, and by late April were playing college and small town teams in Iowa, complete with public camp outs.

By early June, the Indians arrived in the Chicago area, and among their opponents were the Columbia Giants, a prominent "colored" team that in 1900 featured Sol White. Even though the Giants edged the Indians 4-3, the Indians held White hitless. [177]

The Indians headed next to Pennsylvania in July, with multiple games in the Pittsburgh area, and then proceeded across the state. By August, the Indians were in New York State, and, according to their hometown Nebraska newspapers, their record was formidable – having by the end of the August lost just one game in New York, and having won fourteen of their last fifteen games.[178]

Immediately prior to arriving in Waverly for their Labor Day double-header contest, the Indians played Clifton Springs and won 4-3, bringing their hot streak to fifteen wins out of their last sixteen games.[179]

Fred Tucker and his charges were excited by the opportunity to play the great barnstorming Indians before a hometown Labor Day crowd. This was the showcase Tucker had been hoping for – the chance to prove Waverly belonged among the very best semi-professional teams in the country.

Unfortunately, as both teams warmed up to start the morning game, Tucker could not help but notice that the huge crowd he had hoped for was not materializing. The grand stand was not filling up. Only fair crowds were lining up outside the Providence Street and Howard Street gates, and outside the fences. It seemed more like a Saturday than a holiday. Perhaps more people had to work on Labor Day morning than he expected.

Despite the circumstances, Tucker focused on the matter at hand – defeating the Indians. He tapped reliable Ging to pitch the first game, and set the batting order very similar to other recent games during their hot streak: Hanna led off playing third base, then Heine at second base, McDougal in center field, Dwyer at first base, O'Neil at shortstop, Accorsini at catcher, Hughes in left field, himself in right field and Ging batting ninth.

The Nebraska Indians likely dressed in costume and were sufficiently dark-skinned to pass for Native Americans, but if Waverly's players and the relatively few gathering fans had studied recent box scores or been given the names of that day's line-up, they would have noticed that the team appeared to include many non-natives. Among those missing from the spring rosters were "Good Voiced Elk," "Spotted Crow," "Cochita," "Charging Eagle," and "White Eyes." In their place were players with the last names of Haley in left field, Miner at second base, Osborne at third base, and Anderson in right field. Miner could have been Garfield

Miner, the twenty-year-old son of a Civil War veteran farmer in South Dakota, but the author did not confirm whether he or the others had indigenous ancestry. It is certainly possible. Garfield Miner, for example, wrote "yes" in both the "White" and "Indian Citizen" blocks of his World War I Draft Registration card, so perhaps he and the others were of mixed ancestry.

Among those with confirmed identities were Jacob Buckheart at first base, manager Guy Green, his business partner John D. Smith at catcher, steady twenty-five-year-old Jim Corbett (not the boxer), who was born in Canada and moved to a Nebraska farm as a child, at shortstop, and speedy twenty-four-year-old Albert Ninhan, a full-blooded Oneida tribesman from Wisconsin, in center field.

Warming up to pitch for the Indians was the tall, dark-haired twenty-six-year-old Danny "The Terrible Swede" Salene. Salene's nickname was apt, as his parents were actually from Sweden, arriving first in Orion, Illinois in 1869 and then moving to Axtell, Nebraska. Salene's father Erik was a Grain Dealer in 1880 and a newspaper agent in 1900.

The crowd grew slowly in size and enthusiasm as the game began. Salene and Ging each held most of their opposing batting orders in check through the first few innings. Unfortunately for Salene, O'Neil and Heine tagged him for home runs (O'Neil two and Heine one), and Waverly leveraged the big hits to score nine runs. Ging meanwhile seemed to lull the Indians hitters to sleep by scattering eight hits and giving up only four runs, resulting in a 9-4 Waverly victory. Only Miner, who cracked a home run, had an extra-base hit in the game for the Indians.

The first game was "a very sleepy, listless game," the *Free Press* complained. "Neither team seemed to have any ginger,"[180] contemporaneous slang for energy.

The Indians had very little time to recover from the loss, just their second in New York State, since they needed to prepare for the afternoon game. Both teams planned to use similar line-ups in the second game, with McDougal taking the mound for Waverly and Green for the Indians. The rest of the batting orders were identical, with one exception: batting last and playing right field for Waverly in the second game would be Jack Barnett, normally a pitcher. Tucker also switched himself to second base and Heine to center field to substitute for McDougal taking the mound. Tucker, normally a pitcher, had muffed a fly ball in the first game, so preferred not to take that chance in the second. Heine was more reliable.

As the teams set their line-ups and prepared for the game, the hometown crowd continued to increase. Joining the spectators was the Waverly City Band, which planned to entertain the fans between innings. Unlike the first game, this afternoon contest was shaping up to be a grand civic spectacle. Between the band and the crowd, the players on both sides felt the rising enthusiasm, and put more spring into their steps.

As the game proceeded, the crowd grew larger and more boisterous. The resulting difference in play on the field was palpable – not listless like the first game, but energetic and "brilliant." As McDougal and Green went about their pitches, the fielding support behind both was exceptional, with both teams trading leads up to the top of the sixth inning when the Indians went ahead 5-4. The intensity of each pitch rose as the game grew longer and dusk beckoned.

According to the *Free Press*, the attendance "was the largest ever on the local diamond, it being entirely safe to say that 1,800 people were present." Dwyer and O'Neil led the hitting attack for Waverly, supporting McDougal's pitching.

Entering the bottom of the seventh inning still trailing 5-4, Waverly scored twice to take a 6-5 lead. The teams went scoreless in the eighth, leaving it up to McDougal to close the game out in the ninth.[181]

The Band continued to entertain the crowd between the eighth and ninth innings, but the hometown fans were likely nervous and not paying attention to the music. They were well aware that the top of the Indians' order was due up, meaning McDougal had very little room for error.

An experienced veteran of both the Western and Eastern minor leagues, Elmira native Jack Barnett was a longtime friend of Bill Heine's, and a skilled pitcher who gave Waverly's staff an unusual depth of experience. Portrait by Gary Cieradkowski.

The crowd's jitters were well placed, as McDougal opened the ninth by allowing both Smith and Ninhan to reach base.

With two on and no outs, McDougal now bore down, striking out Corbett and then striking out Haley, who had homered off McDougal earlier in the game.

Now with two outs and two on, the Indians' best player and cleanup hitter Buckheart was due up. This "made the crowd of Waverly rooters nervous."

Miner, who had homered in the first game, was on deck.

Baseball strategy in such situations has changed little in the last hundred-plus years, and this was a tough decision. With a one-run lead, two out and two men on base, most managers would not wish to allow the next batter to reach, thus putting the go-ahead run in scoring position. On the other hand, Buckheart was by far the Indians' best hitter, and do you really want the opponent's best hitter to beat you?

Tucker and McDougal decided to walk Buckheart and pitch to Miner.

Buckheart walked to first and Miner came up to bat.

Now, with the bases loaded and the game in the balance, McDougal again bore down. He and Miner competed intensely for each pitch, with the count gradually growing full – three balls and two strikes.

"With two men out and two men on bases he gave Buckheart a pass," the *Free Press* explained. "Then Miner, who made a home run in the morning game, came up and when the umpire called the second strike and the third ball every one held their breath."

McDougal's pitching had been forcing a lot of ground balls, so to help bolster the infield in the late innings, Tucker had switched himself back to center field and put the slick-fielding veteran Heine back at second base. Now he stood at his center field position and watched the action. His line-up was strong, but there were a few potential holes in moments like this. Hughes was solid in left field but the pitcher Barnett was in right field. In other words, he had himself and Barnett, two pitchers, occupying two-thirds of his outfield at the most critical moment of the season.

Tucker watched from center field as McDougal's next pitch sailed in to Miner. It was over the plate.

Miner swung.

A good healthy crack of the bat. Big fly ball. Headed into right field. Maybe long enough to go over Barnett's head or even go over the fence. From his vantage point in center, Tucker could see the trajectory of the ball and measure Barnett's pursuit.

Barnett raced back at full speed into deep right field.

He reached up just before striking the fence.

And caught the ball.

The game was over, and Waverly had swept the double-header.

"Then a high one went over in Barnett's hands, rested there, and the game was ours," the *Free Press* reported. "There was a vociferous applause and the band played a lively tune."[182]

In his journal entries on the season, Green said the second Waverly game "was one of the closest and most exciting we have ever participated in. The right fielder of the Waverly team pulled down a long fly in the 9th inning that looked good for a home run and so saved the game for his boys."[183]

It was a huge victory for Waverly and its hometown fans, and a fitting exclamation point on a very successful season, especially in front of such a large enthusiastic holiday crowd.

After their stop in Waverly, the Indians went on to play Corning, Avoca, Hammondsport, Livonia, and Tonawanda (at Akron) before turning north to Canada and then back into Michigan and Chicago on their return trip west to Nebraska. By the end of the 1900 season, they reportedly had a 90-53 record.

Green would go on to lead Nebraska Indian tours for several more years, but two of his best 1900 players would play only sporadically in future years. Buckheart played a few more years for Green, but was a farmer in Shawnee, Oklahoma (Indian territory) by 1910. Salene played amateur baseball for teams in Nebraska for a few seasons after 1900, but by 1910 was a bartender in Blue Hill, Nebraska, and by 1920 was a laborer for a coal company in Hastings, Nebraska. Salene eventually moved to Inglewood, California. Corbett settled in Lincoln, Nebraska, and in 1920 worked there as a grocery clerk.[184]

Following its contests with the Nebraska Indians, Waverly met familiar foes Susquehanna, Moravia, and Lestershire during the week, splitting the games but continuing to draw just enough spectators to meet expenses. The team had managed to escape the stigma of folding early—a major success in the semi-professional baseball world—but could this success translate into a regular league schedule? "What will Waverly do with the state League teams?" the *Free Press* asked.

Not all local baseball fans appreciated Waverly's success, however. "The Sayre and Athens spectators are very sore and do not fail to insult the players, the umpire, or the decent people on the grounds whenever possible," the *Free Press* complained.[185]

Meanwhile, New York State League action was winding down, with Utica, Cortland, and Rome at the top of the standings, followed by Schenectady, Albany, Binghamton, Troy, and, in dead last place, Elmira. On September 7, Cortland hosted Elmira and lost 6-5, ending any pennant hopes. Lee earned the win for Elmira, while former Elmiran Mal Eason took the loss for Cortland. George Grant, who continued to stick with Elmira after leaving Waverly, started at shortstop and hit three singles to lead the Elmira attack, while Hamburg chipped in a double, and Bottenus, two singles. Phil Nadeau, who at twenty-eight was still a top prospect, went hitless for Cortland in right field.[186] He was reportedly still deeply impacted by late-summer hay fever, as he had been in the New England League. Cortland finished the season with a 70-42 record, and according to the *Cortland Evening Standard*, "kept its men well paid."

The *Evening Standard* praised the Cortland team and management, despite not winning the league championship:

> [Team President Daniel] Riley may justly feel a pride in the success of the National game in Cortland this year, for Cortland never had such a good exhibition of ball before, nor has there ever been a year when the people were so interested in the game and were more willing to help it through the season."
>
> To Manager [J. D.] Roche , who has had the direct supervision of the team, also belongs a great deal of praise. Under his charge the men have conducted themselves well in all places, and they have been sober and orderly. His policy has been to play the game in a sportsmanlike way and never to leave a play ground unless it was absolutely necessary.
>
> The baseball season has closed and the people are satisfied. The prospects for the game next year were never brighter.[187]

With the NYSL season over, many of the league teams vied for games with the local semi-pros. As a result, Waverly tentatively scheduled games with Rome, Binghamton, Cortland, Schenectady, Utica, and Elmira and published the schedule in the *Free Press*. It was an opportunity for the professionals to pick up some extra money and for the semi-professionals to earn both money and bragging rights.

On Tuesday, September 11, Waverly hosted third-place finisher Rome and lost 3-2. Waverly had released many of its players, so played with a make-shift line-up, putting Barnett at first base, Tucker at second, Heine at shortstop, and Tom "Snibs" O'Hara, a 20-year-old Waverly native whose Irish-born father John worked at the local railroad yard, in center field. "Had the regular team been in the field Waverly would have won with ease," the *Free Press* opined.[188]

The next day, Waverly had originally been scheduled to play both Lestershire and Cortland, but Lestershire was concerned about "threatening" weather and cancelled. Cortland, possibly sharing Lestershire's concern, also cancelled.

The cancellations were disappointing, as Waverly was at the same time hosting New York State's annual convention of the Patriotic Order of the Sons of America, and, despite the threatening weather, was looking forward to ball games to accompany the large parade scheduled for that afternoon. The town was well decorated and "the spirit of patriotism prevailed everywhere."

Fortunately, Binghamton replaced Cortland at the Howard Street Grounds, and it was another close contest. Waverly picked up two runs in the first inning against Ernest Crabill and took their 3-1 lead into the eighth. Ging pitched effectively for Waverly but was unable to hold the lead, and Binghamton tied it up, 3-3. Waverly had only managed three hits at that point, with Heine and Accorsini each clouting doubles. It looked like extra innings and darkness would soon come into play. Then, Tucker smacked a game-winning home run to defeat Binghamton, 4-3.[189]

"The Binghamton fans had no thought of anything but victory when they came here Wednesday," the *Free Press* said, "but the Waverly boys did them up brown,"[190] which was contemporaneous slang for doing something thoroughly well, as in cooking.

Although several games remained on the calendar, the colder weather and school's resumption kept the crowds smaller than had been expected. As a result, most of the games were not played at all. "Two games will be played [against] Rome Saturday afternoon for the price of one–twenty-five cents to all," the *Free Press* announced. "This will be the last baseball in Waverly this season and both will be good exhibitions of the nation game. Go and see them."[191]

Waverly split its September 15th double-header with Rome, losing 9-8 in the first game and winning 3-2 after three innings on account of darkness in the second. Ging pitched the first game for Waverly against veteran George Wheeler for Rome, and Tucker pitched the second against Frank Rudderham. Hughes and McDougal each hit home runs for Waverly in the second game. The *Free Press* reported a "large crowd" was on hand at the Howard Street Grounds for both games.[192]

Waverly played a benefit exhibition on Wednesday, September 19 before their hometown fans. Heine won a homerun derby; Hughes won a ball-throwing contest, followed closely by O'Neil, Accorsini, and Hanna; Dwyer won a hundred-yard handicap race; and O'Neil won a race around the bases. "The players received something over $5 each from the proceeds," the *Free Press* said.[193]

Just three days later, Heine's wife, Ellen, gave birth to their third child and first son, William Henry "Bud" Heine. "It is not fully decided what team he will join," the *Elmira Advertiser* reported. The *Free Press* responded, "If he is as good as his daddy, he can come to Waverly."[194]

Two final games against the barnstorming Cuban X Giants were all that remained on the calendar for the Howard Street Grounds that season. The two-game series was scheduled for September 24 and 25, and a good crowd was expected.

The Cuban X Giants were arguably baseball's hardest working team in 1900. Their season started in early February, with a barnstorming tour of Cuba, playing teams in Havana as well as in smaller towns up and down the island. They returned to the U.S. in mid-April, and immediately began playing teams in the New York City area as well as traveling to play teams throughout New England, Western New York and Pennsylvania, on their way to the Chicago area in mid-June for a second consecutive year of "championship" tournaments against fellow African-American powerhouse barnstorming teams -- the Chicago Columbia Giants, the Chicago Unions, and their arch-rivals the Cuban Giants, now sometimes dubbed the "Genuine Cuban Giants" in an effort to minimize confusion.

Although Frank Grant traveled with the Cuban X Giants to Cuba, he quickly joined the Cuban Giants once the club returned to the U.S., and stuck with them until an injury, fatigue or some other unreported circumstance put him out of action. By the time the Giants arrived in Waverly on July 27, for example, Grant was not in the line-up. Sol White, meanwhile, stuck with the Chicago Columbia Giants for the entire 1900 season. Both players figured prominently for their teams in the 1900 Chicago tournament.

Once the Chicago games were finished in late June, both the Cuban Giants and the Cuban X Giants returned to the Northeast, where they resumed their barnstorming tours. Immediately prior to arriving in Waverly, the X Giants played local teams in the Philadelphia area, including a town team in Chester and a YMCA team sponsored by the Pennsylvania Railroad. At the same time, the Cuban Giants played teams in the New York City area.

Several of the Cuban X Giants who traveled to Cuba in February continued to tour with the team in September, including third baseman Robert Jordan, first baseman Ray Wilson, catcher Clarence Williams, center fielder Andy Jackson, and pitcher/outfielders John Nelson, James Robinson, and Dan McLellan. They were joined by second baseman "Big Bill" Smith and shortstop John Hill on the September 24-25 visit to Waverly.

Having played nearly every day since early February, in addition to entertaining fans with "antics" that demonstrated "a decided talent for the burlesque of the minstrel stage,"[195] the hard-working Cuban X Giants must have been weary when they arrived at the Howard Street Grounds that Monday afternoon, September 24. The thirty-four-year-old Williams, a Harrisburg native and team captain, must have been particularly tired of the daily grind of catching as well as leading many of the team's "antics."

Near the end of a grueling seven-month schedule of road games, longtime captain and catcher Clarence Williams and his Cuban X Giants arrived in Waverly for a late September series, and played extremely well. Portrait by Gary Cieradkowski.

Nevertheless, the X Giants were in excellent game shape for the first contest, edging Waverly 3-2 when "Big Bill" Smith, a thirty-one-year-old 240-pound native of Tennessee, scored the winning run in the ninth on a throwing error by Waverly shortstop O'Neil. Accorsini and Barnett each hit doubles for Waverly. Wilson, a thirty-year-old Pennsylvanian, who, at six feet two inches, towered over many of his teammates, hit a double for the Giants.[196]

In the second game, the next afternoon before a crowd of 350, Nelson took the mound for the Cuban X Giants and Barnett for Waverly. Both were veteran workhorses used to winning big games, and the Giants struck first, scoring two runs in each of the first two innings to take a 4-0 lead. Waverly picked up two runs in the third, and the two teams traded scattered runs the next five innings. Assuming that Waverly batted first in the ninth, the Giants headed into the bottom of the ninth with the score tied 5-5.

This time it was the Giants' hitting rather than a Waverly error that won the game, as Andy Jackson smacked a long single to knock in Smith for the winning run, and a final score of 6-5. Jordan, Wilson, Robinson and Williams each had two hits for the Giants, while Dwyer, Hughes, Tucker and Ging each had multiple hits for Waverly. "It was nobody's game until the ninth inning, when Jackson's long hit brought in Smith and the winning run," the *Free Press* reported. "A feature of the game was the tumble of Williams while trying to get away from first, which afforded Dwyer an easy out. Hughes made a fine catch of a difficult fly in extreme left field."[197]

From Waverly, the Giants traveled roughly sixty miles southwest to Wellsboro, Pennsylvania, just west of Mansfield, for a three-game series with the local team. The games were part of Wellsboro's three-day Athletic Carnival, and crowds of well over 2,000 were expected. Even the famous boxer John L. Sullivan was expected to put in an appearance, as umpire for the Giants games. From Wellsboro, the Giants would head back to the Philadelphia area to finish up their long summer.

The village of Waverly, meanwhile, despite the losses to the Giants, basked in its team's success.

A few days after that final game, the *Free Press* reported:

> The players who have justly earned the title of champions of western New York independent baseball teams have

all gone home except Dwyer, who will play three weeks with the Great Bend team. O'Neil has gone to Syracuse, Heine, Barnett, Hughes and Ging returned to Elmira, Accorsini left Tuesday evening for Lynchburg, Va., Hanna went Wednesday to Lock Haven, Pa., and McDougal is at home in Buffalo, where he went two weeks ago.

The boys have been a great credit to Waverly and have played a first-class game of ball all through. The village has been widely advertised by means of the team and considerable money has been brought to the town on account of the games. The bills of the management have all been paid and there is a good prospect for a winning team again next year. The players say they have been handsomely treated here and have expressed their willingness to come back next year. We want them.[198]

Contrary to its opinion of the 1896 season, when gambling, drinking, financial losses and rumors of throwing games dogged the team, the *Advocate* was full of praise for Waverly's 1900 squad. "People generally have a poor conception of ball players," the *Advocate* said, thinking no doubt of the impression left by some of the '96 players. "Their brains have been filled with pictures of toughs, half drunkards. The players who have worn a "W" on their jackets this summer have proved that the ball player is a gentleman not a tough. They have behaved themselves in a decidedly decent manner while in Waverly, and have won the respect of all who have met them."[199]

According to the September 26th edition of the *Elmira Daily Gazette*, Waverly ended the 1900 season with forty-two wins and sixteen losses, an outstanding .724 winning percentage.[200] Game accounts from a variety of newspapers document a record of forty-two wins and eighteen losses. It is very possible that some of the games were not formally documented, but either way, it was a very successful season both on and off the diamond, and portended even greater success for the 1901 season.

CHAPTER 7

Conservative Shrewdness

The 1900 National League season ended with Brooklyn—comprised of former Orioles Ned Hanlon, Willie Keeler, Joe Kelley, and Hughie Jennings—winning the pennant with a record of 82-54. Pittsburgh was in second place at 79-60, while New York was last at 60-78.

The American League, still a minor league at the time, ended its first season with Chicago winning the pennant with a record of 82-53. Milwaukee finished four games behind them in second, and Minneapolis came in last at 53-86.[201]

Although the American League was a minor league, Ban Johnson planned to change that in 1901, and intended to lure the best players from the National League. "Everybody in baseball felt nervous and ill at ease," John McGraw explained. "Neither the players nor the owners knew exactly which way to jump. That a big change was coming was evident. The problem of all concerned was where to land on the new map."[202]

Meanwhile, the Players' Protective Association (PPA), led by Harry Taylor, Chief Zimmer, Hughie Jennings, Clark Griffith, and Boileryard Clarke, formally announced its campaign to obtain specific changes from organized baseball. "Some radical departures from existing conditions are asked for," the *New York Times* reported on October 14. "The main thing is to get the National

League to accept the propositions. Whether or not the major league will do so is a question of considerable doubt. President Johnson of the American League has agreed to the propositions."

The union's requests, as reported by the *New York Times*, were:

1. No suspension of a player for more than ten days at any one time.

2. Clubs to pay all physicians' fees for incapacitation of a player in actual play.

3. Word "assigns" not to appear in the contract, and all services are to be with the club making a contract and no one else.

4. If the club gets out of the league, the player can terminate the contract for any reason by giving ten days' notice.

5. Clubs agree that they will not sell, buy, "farm," &c., any player, or attempt to do so, or make any arrangement or have any understanding with any other club owner to do so or to "claim" or "select" any player in any way without the player's written consent.

6. No right of reservation for a lesser salary than that provided in the contract for the current year, and no reservation in any one city for more than three seasons or parts of seasons without the player's written consent.

7. A provision for a Board of Arbitration, which shall take up and pass on all differences of every kind that may come up between player and owner, to those decision they must submit, and from whose decision there is no appeal to any court of law.

These requests were clearly a departure from current standard practice, especially in light of the fact that the National League owners had total control over the major league game.

Ban Johnson's agreement to accept these requests on behalf of the new American League was part of his approach to differentiate his league from the National League and to establish his league's viability. It also positioned him favorably with the players, which would in turn help him pull them away from the National League once his franchises were fully established.

"Ban Johnson's organization is very strong with the players," wrote Cincinnati's *Sporting News* correspondent, J. Ed. Grillo. According to Grillo, one anonymous Cincinnati player expressed a common player reaction to the National League's high-handed approach to negotiations: "We are willing to listen to any fair proposition, but if the magnates show that they are going to resort to trickery or a bluffing game, you can bet that they will be ones to suffer, not we."[203]

In the midst of big changes in the baseball world, 1900 was also a presidential election year, and it was shaping up to be another contest between William Jennings Bryan and William McKinley. This time, however, there was an added element of excitement: despite months of demurring, in June, New York Governor Theodore Roosevelt accepted the vice-presidential spot on McKinley's ticket and planned to campaign with his typical gusto.

It was a shockingly fast political rise for young Roosevelt: from New York City police commissioner, to Navy Assistant Secretary, to the Spanish-American War hero of San Juan Hill, to New York governor, to vice-presidential candidate, all in less than four years. He had been a relative unknown just a decade earlier at the Delmonico's dinner celebrating baseball's world tour team in 1889.

Roosevelt's rise was attributable not only to his energy and intelligence, but to the fact that although from an elite family and elite institutions, he was aware of the problems of common working people. This awareness was sown during his days as a New York State Assemblyman, when he was so "shocked" at the "evil" conditions of tenement cigar workers, revealed to him by Samuel Gompers, that he reversed his longtime laissez-faire attitude and in 1883 championed legislation to prohibit cigar making in tenement houses.[204] As his political career developed, he continued to work toward a sensible middle ground between laissez-faire and radicalism. He believed in neither the elite Republican adherence to monopoly capitalism nor the radical populist flirtation with "Socialism." During the 1899 fight over a state franchise tax, for example, while he was New York Governor, Roosevelt explained to Owego native and U.S. Senator Thomas "Boss" Platt his support for the tax as a means to correct evils.

"I do not believe that it is wise or safe for us as a party to take refuge in mere negation and to say that there are no evils to be corrected," he wrote to Platt. "It seems to me that our attitude should be one of correcting the evils," he continued, noting that such action should be directed "against improper corporate influence on the one hand as against demagogy and mob rule on the other."[205]

William McKinley and Theodore Roosevelt campaign poster. From the Library of Congress.

As a result of this approach, he was not fully trusted by either extreme, but especially not trusted by the Republican elite. Many Roosevelt biographers have gone so far as to call Platt and Roosevelt enemies, despite a public truce between the two while Roosevelt was governor. Nevertheless, news reporters at the time, including the esteemed Lincoln Steffens, believed Republican leaders would not allow Roosevelt to have a second term as governor, since "the [party] organization doesn't like Mr. Roosevelt as Governor, neither does [Platt friend and Roosevelt foil] 'Lou' Payn, neither do the corporations. The corporations cannot come out openly to fight him; they have simply served notice on the organization that if he is re-nominated they will not contribute to campaign funds."[206]

Historians generally believe that these elite New York Republicans, particularly Platt and U.S. Representative Benjamin B. Odell, were so anxious to get Roosevelt out of New York that they worked with McKinley stalwart Mark Hanna (who had called Roosevelt a "damned Cowboy")[207] to convince the erstwhile Rough Rider to take the second spot on the presidential ticket and "kick him upstairs," since, as Roosevelt himself said, "As Governor, I can achieve something, but as Vice President I should achieve nothing." The vice presidency, he allegedly complained to Platt, is "not an office in which a man who is still vigorous and not past middle life has much chance of doing anything. As you know, I am of an active nature." He would prefer to remain governor or take a job like William Taft's managing the Philippine occupation.

Owego native and U.S. Senator Thomas "Boss" Platt.

Platt did not publicly acknowledge this motivation, and called such speculation "unthinking and superficial," and "actuated more by mugwump malice than by reason."

"When any one talked about shelving Roosevelt, they simply expose their ignorance of the man," Platt wrote.[208]

When Roosevelt arrived at the Republican's National Convention on June 21 in Philadelphia to second McKinley's nomination and finally accept the Vice Presidential nomination, he was greeted by loud chants of "Teddy, Teddy, Teddy," and a "raucous" chorus of "There'll Be a Hot Time in the Old Town Tonight," the official song of the Rough Riders.[209]

Before Roosevelt was completely on board the McKinley ticket, however, Platt and his sons Frank and Harry, a former Owego ball player,[210] devised a plot to ensure there would be no last-second change of heart at the convention. According to Platt's account:

> "Now I want your promise, that if you are endorsed by the New York caucus, you will not refuse, and that, if you are nominated by the convention, you will run," I added.
>
> Roosevelt showed his teeth, paced up and down the room, and chafed as a horse does under a tight rein and curbed bit.

"Well, Senator Platt," finally returned Roosevelt reluctantly, "I will pledge myself not to formally decline the New York caucus endorsement, but I shall certainly urge the caucus to name another," he added.

"And remember I shall pinch you if I see any signs of your getting up and declining," put in my son.

"All right, you may pinch me as hard as you like," answered Roosevelt, as he and Frank hurried to the caucus.

Just as Dr. Albert Shaw, Frederick W. Holls, Nicholas Murray Butler, and others of Roosevelt's self-constituted friends, clustered about him and whispered audibly: "Say you'll decline if nominated, Governor," my son pinched Roosevelt in the leg and said: "Remember your contract with the Senator, Governor."

Roosevelt kept faith. He ignored the solicitations of Shaw and others and sat down.[211]

Roosevelt may have had neither the trust of the true conservatives in his own party, nor of the Democrats, but he did have a level of vigor and popularity with the voting public and the news media beyond what party leaders expected, which helped his campaign speeches generate at least as much energy and excitement as Bryan's. This level of enthusiasm was critical to attracting enough progressive voters to the Republican cause. Roosevelt promised a middle road for dissatisfied working-class voters who were more progressive than true conservatives, but were not as disruptive as Bryan's followers.

Roosevelt offered a type of practical progressive Republicanism that would likely have attracted a young lawyer like Harry Taylor, who was deep in his own efforts to achieve practical progressive labor improvements with an entrenched monopolistic conservative ownership group.

As he had in 1896, President McKinley stayed at home during the 1900 campaign, giving speeches from his Canton, Ohio, front porch. This was customary at a time when candidates were as likely to "stand" for office as to "run." In fact, James Garfield, standing for President in 1880, allegedly complained that he was expected to "sit cross legged and look wise," rather than actually campaign, as he welcomed supporters to his front porch while others campaigned on his behalf. Not only did this help preserve the candidates' dignity and the power of Democratic and Republican Party bosses, but it was consistent with the general nineteenth century concern Americans had with personal health and safety, especially given the onslaught of infectious diseases like yellow fever, cholera, tuberculosis and typhoid that, in the wake of industrialization and urbanization, caused life expectancy to actually drop from 1790 to 1890.[212] Fear of "consumption" and other mysterious communicable diseases prompted a proliferation of "snake oil" cures throughout the period, until reliable treatments became more commonly available in the twentieth century.[213]

As the public's understanding of germ theory improved, candidates were less fearful of open campaigning, and Bryan in 1896 was the very first Presidential candidate to break tradition, traveling himself across the country by railroad and giving hundreds of inspiring speeches on his own behalf. According to Smithsonian curator Jon Grinspan, this new type of open campaigning was dependent on the corresponding revolution in public health. "Basic hygiene—washing hands, clean drinking water, less spitting—cleaned up society well before antibiotics," he explained. "It's no coincidence that political ads and soap ads both filled newspapers around 1890. Presidents really were safer shaking hands."[214]

McKinley would not break tradition in 1900, but Roosevelt was fully prepared to embrace the new campaign approach, and match, if not exceed, Bryan's energy and mileage. Open campaigning, and an educated defiance of disease risk, was consistent with Roosevelt's brand of progressive conservatism, fighting the evils of dirty slums and hazardous working conditions, while promoting public health and hygiene. "Roosevelt carried the entire campaign on his shoulders," wrote historian Doris Kearns Goodwin.[215]

Emotions ran high during the presidential campaign, as each candidate had loyal and enthusiastic support. Bryan tended to do well with the public when he focused on McKinley's foreign policy–particularly the administration's struggles in the Philippines and China. However, because the general economy was going well since recovering from the 1893-1894 depression, McKinley and Roosevelt were more successful campaigning on the concept that Americans had "a chicken in every pot."

"If you legislate to make the masses prosperous," Bryan countered, "their prosperity will find its way up through every class which rests upon them."[216]

In response to this argument, Roosevelt harkened back to his laissez-faire roots, arguing that such "radical" policies would bring "financial disgrace and economic disaster."[217]

Despite the generally favorable economic times, for miners of the anthracite region, 1900 was a time of high tension. A major strike was called in September, this one involving over 260,000 miners across the states of Illinois, Indiana, Ohio, West Virginia, and Pennsylvania. The strike underscored the prolonged conflict between the region's working and business classes.

The prospect of labor violence was ever-present in coal country, especially just three years since local deputies shot and killed nineteen striking miners (wounding between seventeen and forty-nine more, most shot in the back as they fled) near the mine in Lattimer, Pennsylvania.[218] In early October, 1900, as part of a pilgrimage to the scene of the 1897 massacre, the barely five-foot-tall Mary Harris "Mother" Jones, then sixty-three, traveled across the area to encourage miners to strike. According to her autobiography, she marched more than thirty miles along with 150 other women in Pennsylvania from McAdoo to Coaldale in an effort to encourage the strikers. "I told them to leave their men at home to take care of the family," she explained. "I asked them to put on their kitchen clothes and bring mops and brooms with them and a couple of tin pans. We marched over the mountains fifteen miles, beating on the tin pans as if they were cymbals."[219]

At three in the morning one day in the first week of October,[220] in pitch darkness, a local militia patrolling the road to Coaldale halted the band of women. When asked to retreat, Mother Jones refused, and the militia threatened to fix bayonets and charge. The two sides faced one another, neither backing down.

"They kept us there till daybreak," Jones said, "and when they saw the army of women in kitchen aprons, with dishpans and mops, they laughed and let us pass. An army of strong mining women makes a wonderfully spectacular picture."[221]

The longer the strike continued, the better it played into Bryan's hands in the presidential race, and so financier J. P. Morgan—who had a financial interest in many of the region's mines and railroads—urged mine owners to make concessions on wages. Although the mine owners neither recognized the union nor established a structure or approach for future wage increases, the United Mine Workers of America (UMWA) accepted the terms and ended its strike on October 29–just in time for the election.

As October wound down, both candidates made last-minute campaign runs through New York state, making "whistle-stop" speeches from their trains in small towns throughout the state, in addition to the big cities.

Much of upstate and western New York was conservative and Republican—strong McKinley and Roosevelt territory. Bryan's support was especially strong in the big cities, but—though the numbers were smaller—he also had aggressive support in small cities. Bryan's oratory was inspirational and provocative, and his "Cross of Gold" speech in 1896, in which he used religious imagery to turn a complex monetary economics question (the existing Gold standard versus a bimetal Gold/Silver standard) into a simple issue of fairness to working people, was one of the most passionate in American history.[222] His supporters tended to be similarly passionate, often exceeding McKinley supporters in enthusiasm.

Waverly's Tioga county neighbor to the east, Owego, had a long tradition of quiet commerce, conservatism and order; it was not only the home of prominent Republicans Senator Platt and former Navy Secretary Benjamin Tracy, but was also the childhood home of John D. Rockefeller and would become the retirement home of military engineer Henry Martyn Robert, the author of *Robert's Rules of Order*. In contrast, Waverly's Chemung county neighbor to the west, Elmira, was much larger, more boisterous, and had a more activist reputation; it was, for example, the home of prominent Democratic politician John B. Stanchfield, writer Sam Clemens (during the summers) and the Reverend Thomas K. Beecher, who had just passed away on March 24, 1900. Beecher's sister, the anti-slavery activist Harriet Beecher Stowe, was author of *Uncle Tom's Cabin*, the second-best-selling book of the nineteenth century, behind only the Bible. Moreover, in pre-Civil War days, Elmira was an active stop for runaway slaves on the Underground Railroad, via agent John W. Jones. Elmira was also a major Union depot during the Civil War, and Elmira prison, opened along the Chemung River in 1864 just five months after Andersonville prison was opened in Georgia, was one of the Civil War's most notorious prisoner of war camps, holding over 12,000 Confederates (of which nearly 3,000 died), and commanded for a time by Owego's Benjamin Tracy.

Although it is commonly thought today that labor unions always affiliate more with the Democratic Party and industrialists more with the Republican Party, in 1900, ethnic and religious influences were at least as important to political affiliation as class and economics.[223] This tended to be true in the baseball context as well.

Waverly players Jack Barnett and Bill Heine, for example, both children of immigrant Catholic families in Elmira, were not only teammates on the ball field, but were also active together in Elmira Democratic politics, serving as election inspectors for their respective wards–Heine in the fourth and Barnett in the fifth.[224] Bill Ging, also a child of an immigrant Catholic family in Elmira, was also active in Democratic politics. The 1890s were challenging economic times for working-class men and women, and urban Irish Catholics were particularly sensitive to any efforts to roll back their rights. In fact, in addition to the Democratic party, Elmira's seventh ward also contained an "Anti-A.P.A. Party." The American Protective Association, or A.P.A., as it was generally called, was a secretive anti-Catholic and anti-immigration organization. The A.P.A.'s platform called for restrictions on immigration, an extension of time between entry in the country and naturalization, educational qualifications for voter eligibility, a single non-sectarian school system, that public funds and property not be used for sectarian purposes, and that "no person who recognizes allegiance to any foreign or ecclesiastical potentate shall be supported for any official public position whatsoever"[225]–an obvious reference to Catholics and the Pope. Thus, it is no surprise that Irish Catholic immigrants organized to counter the nativist group. Former champion runner and walker Daniel Burns, the son of Irish immigrants and by 1900 the proprietor of Elmira's Columbia Hotel, was among the proud "Anti-A.P.A. Party" leaders.[226]

The Democratic nominee Bryan's campaign was the first to travel through the Owego-Waverly-Elmira corridor in the campaign's final month. According to the *Buffalo Courier*, Bryan's campaign arrived in Elmira on October 20, and Bryan made a speech at nine o'clock in the morning in Wisner Park "to an audience that was large as well as enthusiastic." John Stanchfield, the Democratic candidate to succeed Roosevelt as Governor, accompanied Bryan.[227] Stanchfield had been an effective pitcher for an amateur Elmira baseball team in the 1870s and later pitched for Amherst College.[228] Waverly ballplayers Heine, Ging, and Barnett, active long-time local Democrats, were also likely on hand.

*William Jennings Bryan campaign poster.
From the Library of Congress.*

The *Buffalo Courier* reported on Bryan's remarks:

> You have a large crowd for this time in the morning, and you do not come from curiosity, for you have had so much experience in seeing men prominent in politics that a mere

question of a Presidential candidate would arouse no curiosity. You are the home of Governors. You have had two, and are about to have a third. So I know that you are here this morning because you are interested in the questions which are before the people in this campaign. The people have to sit in judgment upon the issues presented by the parties and I am glad that I live in a country where men can not be elected unless the people want them elected and where no policy can be enforced unless the people want that policy enforced, for up to this time, the Republicans have not yet denied outright to attend to our business, although they deny the Filipino the right to attend to his business.[229]

The last phrase targeted McKinley's policy of waging war against insurgencies in the Philippines, an example of Bryan's effort to fight McKinley on his "imperialist" foreign policy.

From Elmira, Bryan's train proceeded west to Buffalo, stopping for short speeches in eleven towns along the way, including Corning, Bath, Livonia, Brockport, and Niagara Falls. Once Bryan reached Buffalo, the *Courier* was effusive in its enthusiasm, noting that the city's welcome was "the greatest demonstration in Buffalo's history." The sub-headline shouted: "No Man Was Ever Before Given Such a Reception in Buffalo—Over 30,000 Listen to His Speeches and 40,000 More Cheer Him as He Rides Through the City."[230]

"Wild, surging crowds jammed Broadway and side streets," a picture caption read, "and thousands of rockets and red fire illuminated the scene."

"Democrat managers were jubilant last night," the *Courier* reported of the celebration. "When the reception committee … saw the shouting thousands at Broadway Market, they smiled in triumph at the glorious outpouring of Buffalo's East Side population that screamed and shouted hurrahs of welcome to Bryan."[231]

In contrast, the conservative *Buffalo Morning Express*'s commentary was more tempered:

In his speeches Bryan dinned on the trusts, iterated and reiterated his utterances on imperialism, jabbed at Roosevelt, charged the ice trust up to the Republican Party, attacked [Mark] Hanna, defended and glorified the Filipinos, opposed an increase in the standing army and trod blithely and jauntily his well-worn ring of oratory with the issues looming up like hurdles to be jumped one by one, while the spectators lavished their plaudits on the performer. He was full of trite sayings, of quotable sentences, of aphorisms. He spoke more with the zeal of a zealot than with the fire of a fanatic. He made scant reference to free silver, and then what he said chiefly was in the way of escape from the topic. He talked with a gusto, a delight, equally manifest before the smaller country crowd and the larger city throng. He seemed to justify those who heralded him as a voice. The enthusiasts of his own party hailed him as the voice of the Democracy. Others who heard him vowed they heard the distinct murmur of the coming echo of defeat, the vanquishing of a voice.

After Buffalo, Bryan's campaign moved on to Pittsburgh and West Virginia.

Roosevelt's campaign on behalf of McKinley moved into the Southern Tier region just a few days after Bryan's. While Bryan's pace through New York had been impressive, Roosevelt's was at least equal to it. On October 25, the governor made speeches in Syracuse, Auburn, Watertown, Camden, and Oswego. The next day he spoke in Schenectady and New York City, and the day after that, he spoke in Middletown, Port Jervis, and Binghamton.

Roosevelt was no stranger to the Southern Tier. In fact, a year earlier, on October 6, 1899, just days after Ging's successful appearance in New York City, the new governor, just a little over a year removed from being the Rough Rider hero of San Juan Hill, visited Waverly for a much anticipated speech.

Roosevelt arrived in Waverly that day from Elmira, where he had participated in festivities honoring Frederick Douglass. According to the *Waverly Free Press*, Roosevelt's private car was attached to Erie train 24, and the R. A. Packer Band greeted him and his entourage at the depot.

Upon his arrival, Roosevelt went to dinner with twenty-five of the town's leading men, most likely including John Tucker and Fred Talada, at the home of New York State Senator William E. Johnson at 440 Park Avenue, and then was accompanied to the Opera House by the Band, where he gave an address at eight o'clock for the benefit of the Young People's Society of Christian Endeavor chapter of the Waverly Presbyterian Church. In his speech, Roosevelt detailed his experiences leading the Rough Riders in the recent war, and held forth on current events.

The Free Press reported:

> He did not distinguish between men on account of their nationality, creed or color, but measured every man by his merit. He allowed no special favors in the way of rations, etc., to the officers, but taught them that they were to give the men the preference, if any was shown.
>
> "You must be courageous, and that is not all," Roosevelt said. "You have got to have honesty and civic uprightness in your life. Smartness alone does not count. I have no respect for the man who is looked up to because he is smart. A smart man without a conscience is one of the most dangerous foes of our body politic. You have got to be honest.
>
> "Children should not be brought up to think that they should live an easy life," he continued. "This doctrine is one of the greatest curses of our country. It is ignoble and mean. Instill into their minds to live a life that counts; to face strife and overcome; that the easy life is not worth living; to work for the work's sake."[232]

The speech "was interrupted several times with prolonged applause," and Roosevelt followed it up with an informal reception at the Hoadley House, "at which a very large number of ladies and gentlemen met the governor, for each of whom he had a smile and pleasant word as they were introduced by Senator Johnson." Following the reception, the governor left Waverly on Erie train number 12, bound for Albany.[233]

Now, a year later, on Monday, October 29, 1900, Roosevelt was scheduled to swing his Presidential campaign into the local area, speaking at Cortland, Ithaca, and Elmira. The festivities in the first two towns went off without incident. His appearance in Elmira, however, contained a surprise.

On the surface, Roosevelt's reception in Elmira was nearly as impressive as Buffalo's greeting had been for Bryan. *The Waverly Free Press* reported:

> Governor Roosevelt was given a magnificent reception in Elmira Monday evening, conceded to be the greatest political demonstration there in many years. The city was ablaze with electric lights, red fire, and the national colors, and the crowds that paraded and that lined the streets were variously estimated at from 20,000 to 30,000 people.
>
> The parade was a most imposing affair, and the spectacular effect was most inspiring. It was led by 900 mounted rough riders, and there were bands, drum corps, clubs and companies, torches and fireworks galore. Last but not least were the Waverly City Band and the Waverly first voters club, followed by about fifty of our well known citizens.

According to the *Free Press*, Roosevelt spoke for about forty-five minutes at the Lyceum, which was Elmira's old Opera House, located at 150 Lake Street on the northeast corner of Lake and Carroll Streets, just one block east of Bill Heine's saloon. After that, he spoke at the Tivoli Theater for fifteen minutes.

According to the *New York Weekly Press*, Roosevelt also spoke to the overflow crowd in "an enormous mass meeting in the open air," likely in front of the Lyceum:

> "I want to point out to you," Roosevelt said, "that in seeking after models of good legislation as regards both wage-workers and corporations we have gone outside our Nation to communities like New Zealand and outside the nations to communities like Massachusetts, which has had a Republican law-making body for over forty years, in both of which places we found excellent material to help us, but we didn't find a thing on the statute books of [Bryan's home state of] Nebraska which it was worth while to copy, this populistic State not having paid much attention to the laboring man. And the same is true of other States, such as the Carolinas and Mississippi, from which Mr. Bryan expects to get his electoral vote."[234]

Notwithstanding the rousing speeches, the surprise of the day came when Roosevelt and the immense Elmira parade was attacked by—according to the *New York Weekly Press*—a "Hoodlum Gang." *The New York Times* called the attackers "Ruffians" and "Bryan Partisans."[235]

The *Weekly Press* reported that the governor:

> ...was attacked by a gang of hoodlums carrying Stanchfield banners and lithographs, his Rough Rider hat was knocked off by a stick in the hands of an Elmira Bryanite, and six paraders in the campaign garb of Rough Riders were assaulted so viciously that ambulances were called and the reserve police force of the city was rushed to the scene of disturbance in patrol wagons
>
> The mobbing of Governor Roosevelt took place while the parade of the early evening was in progress. A gang

issued from an alleyway and began to hurl potatoes, stones and other missiles at the carriage in which he sat.[236]

The *New York Tribune*, under the headline "Bryanism Breeds Rowdyism," ran a similar account and emphasized Elmira's Stanchfield connection.[237] Regional newspapers also ran corroborating stories. The Williamsport (PA) *Sun-Gazette* reported, for instance, that "Roosevelt was pelted with eggs and vegetables,"[238] while the Rochester (NY) *Democrat and Chronicle* noted that items found in Roosevelt's carriage following the "attack" included "a turnip, an old shoe and a club."[239]

The *Free Press* added its own account:

> While Elmira honored herself in the reception that the better class of her citizens gave to the governor, deep and lasting disgrace was brought upon the city by the violent and disgraceful doings of large groups of toughs and hoodlums, without apparent effort on the part of police to prevent it, and the disgrace is intensified by the fact–as vouched for by respectable citizens of that city, among whom at least one lady of prominence–that the hoodlums who created the disturbances were supplied with torches and banners at democratic headquarters.
>
> One gang followed the carriage in which was seated Governor Roosevelt, Senator [Jacob S.] Fassett and others. The governor was struck with a turnip, his hat was knocked off by a cane, and he was kept busy dodging missiles, and an old shoe, a turnip and what Senator Fassett characterized as "other democratic arguments" were taken from his carriage. The Corning club was attacked near the corner of Railroad Avenue and Water Street, and several of them, among whom was Postmaster J. S. Kennedy, were seriously injured. A half dozen were taken into a nearby drug store for medical treatment. One was so seriously injured that he was unconscious for an hour

at the Erie station, and it was reported that he was dead, but this was subsequently denied. Many windows were broken and decorations were torn down along the line. The Waverly club, and more particularly, the citizens following them were repeatedly pelted with mud and stones, Dr. [Rufus] S. Harnden's overcoat was nearly ruined with the mud, and the writer of this narrowly missed a blow from a cane which struck his torch to the ground.

The Cortland Evening Standard reported that the rioters intended to pull Roosevelt "from his carriage and rotten egg him."[240] Judge Job E. Hedges, who accompanied Roosevelt and Fassett in the carriage, described the attack to the *Evening Standard* as follows:

> We had moved several blocks from the hotel, going quite slowing and stopping from time to time to let the mounted Rough Riders get ahead of us in the parade. The driver of the carriage was a little slow and let them get rather farther ahead of us than was necessary. A large number of grown young men closed in about the carriage. Most of them had Stanchfield lithographs on long sticks which they flaunted into the carriage. They crawled upon the hood of the carriage, which was folded behind. They were flourishing sticks at us and shouting every vile epithet at the governor you could think of. "Scab" was the nicest word I heard them use. There were no police around the carriage, but after this sort of thing had been going on for some time a man not in uniform, who was apparently a special policeman, came up to the carriage and drove back the crowd to a distance of six feet or more from the carriage. This stopped neither their yelling nor the throwing of missiles, which had started before he came. Several handfuls of gravel were thrown. Something passed between

me and Senator Fassett which seemed to me as it passed to be the half of an apple. Then a turnip grazed the top of the governor's hat. The butts of burned red-fire sticks were also thrown into the carriage and other missiles. Senator Fassett told us that we were approaching the roughest part of the city. I noticed that the men who were shouting and making trouble seemed many of them to be older than those who first surrounded us. The senator called out to the driver to hurry up and get among the mounted men ahead. This was done, and we had fifteen or more of the Rough Riders crowd in around us. There was no serious trouble after then. There was some yelling from the sidewalks.[241]

According to the *Evening Standard,* one local man was arrested and implicated in the protest: Daniel Burns' younger brother and fellow ex-champion race walker, Felix "Fely" Burns.[242] Since his days in the mid-1880s as a competitive runner and walker,[243] Felix had repeatedly been in trouble with the authorities; in fact, just within the last month, he had been sentenced to a three-dollar fine or ten days in the local jail for intoxication.[244] Moreover, Daniel and Felix's other brother, James, a barber, had just been killed in a "friendly boxing contest," where "no blame was attached,"[245] so there was no shortage of tragedy in the family. According to the *Evening Standard*, Felix Burns admitted that the gang had formed in Elmira's tough neighborhood, known as "the Patch," and that their intention was to "do Roosevelt up." They were unable to pull him out of the carriage once it "got in among the Rough Riders."[246]

"Burns is the sort of a man who regards such doings as highly humorous features of a political campaign," the *Evening Standard* explained. "He was rather proud of the part he had taken in the plot."[247]

Although contradicted by multiple sources, the *Elmira Daily Gazette* disputed the reports of any political disturbances at the

Roosevelt event, blaming the "outrageously false report" on "Republican press accounts" designed to curry sympathy for Roosevelt and McKinley. The *Gazette* claimed: "Some very ridiculous accounts of Monday night's affair in this city were sent to the New York papers by the young men who were with Roosevelt. None of these young men saw the disturbance."[248]

With respect to Burns, the *Gazette* reported, "Burns absolutely had nothing to do with the affair except to shout derisively at a policeman, for which he was taken in." Regarding the young man's alleged comments to the *Evening Standard*, the *Gazette* assured its readers, "Burns said nothing of the kind."[249]

Instead, the *Gazette* ascribed the "disturbance" not to politics, but to "an old feud between hoodlums" of Elmira and Corning. The *Gazette* acknowledged jeering, fistfights, stone throwing and multiple casualties, including at least six "who had cuts in their heads." The *Gazette* also highlighted an incident involving the Waverly Band, where a "tough" tried to steal the bass drummer's music during the parade. "The hand that reached out from the crowd just touched the sheet [of music] when the base [sic] drum stick came down with a resounding whack," the *Gazette* explained. "The tough dropped in his tracks, the base [sic] drummer continuing his march and playing with only the loss of one beat."[250]

The *Gazette* did not acknowledge, however, any attacks intentionally directed at Roosevelt. One can surmise that the newspaper was attempting to protect the city's reputation (and by extension Stanchfield's) by warding off negative political coverage.

According to the *New York Times*, Roosevelt shrugged off the "attack," declaring it to be the work of "hoodlums" and proceeded apace with his speeches.

Having safely escaped the events in Elmira, Roosevelt continued his campaign the next day in Canandaigua, Corning, Bath, Avon, Livonia, and so on, heading west to Buffalo. He then turned back and went through Jamestown, Dunkirk, Olean, Hornellsville, and multiple other towns—including Waverly, where just as his train was pulling out of the station, "a stone was fired, breaking the glass in the observation window of the Governor's car"[251]–before arriving at the Owego home of Senator Platt on the evening of November 2.[252]

The Indianapolis Journal reported from Owego:

> In eight weeks [Roosevelt] has visited twenty-four States of the Union, made 673 speeches, traveled 21,209 miles, visited 567 towns and cities, and talked to what is estimated to be 3,000,000 people. [He] exceeds Mr. Bryan's record in 1896, which was 599 speeches made and 19,000 miles covered.
>
> "Mr. Bryan is now inclined to laugh at the argument of the full dinner pail," Roosevelt said at his last few campaign stops, in his continuing effort to promote the current economy and paint Bryan as radical and out of touch with common Americans. "Nobody laughed about it four years ago. It was a mighty sight easier to laugh about it when it is full than when it is empty. When it is empty it is serious business. If this Nation chooses to turn bedlamite and put in Mr. Bryan and try his policies, we have nobody but ourselves to thank for the disaster that will surely follow.
>
> "We want not merely to whip Bryanism, but to crush it under our heels. I ask you to stand by the party that succeeds and not the party that fails, for the party that makes financial policies that work, and not the party that advocates financial policies that won't work; for the party that fought to a finish the Spanish war and hoisted the flag in the Philippines and not the party that grumbled about how the war was fought and now wants to haul down the flag in the Philippines."[253]

Following his last campaign stop in Owego, Roosevelt returned home to Oyster Bay for one last speech on Monday, November

5. Thus ended Roosevelt's first campaign for national office.

The next day was Election Day, and McKinley and Roosevelt won handily, collecting 292 electoral votes to Bryan's 155. They secured 51 percent of the popular vote and carried twenty-eight of the then-forty-five states. This was an improvement over 1896, when McKinley collected 271 electoral votes, secured 51 percent of the popular votes, and carried just twenty-three states. Roosevelt had clearly made a difference. The Republican candidate to replace him as New York State Governor, Benjamin Odell, was also victorious, defeating Stanchfield.

"Early in the campaign [Roosevelt] became the national Republican leader who on every occasion was pitted against Bryan and who vanquished the Democratic Presidential candidate off every field," explained Senator Platt. "He answered all of Bryan's questions. Bryan could answer none of his. Besides all this, Roosevelt broke all records as a campaigner. He traveled more miles, visited more States, spoke in more towns, made more speeches and addressed a larger number of people than any man who ever went on the American stump."[254]

Roosevelt's aggressive campaign was indeed impressive, and the end result was that conservative Republicans remained in power. On the surface, the nation's move from monopolism to populism seemed to have stalled.

JUST A FEW DAYS AFTER THE ELECTION AND A SHORT WALK from Senator Platt's Owego home, the Krist murder trial opened at the Tioga County Courthouse, and Waverly was forced to relive the embarrassing public tragedy that the championship baseball season had all but wiped from public memory.

What many in Waverly had hoped would be a quickly and quietly resolved case had not gone away, but had continued to grow in public interest.

The district attorney assigned to defend Fred Krist was

Frank A. Darrow, a Republican graduate of Cornell Law School, who, like Harry Taylor, had enjoyed a quiet rural upbringing as a farmer's son in a largely white, English-speaking, native-born area. In Darrow's case, it was in rural Bradford County, Pennsylvania, just across the border from Tioga County, New York. Darrow had preceded Taylor at Cornell Law School, and would continue to practice law in the village for many years following the Krist trial, serving respectably in a variety of offices.

For the Krist case, Darrow employed the well known—but rare in practice—insanity defense. In other words, Darrow claimed Krist was not guilty because at the time of the crime he was of unsound mind. Not even counting Krist's public statements following the murder, Darrow believed the best defense would be to show that there was sufficient evidence to demonstrate that Krist's behavior in committing the murder was so out of character that it rose to the level of insanity.

District Attorney Oscar B. Glezen, assisted by Frederick E Hawkes, was just as insistent that Krist's behavior was calculated and pre-meditated, and his team accumulated evidence and expert witnesses to make that case to the jury.

Tioga County Courthouse in Owego, NY

Both sides brought their best arguments to the courthouse, and the *Elmira Daily Gazette* predicted, "The murder trial promises to be one of the most interesting and bitterly fought trials in the history of Tioga county."[255]

"People in Waverly are divided in their sentiments," Fred Krist's brother Henry had told the *Gazette* in April. "Many sympathize with Fred, and they include all who knew him well. His wife has not turned against him, and the people with whom he lived remain friendly to him and tell things that add to our own knowledge that Fred was not rational when he shot the girl. He was, as [Krist's brother] Julius says, perfect in morals and conduct, as far as I ever saw or heard."[256]

The *Gazette* went on to explain that the Krist family in Ithaca "has been very much respected as industrious, quiet and religious people, who are receiving the sympathy of all who know them."

"There was a large attendance in court and Krist was the center of attention," the *Gazette* reported as the trial began. "He was finely dressed and had a jaunty, nonchalant air. He does not appear to be affronted by his serious position."[257]

Ball players Fred Tucker and Owen Dunham were among the numerous witnesses who testified at the trial, describing what they saw the day of the murder. They both also repeated Krist's own words to them in his jail cell following the incident.

As a final witness, Darrow brought out Dr. James M. Barrett, an Owego physician. After Darrow provided a long, exacting description of Krist's circumstances and behavior at the time of the murder, Dr. Barrett allowed that, hypothetically, Krist was of "unsound mind."

As an opposing expert witness, Glezen called Dr. Charles G. Wagner from the Binghamton State Hospital for the Insane, who testified that, in his opinion, Dr. Barrett had failed to establish a case for melancholia or insanity, since Krist's behavior was depressed, but not delusional. "I think I have already explained what delusions are," Dr. Wagner explained, "a faulty belief, and error of judgment–out of which the person cannot be reasoned by facts and arguments that ordinarily would convince a man in his station of life." As an example, Dr. Wagner cited patients who must be fed with a "stomach-tube" because they were too delusional to eat.

Glezen then called another expert witness, Dr. J. T. Greenleaf of Owego, who had graduated from the New York Homeopathic Medical College in 1867, and he agreed with Dr. Wagner that Krist was of sound mind. Glezen also called Waverly physician Dr. Rufus Harnden, a witness to the shooting, who said immediately after the shooting Krist was "very cool and collected, and stood and walked as steadily as I ever saw any one."[258]

Darrow's expert witness was outnumbered.

"Mrs. Tobin and Mrs. Donahue, mother and sister of the murdered girl, and Krist's wife and [Krist's wife's] sisters wept and sobbed during his plea," the *Buffalo Courier* noted, "but Krist showed no emotion whatever."[259]

Following the closing arguments, Judge Burr J. Mattice issued detailed instructions to the jurors, and they retired at five o'clock on Friday evening, whereupon Krist was returned to his cell to await the verdict. "Krist left the court with the same smiling air of nonchalance which he has carried throughout the trial and chatted and laughed on his way to the jail, where his brothers expressed great sorrow but Krist maintained the same indifferent air," the *Tioga County Record* reported.[260]

At 8:15 in the evening, the jury returned with their verdict. Krist was brought in, and his two brothers, Henry and Julius, were with him, along with a large crowd. "The courtroom was packed, hundreds of women being present, some of them standing for hours waiting for the verdict and not even leaving the room for a lunch," reported the *Buffalo Courier*.[261]

The tense courtroom braced for the verdict. Judge Mattice asked Krist to stand to receive the jury's judgment. Despite the size and passion of the crowd, the room was rapt with silent anticipation. "The judge warned the audience that he would not tolerate any expression of approval or disapproval upon their part before he announced the verdict and it was heard in almost absolute silence," the *Buffalo Courier* noted.

"Jurors, look upon the defendant," Judge Mattice stated solemnly. "Defendant, look upon the jurors. Gentlemen, what is your verdict?"

"Guilty of murder in the first degree," the jury foreman replied.[262]

Krist received the information with an "air of indifference," and, while the packed courtroom was silent, there is no record of how the broader community received the verdict. One imagines whispers of confirmation and acknowledgment among the crowd outside, as the Judge closed the session, and spectators eventually filed out of the courthouse. According to news reports, Krist's brothers were his "only friends in court when the verdict was announced."[263]

The next morning at 9:30, Krist received his sentence. "Judge Mattice ordered the prisoner to stand, Krist rose, smiling, threw back his overcoat, put one hand in his trousers pockets, running the fingers of the other into his double-breasted flowered vest, and heard with unmoved features" that he was to be executed in early January at the prison in Auburn.[264] After two more nights in the Owego jail, Krist was readied for his train journey to Auburn on Monday morning.

It had been raining heavily for days throughout the region, but especially along the Lehigh Valley Railroad route between Waverly and Auburn. In Ithaca, Krist's hometown, the rain was particularly damaging on the Monday of Krist's scheduled departure for Auburn. The *Ithaca Daily News* reported:

> Farmers say the roads are almost impassable all through the county and that the water has left great gulches in the fields. Fifteen hogs belonging to Patrick Clines, which were penned at his slaughter house south of the city were drowned. A two year old colt belonging to Charles Simms, who lives in the inlet road, was drowned in its stall.
>
> Throughout the immediate country surrounding much damage was done by the water. In many places there were heavy washouts and landslides which have left the railroads in bad condition. Many bridges along the highways are also gone.[265]

Krist, accompanied by Sheriff Abe Thurston, Under Sheriff E. W. Rodman, and reporter S. W. Smyth, took the northbound Lehigh Valley train from Owego and was due to arrive in Auburn at one p.m. Unfortunately, about two and one-half miles north of Moravia, the rails had been washed out by the torrential rains, and the train crashed.[266]

"The party had been playing cards and had just concluded the game when the crash came," the *Tioga County Record* reported. "Sheriff Thurston was seated in the smoker, the rear coach in the train, with his back toward the locomotive and was reaching into his hip pocket, when the shock threw him violently…injuring his left hip and side so badly that he nearly fainted from the pain."[267]

The train was wrecked, and Krist was momentarily out of custody. "The sheriff was pinned under the wreckage, but Krist, who was not handcuffed to the officer, was uninjured," the *Auburn Journal* reported.[268]

Moravia was roughly equidistant between Ithaca and Auburn. Were Krist to escape there, he had an opportunity to make it home, where his brothers could perhaps help him get to Canada. Moreover, with all the confusion surrounding the rain, the flooding, and the crash, it could be hours before his captors would begin the search for him.

Given the opportunity to escape, Krist instead went to the injured Sheriff Thurston and began to assist him. "Krist immediately began to haul over the broken timbers and pieces of iron and freed the man who was taking him to the electric chair. Krist made no effort to escape, although he had every chance in the world. He could have escaped and if he had been recaptured no worse punishment could have been imposed on him, as he was under sentence of death," the *Journal* wrote.

Once Thurston's rescue was complete, the party, with Krist fully back in custody, drove to Cascade, likely renting a local wagon, to catch another train, finally reaching Auburn around four p.m., three hours later than scheduled.[269] The entourage arrived very quietly in a cold rain that "kept the away the curious ones that are usually on hand when a criminal of any note passes through the big gates."[270] Krist immediately took the only open cell of five on "condemned row." The other four cells were occupied by George Smith, who murdered his wife in Churchville in September 1897; Squire Tankard, who murdered his wife's sister and wounded her husband at a camp near Chautauqua Lake in July 1899; Frank Wennerholm, who murdered his mistress in Falconer in September 1899; and John Truck, who murdered a farmer during a burglary in Virgil in March 1899.

A few days after the wreck, his rescue of Sheriff Thurston, and his arrival in Auburn, Krist wrote a long letter to local newspapers expressing his opinion of his trial and sentence. "The jury probably did not stop to consider that I was only a common workingman, and could not afford to engage three experts as did the other side," the letter read in part. "Had I been wealthy a few hundred dollars would have also engaged three experts and the result would have been this: The three for the prosecution would have testified I was sane, while my experts would say I was not. This is another instance where money is a very useful article."[271]

"Goodbye all," the letter ended, "and I hope we will meet in a much brighter and happier world, where there is no sorrow or sin."[272]

Krist was scheduled to be executed the week of January 6, 1901, but his friends and family were already working on an appeal and possible retrial that would at a minimum necessitate postponement of the execution until the summer, possibly in the middle of the 1901 baseball season.

CHAPTER 8

We Believe Baseball Will Take on a New Life

As November 1900 gave way to December, discussions among Harry Taylor's Players' Protective Association (PPA), the magnates' National League, and Ban Johnson's American League continued. The American League's acceptance of the PPA's demands stood in stark contrast to the National League's contempt, which played perfectly into Johnson's hands.

Ban Johnson and his allies continued to hold out hope that an agreement could be reached with the National League that would recognize the American League as a fellow major league. To do this peacefully would require modifying the National Agreement that governed relations between rival leagues, but at their annual ownership meetings in December, the National League owners refused to even consider the idea, snubbing Johnson, and insisting that if there was to be a new major league, it would be a new "American Association," not Johnson's "outlaw" league.

Meanwhile, at the same December meetings, Harry Taylor made the PPA's case to the National League. In their negotiations, Taylor made five principle requests of the magnates:

1. Limit the ability of teams to reserve players.
2. Do not allow sales of players without their consent.
3. Pay physicians' fees for players who are injured in the course of duty.
4. Limit the ability of teams to suspend players.
5. Establish an arbitration committee to manage grievances.

Taylor explained:

> We are not looking for trouble. We are simply moving with an idea of putting this game on a higher plane. The salary of the player, we know, is regulated by the law of supply and demand. If we can make the game more popular financially, then our salaries will increase. The public's idea about the ball player today, under the present contract system, is that a ball player is looked upon as a slave. He is a slave under the reserve rule. We know that the reserve rule is the bulwark of base ball, but it should not be abused. What can be done to modify it? The players suggest that it be limited, and that no player may be reserved by a club for more than five years. [273]

It was a reasonable argument fundamentally different from the demands made by John Ward during his Players' League revolt in 1890, where he advocated profit sharing as well as a total ban on both the reserve clause and salary classification. "Gone were the sweeping, industry-wide reforms" that animated Ward and the Brotherhood, noted historian Krister Swanson. The PPA's requests, by contrast, were pragmatic and cautious, coming from "a group of workers that understood the place of the highly skilled worker in the management-labor hierarchy."[274]

Taylor went on to explain how the suggested changes would work in the best interests of all parties, by growing the game in a just manner that would win over the public. "We realize that you magnates could easily get together and have a secret understanding that would render inoperative the changes we ask for, but we believe you will be fair and square with us," he said. "Do as we ask and we believe baseball will take on a new life."[275]

The National League magnates rejected the PPA and the players' arguments out of hand. "They treated us as if we had been unruly kids who had to be lollipopped and put to bed," explained PPA Vice President Clark Griffith. Zimmer, Jennings and Taylor were all angered by the magnates' condescending attitude.[276]

Players' Protective Association Vice President Clark Griffith in 1901 jumped from Chicago in the National League to pitch and manage for Chicago in the American League, and eventually became the longtime owner of the Washington Senators. Portrait from the Library of Congress.

Meanwhile, the American League (AL) continued to gain public approval, and the likelihood that numerous National League (NL) players would jump to the new league for higher salaries threatened to put the NL owners on the defensive. Nevertheless, the NL owners continued to arrogantly profess public certainty that their players would continue to sign their contracts and fall in line. Boston's owner Soden went so far as to inform PPA President Zimmer that the league would be "pleased" to meet with the players, "provided the lawyer was left out"[277]–an obvious jab at Taylor, but also an acknowledgement of his effectiveness in stemming trickery.

Ban Johnson ended the 1900 season with AL franchises in Chicago, Milwaukee, Indianapolis, Detroit, Kansas City, Cleveland, Buffalo, and Minneapolis–a fair mix of his old Western League and the new major league he was creating. Johnson's first season as newly elected President of the Western League was in 1894, with teams in Sioux City (Iowa), Toledo (Ohio) and Grand Rapids (Michigan) instead of Chicago, Cleveland and Buffalo. Over the intervening years Johnson built it into a formidable circuit, moving gradually East, practicing financial prudence, and catering to the respectable as opposed to the disreputable by reducing rowdy behavior both on and off the field.

For 1901, Johnson wanted to add teams in Boston, Philadelphia, Baltimore, Washington, and Cleveland, moving into direct competition with existing NL franchises, and taking advantage of the cities the NL dropped after 1899. Johnson's belief that fans would come out in greater numbers to see a less rowdy, better organized, less monopolistic game was about to be tested, and his acceptance of the PPA's terms, including a rejection of the NL's $2,400 salary cap, helped to make his franchises attractive to NL players.

Many players remained concerned, however, about being blacklisted by the NL owners. The year started with rumors of NL players jumping to the AL, but nothing was confirmed. To put more pressure on the magnates, Taylor sent letters to all PPA members urging them to maintain "loyalty to the cause," and to not sign their NL contracts until the PPA's terms were accepted, essentially a boycott. He advised that players could sign AL contracts, provided all of the PPA terms, agreed to by Johnson, were included. In so advising, Taylor professed to be favoring neither league, but only looking out for the players' best interests. This letter included a solicitation for member opinion on whether to continue to hold out if terms were not met.[278]

On January 11, 1901, the PPA officers met at Harry Taylor's office in Buffalo, and Boston star Jimmy Collins was in attendance. "The details of the consultation were not given out," the *Buffalo Evening News* reported, "but [PPA President] Zimmer said that there was no doubt that the Players' Protective Association would stick together."

By the end of January, the AL abandoned its hope of conciliation with the NL via a peaceful modification of the National Agreement, and officially declared itself a major league on par with (and at war with) the NL. The competition for players began.

On February 1, Jimmy Collins secretly agreed to jump from the NL's Boston team to the AL's new franchise in the same city for a $3,500 salary and ownership interest. Taylor was likely Collins's agent in the deal. Two weeks later, Nap "Larry" Lajoie secretly agreed to jump from one Philadelphia team to the other for a $4,000 salary. These were stratospheric salaries at a time when the average family in the United States earned $750 a year.[279]

In competing for players, Johnson and the AL owners were especially interested in pursuing the NL's best players, particularly those put off by the magnates' $2,400 annual salary cap. When the NL owners cried foul because they insisted the signing was a violation of the player's contract, Taylor reiterated the PPA's call for the magnates to negotiate terms and supported each player's right to negotiate with whichever league he chose. The atmosphere was a confusing one for the players, as both the American and National sides put out competing information regarding the legality of the player contracts.

In the midst of all these rapid changes and confusion, some players expressed concern that the PPA was only interested in helping the elites, not the rank-and-file players of average ability. PPA Secretary Hughie Jennings' announcement that he was continuing to follow Harry Taylor's footsteps to coach at Cornell and attend Cornell Law School only exacerbated this perception. "Yes, he strung us along beautifully," wrote one anonymous player of Jennings to *Sporting Life* in January, "played us for suckers. He got the job to coach at Cornell. Taylor, an old Cornell man, gets the job of lawyer to the Player's Association. Nice for them, but how about us, who have our bread and butter to look out for? In addition to that, I am sorry that I joined such an organization anyhow. I never have any trouble with any man for whom I have worked, have got my salary regularly and have something to show for it."[280]

Other players expressed support for the PPA. Dusty Miller, for instance, a veteran major league outfielder from Oil City, Pennsylvania, told *The Sporting News* "I hope the [PPA] boys will win." He explained that he was signed to a NL contract but required to play in the minor Western League, "a neat little trick of the mandates. This is an example of what the boys are fighting for," he explained.[281]

Throughout January and February, NL owners and supporters, despite evidence to the contrary, continued to express their belief that both the PPA and the AL were doomed.

Brooklyn manager Ned Hanlon, for example, as both former Orioles manager (whose former players dominated the PPA) and a close ally of John Ward and a champion of the 1890 Players' League revolt, believed the players were asking for too much and risking the same defeat the players suffered in 1890. "Players who do not look before they leap this time are foolish," he said. "They are paid more money for their time and labor than any other class of workers in America." Still, despite this critical advice, Hanlon agreed with the PPA that two healthy major leagues would provide "the public with better sport than ever."[282]

All indications were, however, that Taylor and the other PPA leaders had in fact learned the lessons of 1890, as they studiously avoided even the tiniest tint of radicalism or partisanship. In February, for instance, Harry Taylor began running columns in *Sporting Life* entitled "Taylor's Tips," in which he clarified the PPA's position and stressed that the union was not "in cahoots" with the AL. "We are not fighting that [National] League at all," Taylor wrote. "Our attitude has been this all the time. We have been trying to get some satisfactory answer from the National League, but have failed so far. What is the use of us working any further on it? It is up to the National League."[283]

Meanwhile, Hughie Jennings announced that his coaching at Cornell would not prevent him from playing, as he would "be right in the game after the college term closes in June." Jennings arrived at Cornell on February 10, 1901, and immediately got to work with the school's prospects.

By early February, with the contract boycott still going strong, the NL magnates appeared to be weakening, and five of eight publicly said they were willing to negotiate with the PPA after all, but "not through the medium of a lawyer."[284] Presumably, the magnates believed they could negotiate better terms with Zimmer and other players than with Taylor. The PPA leaders accepted the condition and strategized for the meeting, to be held in Cleveland.

Zimmer, Willie Keeler and "Dirty Jack" Doyle were among the players in Cleveland on February 26 for the meeting between the PPA and the magnates. The old Oriole element was very well represented in the PPA leadership, as evidenced by Taylor, Jennings, Clarke, Keeler and Doyle. In exchange for making some concessions to the PPA, the magnates, represented by John Brush, Arthur Soden and Jim Hart, asked Zimmer for the PPA's help in preventing players from jumping to the AL. Zimmer consulted with Keeler and Doyle, and received instructions from Taylor by wire. The result was the NL's acceptance of PPA's modifications to player contracts in exchange for the PPA's agreement to suspend players from the PPA who jump to the AL. At Taylor's suggestion, Zimmer only agreed to such suspensions, when and if approved by the entire association "as a body," and the NL was fine with this condition.

The resultant agreement represented the first concession made by the NL to the PPA, and gave the players their first taste of power and control in labor negotiations. News coverage was nearly universal in its commendation of Taylor and the players. *The Buffalo Express*, for instance, declared it a "grand victory," and both *The Sporting News* and *Sporting Life* lauded the players' "progress." Taylor was "jubilant," and noted that "the players will hail the result with delight and no doubt the magnates will be rewarded by better service from the men, who should now give the game and their employers the best they possess in return for the recognition of their demands and I honestly believe that they will do so."[285]

In his column following the players' victory, *Sporting Life* writer Francis C. Richter said the PPA's "splendid results" were "due to the patience and loyalty of the players and the skill, intelligence, resourcefulness and disinterestedness of the leaders—particularly Messrs. Taylor, Zimmer and Jennings," noting that "they managed by conservative shrewdness to recover lost ground and prestige to compel the magnates to reverse themselves, to secure nearly all they originally asked for; and, at the finish, to give the League a little of its own 'humiliation medicine.'"[286]

The NL's acceptance virtually guaranteed that Taylor and the PPA would be able to position themselves as unbiased player advocates, despite the fact that many players would jump to the AL. In fact, as soon as both leagues accepted the terms, the PPA let players know they could choose between the contracts offered to them. The PPA did not say that the players would be suspended, but that the entire membership would consider such suspensions at the appropriate time. Taylor sent a special letter to each player to explain the situation.

"The impression seems to prevail all over the country that the Protective Association is in alliance with the American League," Taylor wrote in a letter to PPA members. "This is not so at all. We are doing business with President Johnson and the members of his organization for the simple reasons that they see the wisdom of bettering the condition of the men."[287]

Taylor's letter went on to describe each of the contract changes the players should expect and clarified that each player could go to whichever league or team he chose. "You may now sign the new contract when you please in your League, and if you see fit to go to the American you may be sure that it does not at all necessarily mean that you will lose any standing in our Association, but simply that your case will some time be passed on by our Association as a body, and just as it sees fit. You understand."[288]

The purpose of this language was to assure players that the PPA would not take action against any player for jumping from one league to the other, unless it did so "as a body," or, in other words, as an entire organization. This was specifically directed at players who were concerned about violating the reserve rule of their prior contracts. According to Taylor, those prior contracts lacked fairness, or equity, in that they were slanted too far in the direction of team ownership.

As the AL and NL openly began to battle over players, Harry Taylor continued to argue to NL owners that the PPA was not biased in favor of the AL, pointing out that any player under contract with the NL would be subject to suspension from the PPA if he signed with the AL. However, he also reiterated the important caveat that any suspension would require action by the full PPA "as a body." Thus, Taylor was able to argue to the NL that the PPA would take action in response to contract jumpers, but also reassure players that all members would have to agree to any suspension, virtually ensuring that very few if any such suspensions would ever take place.

The NL magnates "are so dense they never realize when they have made a mistake," noted *The Sporting News*.[289] In response to questions as to whether the PPA's commitment to discipline contract-jumpers "as a body" amounted to a "very cleverly planned" strategy by Taylor and Zimmer, *The Sporting News* explained that "no suspension will probably be made until after the base ball season of 1901 opens, and then the game will not be interested."[290]

To players and owners who complained that the PPA was taking sides, Taylor stressed that the PPA's purpose was, in language either intentionally or coincidentally similar to Roosevelt's, to "correct evils," not "secure positions" for its players. It was a hands-off approach to individual negotiations that garnered the organization few fans during the salary war, but it proved to be extremely effective in establishing a stable middle ground between the two leagues that helped ensure the new AL could fairly compete for players, and that players as a whole would benefit from the resultant increase in opportunities that a competitive two-league system would produce.

Meanwhile, Ban Johnson had successfully lured enough experienced and trusted professionals to the AL side, veterans like John McGraw, Clark Griffith, Charles Comiskey, and Connie Mack, that it made it easier for the AL to persuade younger players to take a chance and jump.

Taylor and the PPA may have claimed a victory for players' rights, but the jury was still out on whether the public would accept two leagues and whether the game would truly flourish under the new system as they claimed. The answer to that question would have to wait for the players to sign, actual baseball games to be played, and the public to decide that the games were worth their time and attention.

Nevertheless, between the AL's calm veteran presence and the PPA's consistent and reasonable advocacy, both the players and the public were being set up to be positively influenced in favor of the new league, increasing the likelihood that Taylor's prediction of baseball "taking on a new life" would come true.

After finishing 1900 with such positive results, Fred Tucker and the rest of the Waverly baseball organization were very optimistic about 1901. To get the team started on as strong a financial footing as possible, Waverly's ownership put together a four-day Baseball Fair, which ran March 18-21 at the Opera House on Fulton Street.

Dozens of businesses sponsored games, food, and entertainment both inside and outside the Opera House, including a very popular Ferris wheel. A popular music group played each night: the R.A Packer Band from Sayre on Monday, the Waverly City Band on Tuesday, the Hosmer Band from Athens on Wednesday, and McGuffie's Orchestra from Waverly on Thursday.[291] Local merchants donated significant door prizes each night, including a quartered oak bedroom set, a bicycle, a sewing machine, a parlor table, chairs, a camera, dresses, suitcases, wire mattresses, "tons" of coal, boxes of cigars, cabinet photos, shoes, opera house tickets, newspaper subscriptions, barrels of flour, pants patterns, "fancy" vest patterns, and cases of oranges. Bill Heine, still a proprietor of the family saloon in Elmira, sponsored the fair's bar.

Among the ball players slated to participate in the fair, as reported by the *Waverly Free Press*, were: John "The Alderman" Barnett, James "Johnny of the Spot" O'Neil, William "Silence and Fun" Hughes, William "Slow" Ging, William C. "Pop" Heine, Thomas "Home Run" Dwyer, John "Red Head" McDougal, and "Syracuse Dad" Maroney.[292]

"Syracuse Dad" Maroney was Stephen Maroney, born in 1876 in New York State to Irish parents. In 1900, the family resided at 508 Schuyler Street in Syracuse, and Stephen listed his occupation as "Day Laborer." Clearly, he perceived baseball as a secondary occupation.

To promote the fair, the *Waverly Free Press* produced flyers that contained pictures of four of the team's expected 1901 players: Tom Dwyer, Steve Maroney, James O'Neil, and Vic Accorsini.

Accorsini was getting used to publicity, having been singled out for his name's ethnicity—and not in a favorable way—in the February 3, 1901 edition of the *New York Clipper*: "What is baseball coming to? For nearly half a century things ran smoothly enough until they began to rope in a few ringers, such as [Eddie] Abbaticchio, [Louis] Sockalexis, [Ossee] Schreckengost and now [Vic] Accorsini."

The inference, without any evidence other than surname, that such players were ruining baseball was flippantly intolerant for such a purportedly urbane newspaper. It spoke to the elite presumption of the *Clipper's* editors, especially given that all four players were extremely capable and that the ethnicities involved (Italian, Native American and German) were not particularly exotic. Unfortunately, such treatment was indicative of a broader societal intolerance for ethnic differences, more obvious and openly expressed perhaps in 1901, given very heavy immigration levels at the time, but still evident in the twenty-first century.

For its part, Waverly was proud to have Accorsini back for the 1901 season, and no less a authority than *The Sporting News* reported that "Victor is remarkably popular throughout Southern New York and refused flattering offers from league teams" to return to "Manager Tucker's strong and independent team."[293]

Despite rain on Wednesday, the fair's crowds exceeded expectations, drawing over one thousand visitors on Thursday and netting $1,200 for the team. [294]

Tucker planned to have most of the 1900 team return for 1901 and was also looking to make improvements where possible. In response to a reporter's question, Tucker stressed the advantages of staying "independent" and the disadvantages of joining a full-time professional league, like the New York State League. "The cost of acquiring a franchise and its maintenance is too high," he pointed out.

"In Waverly, the talk lately has centered mainly on the pro passion that locals enter the state league," the *Waverly Advocate* reported. "Manager Tucker and Secretary [George] Bailey did look into the matter, but have decided to keep the [team's colors] white and red out of the organization."[295]

Despite Tucker's comments to the contrary, hopes were high in Waverly that the team would be given some sort of a league franchise.

Bailey, for example, acknowledged to the Elmira *Gazette* that a rival league comprised of Lestershire, Hammondsport, Waverly, Corning and Hornellsville would "give much more interest to the game," and explained that he and Tucker "have been too busy to formulate any plans as yet."[296]

On April 13, the team showed off its new uniforms: cream white shirts and trousers, with red stockings, belts, caps, and coats, with a red "W" on the left breast of the shirt. Tucker proudly displayed a sample of the uniform in his cigar shop's window.

Tucker's mentor John Doran would likely have enjoyed the pre-season preparations—and perhaps he did enjoy some of them—but on April 11, he was once again sent to the county jail in Owego for intoxication, this time for thirty days.[297]

Waverly's first game was scheduled to be against a semi-pro team from Syracuse on April 29, with a contest against Hughie Jennings' Cornell team the following Saturday still in negotiation.

AT THE MAJOR-LEAGUE LEVEL, SKEPTICS CONTINUED TO criticize the new developments, but it was clear to all that the American League was successfully signing some of the National League's best players. In addition to Lajoie and Collins, the American League signed National League stars Clark Griffith for Chicago, John McGraw and Wilbert Robinson for Baltimore, Cy Young and Chick Stahl for Boston, Kid Gleason for Detroit, Socks Seybold for Philadelphia, and Hugh Duffy for Milwaukee.

And this was just a small sample. According to Lee Allen, a Baseball Hall of Fame historian, of the 182 players who would appear on American League rosters in 1901, 111 had National League experience.[298]

Connie Mack of Philadelphia's American League club thought he had signed Christy Mathewson, but the pitcher stuck with the National League New York Giants, which had just obtained him from Cincinnati. It was at least the second time Mathewson had allegedly changed his mind after agreeing to sign with a club. Mathewson would have an outstanding rookie season for the Giants that year–strong enough to earn him the National League's rookie of the year award; Socks Seybold would earn the same for the American League.[299]

In Baltimore, new manager McGraw, never an avid supporter of baseball's color line, was so eager to build a winning team in the new league in 1901 that he attempted to sign African-American second baseman Charlie Grant, and pass him off as a full-blooded Cherokee named Charlie Tokohama. Grant had played the 1900 season with the Chicago Columbia Giants, so was easily recognizable to many in baseball. Nevertheless, McGraw inserted Grant into his line-up during spring training, only releasing him after Charlie Comiskey and others in the Chicago area who easily recognized Grant objected.[300]

Once his Cornell season was over, Hughie Jennings was interested in joining McGraw with the new AL franchise in Baltimore, but Ban Johnson had other ideas. Johnson visited Jennings at Cornell in late April and told him that McGraw was mistaken in saying Jennings could join him. Johnson wanted Jennings in Philadelphia with Lajoie, where the two would strengthen Philadelphia's AL club in its rivalry for fans and attention with the city's NL club. He told Jennings that McGraw had already signed his limit of four NL players for this year, and Jennings believed him. In fact, McGraw had reserved a spot for Jennings, but Johnson misrepresented the situation.

This deception led to a confrontation in early 1901 between Johnson and McGraw—the first of many that would eventually lead McGraw to return to the NL. But for 1901 at least, McGraw was committed to the new Baltimore AL franchise, and expected Jennings to join him in June when his Cornell season was over. "Johnson can take such action as he sees fit," McGraw said.[301]

As a result of all this, it was unclear to Jennings whether he would be able to play with McGraw or would have to join another team when the Cornell season was over.

In addition, the NL owners had not yet given up on a legal remedy for the salary war. On March 27, Philadelphia's NL team filed a suit against Lajoie, seeking to prevent him from playing for the AL. The winner of the case would have an early leg up in the salary wars going forward. A decision would not be rendered until June, and in the meantime, Lajoie was allowed to play for Connie Mack's AL franchise.

Even as the two major leagues set up their squads to begin the season, questions remained about whether both leagues could draw fans and make money. In 1900, the NL as a whole had drawn just over 1.8 million fans; Philadelphia had the largest average attendance at 4,313 per game. The salary cap was intended to help keep expenses low, but now that it had been destroyed by the salary war, how would the major league teams make enough money?

On June 17, 1901, a Philadelphia court agreed with Harry Taylor and Connie Mack that Napoleon Lajoie had the right to execute his contract with the Philadelphia's AL franchise. The NL continued to appeal, and won a narrow victory in the case almost a year later, but the early victory was an important one for the fledgling league and its franchises.

For his part, Lajoie was one of the league's top performers in the early part of the season. Collins and Young in Boston and McGraw and Robinson in Baltimore were also successful at drawing crowds and generating fan interest. By the end of June, McGraw declared to the national sports media that attendance in the early portion of the season had "proven" that the public could and would support two major leagues.

Despite their new competition, the NL was having success as

well, as attendance was keeping pace with 1900, and in some key cities, like New York, Brooklyn and Cincinnati, was growing. As Harry Taylor predicted, the game itself was growing, as overall major league attendance would almost double from 1900 to 1901.

Honus Wagner remained in the senior circuit and was in his second year with Pittsburgh. He had led the league in 1900 in batting average (.381), doubles (445), and triples (22), and was on his way to another great season in 1901, where he would hit .353 and lead the league in runs batted in (126) and stolen bases (49). Christy Mathewson was off to a strong start with his new team in New York and was well on his way to his first twenty-win season. Former Waverly star Bill Donovan, meanwhile, was having a breakout year with Brooklyn and was on his way to a league-leading twenty-five-win season, a feat that retroactively earned him NL pitcher of the year honors from the Society for American Baseball Research in 2016. Cy Young earned that honor for the AL that same year.[302]

Meanwhile, after being involved in controversies throughout the first half of the season, ranging from his PPA motives, to his Cornell gig, to his situation with Baltimore, Hughie Jennings attempted to join McGraw in Baltimore on June 19, but Johnson ordered the umpires to forfeit to Baltimore's opponent any game in which Jennings attempted to play. Johnson demanded that Jennings either play for Philadelphia or return to the NL, where he was still under contract with Brooklyn.

Stymied by the AL, Jennings engineered a deal whereby the Philadelphia NL club purchased his contract from Brooklyn, and, on June 21, he joined the new club. For the rest of 1901 he helped Ed Delehanty and teammates challenge first-place Pittsburgh, led by Honus Wagner, Jack Chesbro, Chief Zimmer, and Tommy Leach, for the pennant.

Soon after joining Philadelphia, Jennings also resigned his position with the PPA. Despite his friendship with and loyalty to Harry Taylor, the PPA had been powerless to help him navigate a way to join his friend McGraw in Baltimore. Moreover, he likely realized that the PPA had already accomplished much of its professed mission with the formation and success of a rival league that would ensure competition and limit the ability of an entire league to ignore player interests. The subtle issues still at play, involving how the PPA would interact with both the minor and major leagues, were more up Taylor's alley. "It has served its purpose as well as it ever will," Jennings explained.[303]

Meanwhile, the action on the field and the results at the box office were extraordinary. From the beginning of the season, teams in many cities reported record-high crowds. By mid-May, "lively" interest was reported in both National and American League cities, and in early June, baseball writer H. G. Merrill reported that the labor "war has been beneficial to base ball."

"The undisputed fact remains that the national game is enjoying a revival," Merrill wrote. "Very few actually believed that such would be the case, last winter, even though some had the temerity to predict a revival. The fact that the crowds are generally pleasingly large and indisputably enthusiastic, augurs well for a continued good patronage."[304]

But how would these events at the top of the baseball food chain impact the minor leagues? Would independent clubs like Waverly benefit or be hurt in the long run?

THE 1901 NEW YORK STATE LEAGUE (NYSL) WAS SET TO OPEN with eight teams in the towns of Utica, Cortland, Schenectady, Rome, Ilion, Binghamton, Troy, and Albany. The 1900 Elmira franchise, after having started out in Oswego, was now in Ilion, a town in Herkimer County, just thirteen miles east of Utica. Ilion was the home of the Remington firearms plant, not far from the Erie Canal. Remington would also eventually manufacture typewriters, sewing machines, and cash registers at Ilion. The town's manufacturing reputation was so prominent that its team was frequently known as the "Typewriters."

The NYSL was considered to be one of the best-run baseball leagues of any level in the country, due in large part to the conscientious management of league president John H. Farrell. Prior to the 1900 season, the league's "failure was almost universally predicted, but in spite of everything it finished the season. Mr. Farrell's Herculean work was all that made this possible. From a small beginning, the league has gradually grown until it is one of the strongest minor leagues in the country."[305] Farrell's exceptional success with the NYSL was similar to Ban Johnson's with the Western and American Leagues, and placed him in excellent position to move onto even greater jobs in the sport.

John H. Farrell, New York State League President

Farrell was born in Canada in July 1866 to Irish immigrant parents. He married his wife, Louise, in 1891, and they resided at 20 Main Street in Auburn with their two young sons, Frederick and Pierre. In the 1900 census, Farrell listed his occupation as "Telegrapher and Press Agent," but by 1910, his league's tenure was secure enough to list his occupation as "Ball Player" and his industry as "Pres. N.Y. State League."[306]

Utica had won the 1900 league championship with a 75-43 record, two and one-half games ahead of Cortland and just three ahead of Rome. Veteran players Howard Earl and Hank Simon had led Utica's 1900 championship team. Earl, thirty-three, had played in the major leagues with Chicago in 1890 and Milwaukee in 1891. He was a powerful player, but did not get another major league shot. At over six feet, he was tall for a ball player at the time and was nicknamed "Slim Jim." Simon, thirty-eight, was one of Utica's best hitters, having hit .326 in 1899.

In 1901, both players were moving on to other NYSL franchises: Earl to Schenectady and Simon to Albany. Utica would instead defend its championship with thirty-one-year-old Canandaigua veteran Jack Lawlor, a former teammate of Jack Chesbro's with the Middletown Asylum club (and one of the last professional players to field without a glove[307]), thirty-seven-year-old infielder Wally Taylor, and a variety of other players with either prior or future major league experience, including Johnny Siegle, who played for Schenectady the previous years, and Dan Coogan, who played for Cortland.

Cortland finished 1900 with a 70-43 record, and they aimed for similar success in 1901. While they lost Coogan, they retained veterans Phil Nadeau, Mickey Mullin, Jim McCormick, and Jimmy Dean, and picked up Carlton Molesworth from Schenectady. In June, Cortland added Lattimer, Pennsylvania, native Matt Broderick, who had started the season with Buffalo following a successful Villanova college stint. Broderick's friend and Villanova teammate, also from an Anthracite coal mining family, Barney McFadden, had shifted from first baseman to pitcher while at college, and in 1901, was already set to pitch in the major leagues for Cincinnati. This gave Broderick extra motivation to get into the majors himself. In 1898, the two had been known as "the best ball players in the Lehigh region."[308]

Rome finished the 1900 season with a 70-44 record and featured journeyman pitcher George Wheeler and outfielder Cy Coulter. For 1901, Rome added Edward Daley (no relation to the pitcher who had passed away from consumption in 1891), who had played for Troy in 1900, and veteran Charlie Hamburg, who spent 1900 in Oswego and Elmira.

Rome received a scare in mid-April when Hamburg was reportedly injured in an industrial accident while working at his off-season job at Ames Iron Works in Oswego. Professional ball players who kept working all year to make ends meet often ran such risks, especially when they came form working-class backgrounds and did not have the job skills to secure safer employment. The Elmira newspapers reported that Hamburg would miss the entire season, but the *Rome Citizen* reported that Hamburg had provided his uniform size to team management in anticipation of his imminent arrival and mentioned nothing of an injury. Fortunately for Rome, the news of Hamburg's demise was exaggerated, and he wound up joining the club on time for the season.

Binghamton ended its 1900 season with Lee Viau as manager, and retooled its approach in 1901 by bringing in thirty-seven-year-old New Orleans outfielder Count Campau to be the player manager. Born in 1863 in Detroit, Campau spent three seasons in the major leagues with Detroit, St. Louis and Washington, and sixteen in the minors, making him, in one historian's calculation, "the most productive minor league player of the 19th century."[309] Bringing in the colorful Campau, the Binghamton owners hoped, would spark the team to improve its record and attract better attendance.

Upstate and western New Yorkers had much more to look forward to in the summer of 1901 than just baseball, though.

After years of paperwork and months of intense preparation, Buffalo was set to host the 1901 Pan-American Exposition on 350 acres of former farmland a half-hour's drive from downtown. The Pan-American Exposition Company, which managed the exhibition, had been working on the event since 1897 and had received Congressional approval and appropriations in 1898. Buffalo was chosen not only due to its proximity to Niagara Falls, but also for its accessibility by rail and the fact that it contained more paved streets than any other city in the world.

"Coming in the wake of the Spanish-American War, the Pan-American Exposition occurred at a time when the United States was expanding commercially, politically, and even militarily in Latin America," an historical *New York Times* analysis stated. "Its expressed purpose was to promote the economic interests and purported solidarity of the Western Hemisphere. The festival was similar to World's Fairs in emphasizing technology, but differed from them in not celebrating a historical event and in the more limited regional origins of the participating countries."[310]

Although smaller than the 1893 Chicago Columbian Exposition, which took up 690 acres, the Pan-American Exposition was huge for the Buffalo region, and the organizers hoped to lure enough visitors over six months—at an entrance fee of fifty cents per person Mondays through Saturdays and twenty-five cents on Sundays—to meet expenses. This was roughly comparable to professional baseball game tickets, and the same as what was charged at Chicago's Exposition in 1893.

Entrance to the Pan-American Exposition grounds began in February at a lower price (twenty-five cents) while the attractions were still under construction. To help facilitate crowds even before the Exposition's official opening on May 1, the Erie and Lehigh Valley Railroads both began offering special excursion fares to and from the event. Not to be outdone, the Lackawanna Railroad, whose tracks ran just south of the Erie's in Waverly, also advertised special rates, explaining to *Waverly Advocate* readers that it offered "the shortest and cleanest route from your door to the doors of the exposition."[311]

By June, the Exposition would be at its peak. "Of this great exhibition the half has never been and cannot be told," wrote the *Hammondsport Herald*. "It must be seen to be believed. The illuminated rainbow city at night is the most gorgeous sight imaginable. The electrical effects have never been equaled and probably never will be surpassed."

"We would advise the readers of the *Herald*," the *Herald* continued, "to visit the Pan-American Exposition, if possible. As an educator of the resources of the Americas it cannot be over-estimated and one glimpse of the illuminated city is worth the expense of the journey."[312]

CHAPTER 9

Too Fast for an Independent Club

Back in Waverly, the villagers were eager to embark on their own triumphant summer as the 1901 baseball season got underway.

In preparation for Opening Day on April 29 against the Syracuse Shamrocks, team officials further enhanced the Howard Street Grounds beyond the improvements made the previous year. They enlarged the grounds, re-graded the field, doubled the size of the grandstand, and erected a new ticket office. They also improved the grandstand's seating arrangements, and even provided several seats for the press. The players practiced on the new playing surface the Wednesday prior to opening day and found it to be muddy. Nonetheless, "some work was done" by the team, and all were optimistic the field would be ready.[313] "Manager Tucker is personally supervising all the improvements," the *Waverly Free Press* reported, "and he may be depended on to give the public the best of everything."[314]

In addition to improvements to the grounds themselves, the team added a walkway from Broad Street to the grounds' entrance on Howard Street.[315] This would help ensure that Broad Street businesses profited from a successful season as much as the team would.

Opening Day began with appropriate pomp, as a large crowd gathered to watch the teams promenade onto the grounds amid a festive atmosphere. "The teams marched to the grounds under the escort of the City Band and Village President [Hugh] Baldwin formally opened the season by tossing the first ball over the plate."

Roughly 1,500 fans crowded into the Howard Street Grounds to witness the festivities.[316] Although major league crowds were improving in 1901, this was still not too far from Brooklyn's average 1900 attendance of 2,507, and matched or exceeded 1899 average attendances for Baltimore, Cleveland, New York and Washington.

As in prior seasons, among the most enthusiastic was Waverly's unofficial cheerleader and mascot, Charles Boggs, the African-American porter at the Warford House. His rally cry, "You've found the ball," and other chants combined to excite the players and the crowd.[317]

Ging, still without a professional organized gig, resumed his starting pitcher role for Waverly against Dineen for the Shamrocks. Waverly's Opening Day starting line-up reflected only minor changes from 1900, with Steve Maroney in center field, Bill Heine at second base, James O'Neil at shortstop, Tom Dwyer at first base, Dell Hughes at third base, Vic Accorsini at catcher, Fred Tucker in left field, and Jack Barnett in right field.

Waverly took a huge lead right away–scoring ten runs in the first inning–and cruised to a 28-8 victory. The game was "loosely played," reflecting the players' early season lack of readiness. Everyone in the Waverly lineup had at least one hit, but Maroney stole the show for the home team, hitting for a cycle (a homerun, triple, double, and three singles) and scoring five runs. The Shamrocks did not help themselves, committing thirteen errors.[318]

The Shamrocks stayed in Waverly for a rematch the next day, which was a much closer game. This time, the visitors committed just ten errors and lost 10-8. Barnett started for Waverly and pitched the entire game to earn the win. Maroney followed his cycle of the previous day with another big performance – a triple, single and two runs scored. Prior to hitting his triple, Maroney "took a look at the delivery of [Shamrock pitcher] Dineen and another at the upper left hand hinge on the Providence Street gate and then – well, the ball did not miss it much and he galloped around to third amid the yells of the crowd."[319]

A speedy centerfielder from the Syracuse Shamrocks, Steve Maroney gave Waverly an immediate boost on the base paths and solidified the outfield. Portrait by Gary Cieradkowski.

Cornell was originally next on Waverly's schedule, but negotiations with Hughie Jennings' boys did not work out, so Ithaca High School visited Waverly instead and was beaten, 18-0. "The visitors played their best, but they were outclassed and they did not succeed in getting anybody around the bases," the *Waverly Free Press* reported. "The features of the game were the field work of Heine, Hughes and Maroney, the pitching of Ging and the batting of O'Neil and Hughes."[320]

Waverly's next test came on May 6 and 7, when the NYSL Binghamton team came to town.

Although Tucker in public indicated a preference for remaining "independent," many locals wanted Waverly to compete for an NYSL franchise, and they believed contests like this set the stage for proving Waverly belonged, especially if one of the existing eight franchises stumbled financially. Even some national baseball writers, like H. G. Merrill, felt that Waverly's "independent team is strong enough for the New York circuit."[321] Merrill, in an earlier spring article for *The Sporting News*, lauded Waverly as "that lively railroad town."[322]

In anticipation of possible league play, and as a replacement for George Grant who had returned to the New England League, Tucker added veteran William Vought to the squad. After playing with Grant and Mathewson for Taunton in 1899, Vought had played for Rome in 1900.

Binghamton had finished second-to-last in 1900, just ahead of Elmira, and was eager to improve its position in 1901. Among those returning from the previous season, three were in Binghamton's starting lineup: Harry Croft at center field, Jim Collopy at third base, and Sam Woodruff in left field.

A twenty-five-year-old Chicago native, Croft had already played a couple of games with Louisville and Philadelphia in the National League and was hoping to return to the majors soon. At thirty-one, Collopy was a veteran minor leaguer who had batted .313 for Bristol in the 1899 Connecticut League; he still hoped to prove himself on bigger stages. Woodruff, twenty-four, was, like Croft, still a young prospect, and he had several minor league seasons under his belt with .300 and higher batting averages. Veteran player and manager Count Campau was also in the starting line-up.[323]

Waverly scored five runs in the first inning and ran its lead to 10-0 by the fifth behind Barnett's shutout pitching. "Barnett's puzzling curves were mostly responsible for the down fall of the visitors," the *Elmira Daily Gazette* reported. Just nine years earlier, Barnett, along with Heine and Keeler, had been among the key contributors to Binghamton's championship season.

Sam Woodruff and Dutch Jordan eventually managed to score three runs between them for Binghamton before ultimately losing, 10-3. The attendance was again estimated to be 1,500. The *Waverly Free Press* said of the game: "Monday's contest with the Binghamton state league team was the best yet played and the victory of the locals over this strong aggregation brought great joy to the hearts of the Waverly fans. Barnett pitched great ball for five innings and was then relieved by Ging."[324]

The next day, Waverly played its first road game of the season, traveling to Binghamton for a rematch. Ging started in the box for Waverly, and Maurice Wolfe, for Binghamton. The score was a repeat of the previous day: a 10-3 victory for Waverly.[325]

On Saturday, May 11, Waverly hosted Wyoming Seminary and won 12-2. Wyoming managed just four hits against Ging and Tucker. Accorsini and Tucker each clouted doubles to lead Waverly's hitting attack.[326]

Five games into the new season, Waverly remained undefeated.

On Monday, May 13, with no game on the schedule, Waverly residents received entertainment of a different sort when Gorton's Minstrels were in town. Joseph Gorton, a former Civil War bandleader from Friendship, New York, was the group's founder, chief composer, arranger and leader. To market their evening show, several of the minstrels gave free exhibitions outside the Opera House near the town clock at the corner of Broad and Fulton. Sam Lee from Lexington, Kentucky, presented a cornet solo, and Joe Gorton, the founder's son, a baritone solo of "Sally in Our Alley," both of which were "loudly applauded."[327]

Waverly and other independent teams continued to avoid games on Sundays, as local ordinances still prohibited them. However, the pressure to play on Sundays and give fans who had to work the rest of the week an opportunity to watch remained intense. "It is hardly likely that ordinary working men could get away on weekdays," wrote historian Harold Seymour, "except for bricklayers, longshoremen, carpenters, and various part-time workers who might have some days off between jobs. But it was working men who swelled the Sunday crowds."³²⁸

Some teams in the region were willing to risk arrest and play on Sundays in order to test law enforcement, and some communities simply refused to enforce the state laws. The Rome and Schenectady NYSL teams, for instance, scheduled many Sunday games, because of lax enforcement in those towns. The Sunday following Waverly's victory over Wyoming, Schenectady hosted Cortland and lost 1-0. Lee pitched for the win, Molesworth scored the lone run for Cortland, and Nadeau led the offense with three singles. The attendance was 3,500, a very appealing number to franchises at any level of professional baseball.

Waverly's next visitor was another club from Syracuse, not the semi-pro Shamrocks, but the Eastern League's Syracuse club. Several Waverly players had played with Syracuse in pre-season contests, so the teams were somewhat familiar with one another. The Eastern League was a higher level league than the New York State League and was comprised of larger cities–Syracuse, Rochester, Worcester, Buffalo, Montreal, Toronto, Hartford, and Providence–so this was truly a difficult challenge.

For Waverly's veteran professionals, like Heine, Barnett, and Vought, this level of competition was nothing new. Waverly took a 1-0 lead in the second inning, and Barnett held it until giving up two in the sixth and two more in the seventh. Waverly was unable to mount a comeback and lost for the first time in the season, 4-1. Maroney led Waverly with three hits, and Accorsini scored Waverly's lone run. Henry Lynch and Lee DeMontreville led Syracuse with two hits each. Walt Woods, who, at twenty-six, already had three years of major league experience under his belt, earned the win.

A crowd of one thousand was on hand, and the New York sports media noticed Waverly's popularity with its fans. "Syracuse played in Buffalo Monday before 100 people and in Waverly yesterday before 1,000," noted a reporter for the *Oswego Daily Times*. "The towns that have the most people are not always best for baseball. Let's take Waverly, Tioga County, New York, in the league in place of Buffalo."[329]

Waverly had put together a lineup good enough to give an Eastern League franchise a competitive game, and it was drawing nearly as many fans as much larger cities. With a record of 5-1, Manager Tucker had a lot to be optimistic about, especially since one of his most experienced pitchers, Sandy McDougal, did not even join the team until May 16, two days after the Syracuse game. McDougal was not recorded as having another baseball job at the time, so his delay was presumably due to business and/or family matters back home in Buffalo.

On Saturday, May 18, Waverly hosted St. Bonaventure, before a crowd of eight hundred spectators. McDougal took the mound for Waverly and held the Bonnies to just one run for the first seven innings. Waverly scored one run in the first inning, and then five more in the fifth to take a 6-0 lead into the eighth. The Bonnies scored three runs in the eighth, but no more, and Waverly won, 7-4. Accorsini had a triple and a single, Tucker had two doubles, and Maroney three singles to lead Waverly's fourteen-hit attack. According to Tucker's calculations, the six leading hitters over the season's first eight games were McDougal (.500), Tucker (.439), Dwyer (.419), Maroney (.390), and O'Neil (.368).[330]

That Saturday evening after the game, Tucker and McDougal were in Tucker's cigar store, likely reveling in the glory of their baseball victory, when Frank W. Preston, a forty-two-year-old traveling solicitor, entered the store and sought to collect what he claimed was an overdue bill that Tucker had incurred for advertising his store in a Corning hotel registry. Tucker said he had paid the bill directly to the hotel, and the two men argued. Preston, according to witnesses, appeared to be intoxicated, used abusive language and walked out of the store. Whether or not Tucker and McDougal had been drinking themselves was not reported, but Preston's remarks were provocative enough that Tucker, normally a jovial sort, followed him out to the sidewalk, confronted him, and either shoved or struck him in the jaw, knocking him to the ground. Upon dropping heavily to the ground, Preston was unable to rise.[331]

"Ain't I a great hitter?" Tucker reportedly joked to McDougal and other witnesses at the scene.

Witnesses assisted Preston to Hanford's furniture store, where Doctors Tucker and Harnden examined him and discovered a broken left hip. He was taken to the Packer Hospital in Sayre for treatment.

As if the Tobin murder a year earlier had not been enough, it was a busy spring for violent confrontations in Waverly. One ongoing story in the *Waverly Free Press* involved Waverly mayor Hugh J. Baldwin's alleged attack with an umbrella on postmaster and newspaperman George D. Genung due to an editorial criticizing Baldwin for appointing his son chief of the fire department. Genung had sued the mayor for $10,000 in damages.[332]

Preston remained at the Packer Hospital overnight, and no change in his condition was reported on Sunday. The next day, Monday, Tucker and his team traveled to St. Bonaventure for a rematch and won 7-4. McDougal again pitched for Waverly and earned the win. After the game, Tucker and several of his non-baseball friends went on a multiday fishing trip.

On Tuesday, while Tucker was out of town, bad news emerged from the Packer Hospital: Preston was dead.

The official cause of death was in dispute, but all agreed that Tucker's blow had something to do with it. Rumors that Tucker would be arrested on murder charges ran rampant. Preston's widow arrived in town and demanded that autopsies cease and that the body be turned over to her for burial.

Meanwhile, without Tucker, Waverly hosted Jamestown before a crowd of seven hundred on Thursday, May 23 and won 11-6. McDougal and Heine led Waverly's attack with two hits each, while Barnett earned the win.[333] Heine likely served as Manager in Tucker's absence.

The next day, local officials issued an arrest warrant for Tucker, charging him with second-degree assault. Tucker returned from his fishing trip, turned himself in, posted bail, and was released. A trial, should it be necessary, would likely not occur until after the season was over. Meanwhile, he also faced possible civil charges from Preston's widow. The negative publicity was not good for his business, the town or the team.

The town's lurid news was compounded by the announcement that Fred Krist, originally scheduled to be executed in early January for his murder of Katie Tobin, had again succeeded in having his execution delayed while the case was under appeal, ensuring more weeks and months of scandalous discussion and speculation.

Among Krist's supporters was Republican activist Reverend Thomas Hendrick, pastor of St. Bridget's Catholic Church in Rochester and a "close acquaintance" of former Governor, now Vice President, Roosevelt. Hendrick, born in 1849 in Penn Yan, New York, had been the pastor at St. Bridget since 1891, and he took a personal interest in the case. Krist's attorneys no doubt encouraged the interest, since it would help Krist both politically and in the realm of public opinion. In addition, an Auburn Sister of Mercy, Sister Teresa, who was one of Krist's former teachers and visited him while in prison, may have encouraged Hendrick.[334] Hendrick's political connections would eventually lead him to be given important church relations duties for the U.S. insular government in the Philippines.

"Governor [Benjamin] Odell is about to be asked for a commutation of Fred A. Krist's sentence," reported the *Penn Yan Democrat*. "He is sentenced to be electrocuted during the week of August 28th, and the crime deserves the death penalty. *The Owego Gazette* says Rev. Thomas A. Hendrick of Rochester, is working for a change of sentence, and George Raines has been engaged to make an argument in favor of it."[335]

Krist's execution was successfully delayed until later in the fall. In the meantime, he remained in Auburn on death row.

DESPITE THE VARIOUS DISTRACTIONS, WAVERLY'S BASEBALL team continued to win and have success drawing competitive opponents and good crowds.

On the Monday following Tucker's arrest and release, Waverly defeated Binghamton for the third consecutive time, 16-3, with Ging getting the win.[336]

This was followed by a doubleheader against Syracuse University on Memorial Day. Unfortunately, unlike in 1900, the 1901 baseball and Memorial Day schedules were not well coordinated, and the crowd and coaches at the Howard Street Grounds were too loud for the solemn ceremonies taking place directly across Providence Street at the cemetery. The noise was particularly annoying when the City Band was playing a dirge in honor of the village's Civil War veterans. "It was probably thoughtlessness on the part of the boys, but it ought not to have been done," the *Free Press* said, noting, "The ball grounds almost adjoin the cemetery." Despite the unfortunate scheduling mishap, Waverly won the first game 10-1, and the second game ended in a 6-6 tie when the Syracuse team needed to leave early to catch its train.[337]

Waverly followed up with a 22-2 victory over Corning, with Tucker earning the win;[338] another doubleheader against Syracuse University, this time a clean sweep; and a split against the Brownson Athletic Club in Wilmington, Delaware. They then lost two straight games at Chester, Pennsylvania, bringing Waverly's season record, as of June 17, to 15-4-1.

Their winning record and extraordinary attendance numbers brought regional attention to Waverly's team, and it was thought that some of the better players might be lured to higher-level teams. This proved to be true when Barnett moved to the Eastern League's Syracuse club in the first week of June.

On June 17, Waverly traveled to the Owego Fairgrounds to play the Genuine Cuban Giants. These were John Bright's Cuban Giants under the "Genuine" name to distinguish them from the

Cuban X Giants. The 1901 Genuine Cuban Giants were the same franchise that Waverly played in 1896 and 1900, and were a strong team, led by "the wonderful" Frank Grant, who, at thirty-five, was the team captain and the club's most well-known and talented player. Grant had unfortunately not been in the line-up when the Giants met Waverly in 1900, but he was back at full strength in 1901. It had been over a decade since he starred for integrated minor league teams in Buffalo and Harrisburg, prior to the color line being drawn, but Grant's magnificence on the field was still evident. "Age has not impaired the ability of Grant to play the second bag," wrote the *York Daily* of Grant's 1901 performance.

Despite being prevented from playing on organized professional teams due to his race, Frank Grant was typically the most outstanding player on whatever diamond and against whatever opponent he played. Waverly was no exception. Portrait by Gary Cieradkowski.

In addition to Grant, the Giants' lineup continued to feature some of the most prominent African-American players in the country, including forty-four-year-old John "Pop" Watkins, outfielder William "King" Kelley, Clarence "Clem" Sampson, Eddie Day from Reading, and twenty-five-year-old catcher John Garcia, likely the only actual Cuban on the team. Others in the lineup were Joe Green, Joseph "Cannonball" Miller, Ed Wilson, and Wallace Gordon.

The Giants were in the middle of their usual summer swing through New York and Pennsylvania, ranging from the New York City suburbs; west to Buffalo and Jamestown; south to Philadelphia, Harrisburg, and York; and north to Ogdensburg, Potsdam, and Malone. Along the way, they brought their unique brand of baseball and showmanship to towns and villages of all sizes. Early advance promotion was the best way to ensure a large crowd, and the Giants were masters of promotion. They even promoted the availability of their singing "quartette" for special occasions; once, in an impromptu moment at the Jamestown Erie Station, their quartette entertained and amused an otherwise impatient and "good sized" crowd awaiting a late evening train.[339]

In 1901, the Giants were in a transitional phase, with veterans like Grant and Watkins becoming less prominent, and competition for young talent with other traveling colored teams, like the Cuban X Giants and clubs from Chicago, picking up.

Compared to much of the rest of their circuit, the Giants found the Finger Lakes region, especially around Bath, Hammondsport, and Penn Yan, to be hospitable and profitable, with healthy enthusiastic crowds. After a ballgame and two "very enjoyable vocal concerts in the park" given by various Giants players, for instance, one Giant remarked that Hammondsport was the best town they visited, especially since "you hear no 'nigger' there."[340]

Unfortunately, this was not true of all New York towns. Even in friendly Lockport, about thirty miles north of Buffalo, a local paper felt it necessary as part of its advertisement for the upcoming game to add, "They will have with them Frank Grant, the famous 'coon' second baseman."[341]

The Giants rolled into the Owego Fairgrounds on the afternoon of June 17, ready to take on the Waverly club in the first of a much-anticipated three-game series. Unfortunately for Grant and company, they were unable to keep the Waverly hitters under control, and lost 20-6.[342]

The next day, the Giants traveled to Waverly's Howard Street Grounds for the second game of the series. Ging started for Waverly, and Joe Green, the victor in the 1900 Waverly contest, for the Giants. Waverly scored four runs in the first four innings and again easily defeated the Giants, this time 10-1. Kelley, Day, and Green were the only Giants hitters who could figure out Ging's mix of pitches, while several Waverly hitters got to Green, especially Maroney, Heine, and Hughes, who scored two runs each. Grant got on base, but had no hits or runs in two trips to the plate. [343]

The Giants faced Waverly again on the Howard Street Grounds the next day for the final game of the series. For the second straight day, a rainstorm, putting a damper on the crowd size, preceded the game.[344] McDougal started on the mound and Tucker behind the plate for Waverly, and Wilson pitched for the Giants. The Giants took an early 3-0 lead and held it until the fourth inning, when Waverly exploded with five runs, taking a 5-3 lead. Waverly then expanded that lead to 6-3, but the Giants fought back and took a 7-6 lead going into the sixth.[345]

There had been talk in other towns during the summer of the Giants losing on purpose in order to "bait" local gamblers into increasing their wagers, and once the coffers were full, the Giants would turn on the gas and prove victorious. Following a Giant victory in the second game of a two-game series against Clifton Springs, New York, for instance, the local newspaper noted, "Reports indicate that the colored gents deported considerable cash wagered on the bait of the first game,"[346] presumably a loss.

If such a gambit was the Giants' intent against Waverly, the plot was foiled, as Waverly scored seven runs in the sixth inning, four in the seventh, and seven more in the ninth, against just three more Giants runs, winning 24-10 and sweeping the series.[347] "There were more hard hits in the game Wednesday than has ever been seen on the home ground before," the *Waverly Advocate* reported.[348]

Unlike in the first two games, the legendary Grant was very strong in game three, with two runs and two hits. It was by far his best performance on a Waverly diamond.

The Giants' owner, John Bright, praised the Waverly team effusively. "I will now have to own up," he told the *Waverly Advocate*, "you have the best club. In fact, it is too fast for an independent club. You should be in the Eastern League."[349]

Waverly's victories over the Giants brought their season record to 18-4-1.

At the same time, rumors were pervasive—both in town and throughout the region—that the Cortland NYSL franchise was about to fold due to financial troubles and that Waverly was first in line to take over. Still, not everyone was enamored with Waverly. H. L. Fry, Albany's correspondent for *The Sporting News*, was not impressed with the village as the potential home for an organized baseball franchise, as he noted in his July 13 column: "Cortland, after various conflicting rumors, has decided to hang on a while longer. There was some talk of transferring the team to Waverly. The said town of Waverly could be put under a postage stamp and would be no better than Cortland. They have a good independent team there, playing a game or two a week. That is about all the base ball the town can pay for."[350]

Tucker had expressed a similar sentiment before the season had started. Even if Waverly were able to lure a franchise like Cortland's, would it be able to sustain its expenses (salaries) and revenues (attendance) over a much more intense NYSL schedule? In addition, with Tucker facing assault charges, the team's future under his direction was not necessarily secure.

Like most town teams at the time, Waverly's revenues were severely limited due to their inability to play on Sundays. A few towns did allow Sunday baseball and others tried to play despite the law. On Sunday, June 23, for example, Waverly traveled to Syracuse and defeated the Shamrocks 14-0 before a crowd of two thousand, but multiple players from Syracuse and one from Waverly were arrested in the process.[351] It was Waverly's last attempt as an independent team to play a Sunday game in 1901.

Whether or not games occurred on Sunday, they frequently attracted gamblers who were far from subtle. This was not necessarily bad for the sport, since, as historian John Thorn once noted, "Gambling was not the impediment to the game's flowering but instead the vital fertilizer."[352] Nevertheless, to many, as Waverly learned from its 1896 experience where some of their players were rumored to have been paid by gamblers to throw games, gambling could grow into a fertilizer of a distinct and undesired odor.

The same people who disdained gambling and advocated baseball-free Sundays also tended to be antithetical to other immoral "entertainment" pursuits. Chief among these crusaders in the U.S. at the time was fifty-four-year-old six-foot-tall Kentucky native Carrie Amelia Moore Nation.

In 1899, Carrie Nation, an active member of a local Women's Christian Temperance Union in Kansas, began her anti-saloon activism by entering saloons singing temperance hymns. By 1900, she escalated her activities by entering saloons with friends—all of them carrying bricks—and using the bricks to smash bottles, furniture, and any "immoral" pictures. Nation's activities continued to escalate into 1901, vandalizing saloons and earning at least thirty short jail sentences throughout Oklahoma, Kansas, Missouri, and Arkansas. In the process, her approach advanced from bricks to easier-to-use tools, such as axes. At a minimum after the attacks, the saloons were required to close temporarily in order to make repairs, and in some cases they were unable to collect insurance and were forced to file for bankruptcy. As a result, many saloon owners hired armed guards to defend against the attacks. In the summer of 1901, Carrie Nation began a well-publicized tour of the eastern states, including at least one visit to New York's Southern Tier and to the Pan-American Exposition.[353] Given the risks of financial loss and bad publicity, saloon owners in Waverly and neighboring towns kept a watchful eye on her travels.

Following their Sunday game in Syracuse, Waverly played three games against Lestershire and won all three. Lestershire continued to be dominated by its association with the local shoe factory, and its team had been bolstered in May by a one-thousand-dollar contribution from George F. Johnson, general manager and half-owner of the Lestershire shoe company and the vice president of the Lestershire Athletic Association.[354] Johnson had risen from the Lester Brothers' factory floor to become a foreman and, in 1899, was made a partner when Henry Bradford Endicott acquired the company. By 1904, the shoe company would be renamed Endicott-Johnson Shoes, and in 1916 Lestershire would become Johnson City. Johnson would continue to be a big booster of baseball as well as his shoe company, eventually becoming a personal friend of baseball Commissioner Kenesaw Mountain Landis,[355] and in 1912 financing the construction of Johnson Field, which for decades was the Binghamton-area home of powerful Yankee farm teams.[356]

Johnson, like most corporate leaders, was extremely skeptical of and antithetical to labor unions. As someone who started as a workingman, he believed each individual had the ability to succeed without the help of a union. A 1906 profile described his rise from shoemaker's bench to company ownership as "a lesson to every ambitious boy of how a man with no great wealth but his talents and no especial instrument save a vigorous and honest manhood can force his way to the front of one of the greatest industries in the United States."[357]

Johnson's story was similar to Andrew Carnegie's and consistent with the self-made-man theme made popular in nineteenth century America by the writer Horatio Alger, Jr. In Johnson's case, however, whether out of self-interest or empathy, he was sympathetic to working conditions, and sought to counter the unions by making living and working conditions satisfying enough for the workers that they would be disinterested in union membership, an approach he termed his "Square Deal." Johnson was extremely active in the community, and his Square Deal provided employees with E-J-built and -financed homes, a profit sharing plan, health care from factory-funded medical facilities, and worker recreational facilities. He did what he could to make sure that employees and their families were happy, productive, and loyal. The author's paternal grandparents, for instance, both worked for E-J, and they raised their family in company-built housing on Grand Avenue in Johnson City.

Johnson's brand of local corporate leadership stood in marked contrast to J.P. Morgan's brand of monopoly leadership. While Johnson continued to lure workers to his local factory, Morgan's U.S. Steel was closing local factories in the name of consolidation and efficiency. The consolidations hit New York and Pennsylvania towns particularly hard. For example, U.S. Steel's subsidiary, American Bridge, took over twenty-nine relatively small, locally-owned bridge companies, including the Elmira Bridge Company, the Union Bridge Company in Athens, the Horseheads Bridge Company, the J.B. & J.M. Cornell Company in Ithaca, and the Groton Bridge Company, not far from Cortland. As a part of this consolidation, the Groton Bridge Company was closed on August 15, resulting in displaced local employees. "The plant employs 400 men," the *New York Times* reported, "and for fourteen years has been the sustaining industry of Groton. Most of the employees have built houses for themselves, and if the mills are removed, it will be a severe blow to the men. Until the time the plant was absorbed by the corporation, the plant had all the work it could handle."[358]

These circumstances, and similar ones impacting other industries, led many workingmen to feel helpless, to fall prey to conspiracy theories, and to look more urgently to organized labor leaders for guidance. Samuel Gompers of the American Federation of Labor spoke out in opposition to the closings, as did Emma Goldman and other activists. As with her speeches concerning the Lattimer, Pennsylvania, massacre of striking coal miners four years earlier, Goldman's 1901 speeches informed and inspired would-be labor activists throughout the region.

The line between activism and violence was always tricky in such tense times. That spring, for instance, Goldman gave a speech in Cleveland that inspired a disgruntled Polish-American steel worker named Leon Czolgosz, who within just a few months would become arguably the most infamous anarchist in world history, and an assassin on par with John Wilkes Booth in American history. In July, Czolgosz met Goldman, this time in Chicago. Czolgosz, using the alias "Nieman," told Goldman he was in a socialist club that was too passive and wanted to network with a more active group. Goldman connected him to her associates in Chicago, but by late August Goldman's associates grew suspicious of "Nieman," and issued a warning in the journal "Free Society" on September 1st to be on the lookout for him, as he was "asking for names, or soliciting aid for acts of contemplated violence."[359]

At twenty-eight, Czolgosz was from the same generation of miners, steel workers, furniture makers, blacksmiths, and ball players that was struggling to navigate an economic landscape where increasing numbers of workers were moving from farms and small towns to factories and larger towns, often in competition with recent immigrants, and often under the control of monopolistic oligarchs, who, at a whim, could close dozens of factories and send their workingmen and women into destitution.

Czolgosz's father and brothers, for example, were having a go at farming in the Cleveland area after escaping factory work in the city. For Czolgosz himself, however, farming held no interest, and the unfairness of the capitalist system loomed large in his psyche. When his brother Jacob suggested he go to the hospital to seek treatment for his obvious emotional distress, Czolgosz's alleged response perfectly illustrated his frustration: "There is no place in the hospital for poor people; if you have lots of money you will get taken care of."[360]

Like Krist writing about his trial, Czolgosz singled out money as the thing that made all the difference in outcomes in America— it meant the different between conviction or acquittal, medical treatment or being turned away from the hospital. In Czolgosz's case, Goldman's speeches had convinced him that his circumstances were part of a much larger problem–the unfair capitalist system.

Signs of heavy-handed corporate dismissals of worker concerns existed throughout society, and the baseball business was no exception. Despite granting concessions to the Players' Protective Association (PPA) in February, for instance, organized baseball's owners distanced themselves from organized labor and would continue to do so for decades, epitomizing the worst stereotypes of unfair capitalism. President Soden of Boston, explained his view in mid-1900 to *Sporting Life* as follows:

> I do not believe in labor organizations or unions. As soon as the players join the Federation they cease to become free agents, and have to do just as they are told. I do not see the need of any such action. For myself, I feel that when a player ceases to be useful to me, I will release him. Even if the players join the Federation does not bind us to hire players who belong to the Federation or pay any prices dictated by that organization. We shall continue to hire whom we please, and pay as we please.[361]

Philadelphia's owner, John Ignatius Rogers, a graduate of the University of Pennsylvania, expressed similar sentiments at the time: "Base ball is not a trade or industry that can be classified under the head of labor. It is merely a sport and has no legitimate place in a federation of labor. When the players band themselves together in an effort to dictate to us the manner in which we shall conduct our business it will then be time for the magnates to retire. And under such circumstances I should like to know where the players will find capital willing to risk a resumption of the enterprise."³⁶²

The baseball players' response to this position, successful in moving to abate the most urgent evils in their industry, was aligned with reformist Republicans like Theodore Roosevelt rather than Democrats like Bryan or activists like Gompers or Goldman. Despite the hardened opposition of the National League's monopolistic owners, baseball's new union activists learned from their past failures to seek more gradual solutions. As explained by Robert Burk: "In contrast [to the brotherhood of a decade earlier], the Protective Association embodied the more restricted horizons of the 'new' trade unionism in its self-proclaimed emphasis upon pragmatic negotiation, designed to promote incremental bread-and-butter gains rather than open defiance of management prerogatives."³⁶³

Many workers, both within and outside of baseball, were resourceful enough to do whatever was necessary to navigate the new economic realities. Some Groton-area workers who were out of a job due to Morgan's creation of the U.S. Steel monopoly, like Orlando Hemingway, the author's great-grandfather, took the changes in stride. In Hemingway's case, he left his family in the Groton area and worked remotely for a time at corporate headquarters in Ambridge, just up the river from Pittsburgh.

The experience of moving from a rural to an urban area brought new challenges in figuring out how to make ends meet. "I…don't think one can ever make money here," Hemingway said of Ambridge, "as it costs all you get to live. The wages here are never going to be very high, except for a very few at the heads of departments."

Hemingway's description of the big industrial city vividly depicts how different the urban industrial environment was from the more rural community he had left behind: "I saw 'Dark Pittsburgh' yesterday for when I got there at 2 PM it was most dark. Lights everywhere same as at night, the smoke and fog were so dense."

Hemingway's letters to his parents from Ambridge also noted the impact of the current economic system on commodity prices: "It seems queer that potatoes are so low there, as they are 75 cents here, but suppose that the freight and commission men and retailers are what make them so high, most of the potatoes here come from Ohio."

Notwithstanding the best efforts of individual workers, especially those at the higher wage levels, to adapt to and thrive in challenging circumstances, there remained that feeling of helplessness at the lower wage levels. Labor advocates like Bryan, Gompers and Goldman had a common message for industrial magnates: you can only crush workers so far before it leads to negative results for yourselves and the economy as a whole. As if taking a cue from such advocates, Mother Nature in the summer of 1901 brought the Twin Tiers more than a typical amount of rain, which in turn presented some communities with an unusual and unpleasant phenomenon that to the advocates would have been an apt metaphor for labor disputes: frog infestation.

"The frogs have appeared in great numbers," the *Elmira Daily Gazette* explained. "The ground in Renwick park [in Ithaca] is covered with them. A train which left for Auburn late Sunday night had difficulty in working its way through the myriads which appeared on the track, which became so slippery from the ones killed that the wheels would not take hold of the rails."[364]

CHAPTER 10

Into Its Proper Class At Last

Baseball continued to be played in the Southern Tier whenever the summer rains stopped long enough, and on July 11, after months of wrangling and speculation, lively Waverly officially took over the Cortland franchise and became a member of the New York State League (NYSL).[365] It was a stunning development for the village, which was now the smallest town in the league. Waverly was officially a professional organized baseball town.

"Waverly's champion base ball nine is now a member of the State league and all doubt as to the future of the National game here the rest of the season is settled," wrote the *Waverly Free Press*, noting that the change put the team "into its proper class at last," and produced "great joy among the local fans."[366]

Waverly had twenty-three wins on the season and Cortland had twenty-one at the time the franchise was transferred, but Cortland had thirty-four losses to Waverly's four–and as a condition of entry, Waverly was obligated to take on Cortland's existing record. This was difficult for the excited town to accept, but it was not nearly as challenging as taking on Cortland's schedule. Over the first seventy-three days of the season, Waverly had played twenty-five games. Over the next twenty-seven days, Waverly would play twenty-six games–each one against another competitive league team. There would be no more games against Lestershire, Corning, or the Cuban Giants. Also, the way Cortland's season schedule unfolded, a majority of Waverly's remaining games would be on the road.

At the time of Waverly's entry into the NYSL, Schenectady was in first place followed closely by Albany, Utica, Troy, Binghamton and Rome. Waverly was next followed by last-place Ilion.

Turning to experienced organized baseball hands, the team gave the managerial reins to Bill Heine and the team captaincy to Vic Accorsini, who took the name "Andrews" for purposes of official game records. It's unclear why Accorsini used a different name, since he did not appear to be under contract elsewhere, and he was already known throughout the region. Also unclear is what role Tucker played in the new organization. He continued to be a financial backer and to play for the team on occasion, and it is assumed he also continued to play an on-field leadership role, albeit more behind the scenes than before, perhaps on account of the legal entanglements and bad publicity associated with the Preston case.

Waverly had the option of retaining whichever of the existing Cortland players it wanted. Initially unhappy with the transition, Cortland's Phil Nadeau, the team's best hitter and a veteran of many professional seasons, attempted to switch to Binghamton, but was hauled back. Also retained from Cortland were third baseman Jim McCormick, pitcher Jack Lee, and pitcher Mickey Mullin.[367] The remaining players, such as shortstop Matt Broderick and outfielder Carlton Molesworth, were free to sign with other clubs, pending any other reservations.

"The expected removal of the Cortland team to Waverly has taken place," wrote *Sporting News* baseball columnist and Waverly skeptic H. L. Fry, "and Billie Heine, an old-timer, has been made manager and captain. His first action was to release [George] Cooper, [Bill] Gannon, Dean, Molesworth, Townsend and Coogan, filling the vacancies with members of the Waverly independent team. I presume Heine knows his business, but he certainly must have something good up his sleeve when he can afford to let such men as Gannon and Molesworth go."³⁶⁸

Countering Fry's negativity, Wilkes-Barre correspondent H. G. Merrill said, "Waverly, NY, ought to prove a better place than Cortland for Mr. Farrell's circuit."³⁶⁹

Waverly celebrated the opening of its NYSL season on Friday afternoon, July 12, with a "fast, snappy" 7-4 home-field victory over last-place Ilion, with McDougal earning the win. O'Neil hit a double and two singles and McDougal hit a home run to lead Waverly's attack. Waverly's first fully professional lineup featured Maroney in center field, O'Neil at shortstop, Nadeau in left field, Dwyer at first base, Heine at second base, McCormick at third base, Hughes in right field, Accorsini (under the name "Andrews") at catcher, and McDougal on the mound.³⁷⁰ The game's box score did not report the crowd size, but it was likely between 500 and 1,000, and would have been larger had the game occurred on a holiday or Saturday, or had Waverly's civic organizations, such as the band, been given enough advance notice to organize a formal celebration.

The winning streak was short-lived, however, as Ging took Waverly's first NYSL season loss the next day before a "large" Saturday home crowd versus Ilion, 3-2.³⁷¹

After taking Sunday, July 14, as a day off, Waverly hosted Rome with newcomer Lee on the mound. It was veteran first baseman Charlie Hamburg's first recorded visit to Waverly's Howard Street Grounds, but the field was familiar to Rome's right fielder, former Lestershire star Harry Lumley.

Waverly took a first inning lead thanks to a hit by Maroney and a double by Dwyer. Lee scattered seven hits and shut down the Rome lineup until giving up a scratch run in the fifth. After that, the two teams battled at 1-1 until the tenth inning, when Lee hit a single against Rome pitcher Willard Mains and made it to second on Maroney's out.

Nadeau came to the plate with a chance to win the game for Waverly, and he slugged a double, scoring Lee. Waverly won 2-1. Hamburg went hitless in four trips to the plate against Lee.³⁷²

Outfielder Phil Nadeau, a veteran of the Eastern, New England and New York State Leagues, was among the NYSL's best hitters, and greatly improved Waverly's run production capability when he joined the team. Portrait by Gary Cieradkowski.

After that victory, hard-hitting Utica was Waverly's next victim, losing 15-11, with Mullin earning the win. Heine led the hitting attack with two triples, two doubles, a single, and four runs scored. Among the Waverly players in the line-up was Tucker, who substituted in the outfield after Maroney sprained his angle. Tucker rapped a single, while Mullin chipped in a homerun and single to help his cause.[373]

"Those Waverlyites are playing the real article of ball now," reported the *Binghamton Republican*.[374]

After Maroney sprained his ankle, Nadeau shifted to center field for the next day's game against Utica, while McDougal played right field. Ging was on the mound and held Utica to just five runs, but he did not get the same support Mullin had gotten the day before–and lost 5-4 as a result. Nadeau, Dwyer, Hughes, and Accorsini each hit doubles for Waverly.³⁷⁵

Waverly started its first NYSL road trip over the weekend, traveling to Rome and losing three straight games by close scores. Waverly then traveled to Utica for two straight losses, the second before a reported crowd of 300, to Schenectady for a two-game split, and to Ilion for two wins out of three games. The attendance in Ilion for the Saturday double-header on July 27 was reported to have been a decent 700, which was higher than many of the crowds reported around the league at the time, but still not tremendous for a Saturday. Waverly's total record for the road trip was 3-7, and their overall NYSL record, a respectable 6-9.

The NYSL schedule rolled on, game after game with little rest.

Waverly began a home stand on July 29 with a two-game series against Albany. This was Waverly's first look at the Senators, who recently took over first place from Schenectady.

A healthy Monday crowd of 750 at the Howard Street Grounds welcomed the clubs for the first game of the series. Ging started on the mound for Waverly, and had trouble handling Albany's top four batters, especially veteran left fielder Hank Simon, who wound up the day with a triple, a single and three runs scored. The thirty-eight-year-old Simon had been playing minor league ball in New York for years, including an 1887 stint with Syracuse, where he and Doug Crothers refused to pose in a team picture with African-American pitcher Bob Higgins, one of several 1887 incidents that signaled the sharpening of the color line in professional baseball.³⁷⁶ Simon seemed to especially feed on Ging's type of tricky off-speed pitches. Hughes relieved Ging at pitcher in the late innings, and did not have much better luck. Simon and the other top four Albany hitters combined for ten of the team's thirteen hits, three of them triples, and seven runs in defeating Ging and Waverly 11-6. The *Free Press* reported that Albany was "more than we could handle," and *Sporting Life* called the game "slow and uninteresting."³⁷⁷

The next day Waverly got another shot at the league leaders. Lee started on the mound for Waverly versus Charles Baker for

Albany, and after four innings the two were locked at five runs apiece. Simon and the others in the top of the order were getting nowhere near as good a look at Lee's pitches as they had at Ging's. Waverly scored one in the fifth, two more in the seventh, and held Albany to just one more in the seventh to earn an 8-6 victory. Manager Bill Heine, the Waverly player with the longest and deepest professional experience, did everything he could to carry the team on his shoulders, scoring three runs and fielding flawlessly at second base. "Heine won special honors with four hits, two of them two-baggers," the *Free Press* reported. Tucker, who relieved Accorsini at catcher, picked up two singles and "caught a good game" in support of Lee's victory. "Fine team work at critical stages was responsible for Waverly's victory," *Sporting Life* reported.

It was a brief burst of sunshine in an otherwise bleak streak of ball, however, as Waverly hosted Troy in the first game of a two-game series the very next day, and lost 4-3.[378]

During the Troy series, the baseball club shared the limelight with hundreds of others in town, as Waverly hosted the regional Emancipation Day festival, which brought African Americans into Waverly from all over the Twin Tiers. "Thursday [August 1] was a gala day for the colored people of Waverly and vicinity," the *Free Press* reported. "It was up to them to celebrate Emancipation Day and they did so in a very successful manner. The program of the day was elaborate but it was carried out without a break and was complete in every detail."[379]

Even after the Civil War and implementation of the Emancipation Proclamation, African Americans in New York and other nearby states continued to celebrate August 1st as "Emancipation Day," since it was the day in 1834 that Great Britain emancipated slaves in the West Indies. Frederick Douglass, for instance, in a speech at Canandaigua, New York, in 1857 explained that, in contrast to continued slavery in the U.S., the West Indian emancipation was a "great deed of justice and humanity which has made the first of August illustrious among all the days of the year."[380]

To open the celebration, the Waverly City Band gave a concert to the early arrivals on Wednesday evening [July 31] on the balcony of the Norwood Hotel—the celebration headquarters–and the official celebrations began Thursday morning with a thirteen-gun salute in the city park. "The morning trains and street cars brought hundreds of people and by ten o'clock great crowds were on the streets and the various musical organizations were marching about lending melodious emphasis to the celebration."[381]

The first event of the day, before the official parade, was an early morning baseball game on the Howard Street Grounds featuring the Keystone Nine of Watkins and the St. Mark's Club of Syracuse, "the champion amateur colored teams of the state." Watkins won 23-16 in an "exciting contest."

Following the game, a parade began at two o'clock. Participating in the parade were the Waverly City Band, the Ithaca Colored Band, the Excelsior YMCA Band of Elmira, the Rough Riders Colored Drum Corps of Binghamton, uniformed clubs from Elmira and Binghamton, and "prominent visitors and others in carriages."

Although there were reportedly hundreds of African American visitors, the majority white population of Waverly and surrounding towns also participated. "The procession made a very creditable showing and the fine music of the bands and drum corps was applauded on every side. Most of the homes and stores along the route were decorated with the national colors and a very genteel display of flags was made throughout the village. Broad and Fulton Streets were crowded with people who came out to see the parade."[382]

Upon the parade's arrival at the city park, a series of orators and music was presented. Among the orators was Charles W. Anderson of New York City, the Reverend E.A.U. Brooks of

Elmira, and postmaster G.D. Genung. According to the *Waverly Free Press*, Anderson, a close confidant of Booker T. Washington, gave a history lesson that pointed out the power emancipation gave to Americans of all races:

> "The fathers founded this great republic on two contrary principles–liberty and slavery. They defended their work with the assertion that the germs of liberty would inevitably exterminate slavery; but it was a delusion. Instead, slavery, like the deadly upas tree of the tropics, subdued and poisoned all who came near it. Slavery soon became interwoven with commercial interests. It controlled conventions, dictated politics, elected presidents, subsidized the press, corrupted the judiciary, and proscribed the pulpit. Timid souls became alarmed and feared that the country could neither carry nor shake off this great weight. It rode the republic as the Old Man of the Sea rode Sinbad the Sailor. This perplexing question presented itself at the very foundation of the republic."

Anderson reviewed the early history of slavery in the U.S. before turning to his peroration:

> "Then came the great conflict. At first our victories were few; but when the call for colored troops was made and the cause for freedom was baptized in negro blood, the tide of battle changed. When Lincoln freed the negro he freed the white man as well. Before the war the white man did not dare to express his opinion of slavery, especially in the south. Now all is different. Wherever the glorious flag of our country needs to be defended there you will find the colored man.
>
> "If I am to leave a message to you to-day it is this: Live up to your opportunities. Equality of rating is never given to us, it must be won by hard work. We cannot all be great

speakers but we can all speak the truth. We cannot all be great scholars and great thinkers but we can all be honest men. We live in the grandest century of the world, among the greatest people in the world, in the greatest country in the world, and we should strive to prepare ourselves to meet the grave responsibilities which this brings to us."[383]

The *Free Press* reported that the speech was "undoubtedly one the best ever delivered on the park. It frequently brought forth great applause and made a deep impression."

Following the speech, the Ithaca Band, under the leadership of John C. Wye and cornet soloist, C. M. Johnson, gave a concert. The celebration concluded that evening with a "cake-walk and ball" at the Opera House, with music by the Arion Colored Orchestra from Ithaca. The cakewalk, featuring five couples, "was artistic and graceful and brought forth much applause." It was followed by a program of twenty-four dances "enjoyed by a large number of colored trippers of the light fantastic."[384]

Between the speech at the park and the evening dances at the Opera House, Waverly lost to Troy 6-5 at the Howard Street Grounds, before a huge holiday crowd of 2,000, when Ging could not hold off Troy's winning run in the ninth.[385] Despite the loss, the *Daily Gazette* said the game produced "the greatest enthusiasm ever seen on the local grounds."[386]

THE FESTIVITIES AND HOME STAND AT AN END, WAVERLY traveled to Binghamton the next day for a game on Friday, August 2, and lost 6-4. Campau smacked two doubles off of Lee to lead Binghamton. The next day, August 3, Binghamton traveled to Waverly for a double-header before a strong Saturday crowd of 1,200. Mickey Mullin started the first game, and pitched a 3-0 shutout, holding Binghamton to just five hits, including another double by Campau. In the second game, Ging and McDougal combined to lose, 10-1. McDougal gave up seven runs in the first three innings, and although Ging pitched solidly the rest of the way, Binghamton's Crabill held Waverly to just two hits.[387] Waverly's record for the week was a disappointing 2-5, bringing Waverly's NYSL record to 8-14.

Despite the record, Waverly's healthy crowds brought out encouragement from the national media. "The Waverly Club, successor to the defunct Cortlands, is doing pretty well since becoming full pledged State leaguers," noted George Harrison of *The Sporting News*. "Waverly is a small town, but overflowing with love for the national game."[388]

The road schedule in particular was becoming a grind, and the team often seemed to be going through the motions, rather than playing with intensity, despite manager Heine's efforts to get them focused. Mullin was 4-2 during the NYSL stretch, compared to Lee at 3-3, McDougal at 1-3, and Ging at 0-6. It was an extremely frustrating time for Ging, whose major league prospects continued to decline amidst his lack of success against NYSL hitting, and poor run support.

The following Monday, the team traveled to Binghamton for another double-header before a crowd of 700, and was swept 4-3 and 8-5. Lee took the first loss, and Ging, the second.[389] Campau continued to pound Waverly's pitching, hitting another double in the first game.

Mullin had been the team's most effective pitcher, and he was frustrated when his scheduled pitching start the next day against Binghamton was rained out. He had been having a good run of luck and was an eager competitor with a reckless streak. In fact, a fight against Hughie Hearne in the previous season, "after great provocation," had resulted in a blow from Hearne that "forced" two of "Mullin's teeth down his throat" and earned Hearne a twenty-five dollar fine and a week's suspension.[390]

The team remained in Binghamton Tuesday night in anticipation of traveling to Troy the next day. They slept at the Lewis House, near the Erie Railroad station.

The Lewis House in Binghamton

Like baseball players today, players in 1901 tended to be very superstitious, and few objects were more associated with superstition than the number thirteen. At that point, Waverly was traveling with thirteen players, and Ging and Mullin were roommates in the Lewis House, assigned to room thirteen on the fourth floor. According to *The Leader*, that night's events were all ascribed to "unlucky 13."

Very early Wednesday morning, while sleeping, Mullin dreamt he was playing in a big game. Around two-thirty, Mullin yelled out, "Thirteen, my God!" as if celebrating a victory, which awoke Ging.

Ging shouted his roommate's name and watched helplessly as Mullin jumped out of bed and started to act out a slide into home, diving head-first straight over a chair and out through their fourth-floor window.

Mullin plunged onto a veranda below, and then dropped in a clump onto Prospect Avenue.

J. W. Stevens, the baggage master of Erie train number thirteen was the first to find Mullin in the street, his head in a ditch, blood everywhere. To both Stevens and a hotel clerk, Mullin appeared to be dead. Stevens left to retrieve the police. By that time, Ging and a local barber staying in the neighboring room had run down to the street.

Upon his return with the police, Stevens saw that a group had gathered around Mullin and witnessed the aggrieved pitcher groaning and turning over. Mullin was carried into the hotel lobby, and hotel workers summoned an ambulance and doctor. Manager Heine by that time had also run down to the lobby. Upon seeing Mullin's injuries and blood, and being told that Mullin had fallen four stories from room thirteen, Heine fainted, and had to be revived with smelling salts.

Mullin continued to groan and move, and after an initial medical exam, was found to have "three deep gashes on his left leg, some bad bruises on the head and body and a broken collar bone." He appeared to be on course for surviving the fall, although further examination would be necessary to determine the extent of any internal injuries. His wife in Cortland was contacted, and his baseball season appeared to be over.[391]

The fact he survived the dive prompted newspapers to position the story more as a curiosity than as a tragedy.

"In a fit of somnambulism, Pitcher Mullin of the local team leaped through the closed window of the room on the four floor of the Lewis house, in Binghamton, occupied by himself and Pitcher Ging, at three o'clock Wednesday morning," the *Waverly Free Press* reported, "breaking his left collar bone and sustaining serious bruises that will keep him from the diamond for some time."[392]

The Binghamton Republican jovially reported:

> "Mickie" Mullin, the State league pitcher, was playing ball when he dived out of the fourth floor window at the Lewis house yesterday morning. The game as well as the opposing team was an imaginary one but never was there a game into which Mr. Mullin put more spirit than in the one yesterday morning. When Mullin let go those jubilant cries signaling a victory, which awakened Pitcher Ging, his roommate, he was sliding home, but the plate was never reached, for Mullin landed four stories below on the sidewalk. It was the longest slide the Mullin ever took, but nevertheless the collar bone

was the only bone broken and he is now resting quietly at the City Hospital. It is expected that he will recover.[393]

"Mullin had made a straight dive out of the window and with sufficient force to clear a chair in front of the window and to carry him over the railing three feet beyond the window and on the same level," the *Elmira Daily Gazette* reported. "He landed on the porch roof even with the third floor window and from there rolled off onto the sidewalk. His head lay on the walk and his body was in the gutter."[394]

"Pitcher Mullin arose in his sleep and walked through a window, glass and all, in the fourth story of the Lewis House, Binghamton," H. L. Fry told a national baseball audience in *The Sporting News*, "and was precipitated to the sidewalk. Billy Heine was so overcome by shock at the sight that he fainted." [395]

Fortunately, upon further inspection, Mullin's internal injuries were not sufficiently severe to threaten his survival, but he remained too banged up to pitch again in 1901.

Grateful for Mullin's likely eventual recovery, Waverly resumed its schedule, traveling that Wednesday afternoon to Troy and losing 11-1, with Lee taking another loss. Thursday's game with Troy was rained out.[396]

The team now headed to Albany for a Friday double-header. Mullin was out, and Lee had just pitched. This meant that, despite having just witnessed his roommate's four-story tumble and carrying a 0-7 record, Ging would have to pitch the first game of the double-header against Albany, the NYSL's first-place team.

And, given the lack of any other available pitchers, he might have to pitch the second game as well.

Friday, August 9 in the New York state capital was a fair and warm day. The day's *Albany Evening Journal* included the latest news on the Boer War in South Africa and also called attention to the big William H. West minstrel show scheduled for Albany's Empire Theater on Saturday. Blackface minstrelsy, popular for decades, was by 1901 facing competition from other types of variety shows, patterned on French Vaudeville, that attracted a broader, hipper (and an inferred more sophisticated) audience. Mindful of this competition, the *Journal* promised this would not be your father's minstrel show:

> Minstrelsy as exemplified in Mr. West's big jubilee, which he is about to present here, retains the black faced end man as a concession to sentiment, but is an up to date end man, not entirely dependent on burnt-cork for his favor with the audience. Between him and his fellow comedian at the other end of the semi-circle are seated a score of other and well known men whose splendid voices are familiar in the capitals of Europe. Associated with them are still others, whose daring feats or novel specialties would supply a dozen vaudeville houses with "top-liners."[397]

Waverly arrived at Riverside Park on Friday morning well aware of the odds against them for the day's double-header. Riverside Park was located in Renssalaer, directly across the Hudson River from the capital city, and a large crowd of 1,200 gradually streamed into the Park from all directions, including many in boats. They were eager for two easy wins that would increase the daylight between them and second-place Schenectady, with third-place Utica close behind. They had little respect for the visitors, whom the local press dubbed "babies" and "orphans" on account of their newly found league status.

While Heine and the other old timers on the team took the disrespect in stride, Ging warmed up before the hostile crowd, and likely steeled himself by recalling his big Polo Grounds appearance two years earlier in New York City. The odds had been long against him in that game as well. The difference this time was that the Albany hitters had just lit up Ging ten days earlier, and they must have been extremely eager to get into the batter's box against him again, especially as they watched him warm up. One ray of hope for the resourceful Ging was that perhaps he could use their eagerness against them.

Opposing Ging for Albany was left-hander Bill Cristall, who had grown up in Buffalo after having emigrated as a child with his family from Ukraine. Cristall was having an outstanding season and would soon receive a late-season call-up to Cleveland.

Albany's starting lineup behind Cristall was nearly identical to the line-up that rocked Ging on July 29. Up first in the order was Chick Cargo at shortstop, then Hank Simon in left field, Curt Bernard at second base, John Duffy in center field, Jim Jones in right field, Jimmy Tamsett at third base, Tom Hess at first base, and Pat Millerick behind the plate. Waverly's starting lineup behind Ging had Maroney in center, O'Neil at short, Nadeau in left, Eddie Hill in right, Dwyer at first, Heine at second, McCormick at third, and Accorsini at catcher. Hill, who had opposed Waverly as a member of the Binghamton team in 1900, started 1901 with Albany and only recently joined Waverly, so was eager to face his old squad.

In addition to Cristall, Albany's line-up featured two other players who would receive late-season 1901 call-ups to the major leagues, in their case to New York: right fielder Jones, who was among the NYSL's hitting leaders, and the left-handed hitting Bernard, reported to be a McGraw favorite. As Ging well knew, a summons to the major leagues was the ultimate reward for excellent minor league performance, the goal of nearly every player on the diamond, but only realized by a fortunate few and capitalized on by even fewer.

Game one began with the two starters picking carefully through the lineups. Ging gave up hits to Cargo and Duffy, just like in his last appearance against them. Only this time in the early going the hits were scattered, not bunched, and they were mainly singles, not triples. He also walked four batters, including Simon, in an effort to keep his pitches from being too hittable. Meanwhile, Cristall's tosses kept the Waverly hitters off-balance as well, and the two remained scoreless through five innings.

Bill Ging pitches for Waverly versus Albany, August 9, 1901. Portrait by Gary Cieradkowski.

Cristall's luck ran out in the sixth, when he gave up one run. This was followed by two more in the seventh, for a 3-0 Waverly lead. Over the two innings, Nadeau and Hill each cracked two singles against the lefty, Albany committed infield errors and Nadeau, Ging and McCormick scored the runs.

Heading into the eighth with a 3-0 lead, Ging only had to hold the Senators a little longer. Unfortunately, Cristall stood tall in the left hand batter's box against Ging. Ging delivered a pitch that found too much of the plate, and Cristall belted a single, his third of the day.

The crowd roared its approval as Ging had to face Simon again, whom he'd walked once and managed to retire twice. His catcher Accorsini had called a terrific game to this point, and so Ging focused firmly and peered into home plate. They agreed on the pitch, Ging wound up and tossed the ball to Accorsini's mitt, but the ball was a little too straight. The old timer jumped on the pitch and smashed it into the outfield. Cristall scored, making the score 3-1, and Simon stopped at second with a double.

Withstanding the threatening cheers of the crowd and the looming comeback, Ging took a deep breath and managed to pitch his way out of the rest of the inning without allowing another run. He then completely shut Albany down in the ninth, quieting the crowd, and earning a 3-1 win.[398]

Through nine innings Ging gave up ten hits, walked four and suffered one error by Dwyer, but gave up only one run. It was a masterful victory, nearly the complete opposite of most of Ging's hard-luck appearances during the season.

It was strong enough that Heine was comfortable throwing Ging again in the second game of the double-header. In order to fit in two games, the teams needed to be conscientious about the remaining sunlight. Since the first game had taken two hours, there was only time for a brief intermission before game two.

One bright side of pitching both ends of the double-header was that Ging did not need much of a warm-up. Each team fielded the same line-up, with Albany pitching Charles Baker, whom Waverly defeated on July 30. Nadeau, Hill and Heine feasted on Baker's pitches in that game, and jumped on him right away in this one as well, bunching hits and stolen bases to score two runs in the first inning and take a 2-0 lead.

Pitching with a lead, Ging went right back to work on the Albany hitters, continuing to give up base hits, but strategically scattering them so as to keep the base runners away from the plate. His control was better as well, and, although Simon again managed to rip him for a double, Ging whitewashed the Senators through all nine innings, earning a 2-0 shutout victory and a doubleheader sweep,[399] sending the large crowd home disappointed.

Ging's only two wins of the NYSL season thus far came on the same day–and were against the league's best team! The sports media's accolades quickly poured in.

Ging "pitched great ball and was given fine support," noted the *Cortland Evening Standard*.[400]

"The strong feature of the games was the pitching of Ging for the visitors," reported the *Albany Evening Journal*. "He was on the rubber for 18 innings and finished, apparently, as strong as he began."

The Albany Argus waxed poetic:

> When the Babies of the State League grow so precocious that they can trounce the leaders twice in the same afternoon, and on their own grounds, it is time that they were called something besides Babies. Hereafter, in Albany at least, the title will carry with it nothing but respect, for a better game than these same Babies put up at Riverside yesterday one would have to travel through many a National League city to see.
>
> Particular honor is due that wiry, tireless young man named Ging, who pitched eighteen superb innings for his team, and, far from weakening, toward the last grew stronger and more effective every minute. Ging's support was good, but by no means marvelous, and to him most of all belongs the credit of standing up against the

batsmen who have raised the Senators to their present position and fooling them for four long hours, allowing only one run and fourteen hits during the whole time. Compared singly with either Cristall or Baker, Ging did not shine with such stellar light, but when it is considered that he pitched two games to their one, his performance is remarkable.

Every man who saw Waverly play wonders why it occupies the place it does next to the tailenders.[401]

"We still lead," reported *Sporting News* Albany correspondent H. L. Fry, "although our margin has been materially reduced mainly through the great pitching feat accomplished by Ging of Waverly on Friday last. In a double-header this tireless gentleman allowed the usually hard-hitting Senators exactly one run and 14 hits. The first game was lost on infield errors, and in the second game, Ging, who seemed to grow stronger as the afternoon waned, was invincible, and our five scattered hits resulted in a symmetrical row of ciphers."[402]

Ging and teammates celebrated the doubleheader win that night in Albany, but they may have imbibed too much or too late, as the very next day they returned to Riverside Park and were listless in a 2-0 loss. They then returned home to lose to last-place Ilion, 8-4, on August 12, with Tucker striving to help the short-handed pitching staff, but needing four innings to find his pitching arm "owing to lack of practice."[403] Rather than changing the team's momentum, Ging's double-header victories appeared to represent a merely a joyful blip in an otherwise rough stretch of August's dog days.

In the midst of these dog days, newspapers around the region began to speculate which cities would have NYSL franchises in 1902. None of the teams were doing tremendously well financially, and *Sporting Life* reported that all of the clubs other than Albany, "are having trouble to pay salaries and other expenses."[404] One prominent rumor was that Waverly, Rome, Troy, and Ilion would be dumped in favor of larger cities like Rochester, Syracuse, Scranton, and Wilkes-Barre.[405] Rumors like these tended to diminish enthusiasm in the impacted towns, which only made it harder to draw crowds and meet expenses.

In Waverly's case, as in Ilion and Schenectady, whose reported average attendance ran less than Waverly's, the rumors and mediocre record led to financial challenges. In the hours leading up to the Ilion game on August 13, the situation was particularly dire. "The attendance has not been large of late," the *Waverly Free Press* pointed out. In addition, there was a rumor that Heine and Accorsini were mismanaging the team's receipts.[406] Accorsini vehemently denied his involvement in any mismanagement, and no further word of or action on the matter was reported. Given Tucker's financial stake in the team, it is unlikely either Heine or Accorsini could have acted on their own to their teammates' detriment.

McDougal started the August 13 game for Waverly and held Ilion to seven hits, while Waverly scored three runs in the first inning and two more in the second to take an early lead. Ilion battled back to pull within one run in the fifth, but Waverly scored six more to take a 12-6 victory. Heine and Dwyer both hit doubles for Waverly.[407]

Although victorious, Waverly reportedly failed to draw enough fans to pay Ilion its guarantee or make the home players' payroll, causing "great dissatisfaction."[408] This is the first time such an incident was reported involving Waverly's team. The situation was particularly irksome to Ilion, since it was having its own financial problems, having found itself $250 short of obligations in a recent game against Schenectady.[409] "Waverly's nine seems to have struck an incline that some one has been unkind enough to grease," the *Waverly Free Press* noted. [410]

Waverly was reportedly short $350, and local investors were willing to provide that amount if the league would guarantee the village a franchise in 1902. Tucker and his partners clearly had the money, so it's possible that they set up the incident intentionally in order to force the NYSL's hand for 1902 and put to bed rumors that were stifling attendance. Given that NYSL President John Farrell wanted to finish the season without any failures, Waverly's baseball committee may have felt it had some leverage. With this guarantee and leverage in mind, they arranged a meeting with Farrell. In the meantime, due to the deficit, scheduled games with Schenectady were canceled.

As a result of the situation, the Waverly team teetered on the same precipice of financial failure that had taken down its neighbors in Elmira and Binghamton–not to mention its immediate predecessor in Cortland—many times in the past few years. "Owing to a lack of funds, the Waverly team decided not to play until its financial status was more clearly determined," *Sporting Life* reported. "The game [versus Schenectady] was therefore declared off."[411]

"The players freely express their indignation at the unsatisfactory turn of affairs," the *Free Press* reported. "No plan has yet been suggested for raising the money to pay them." While awaiting management's meeting with Farrell, the better players, such as Accorsini, Heine, and Nadeau, began to play elsewhere. Accorsini headed to Buffalo, Heine was picked up by Brockton in the Eastern League, and Nadeau was picked up by Binghamton. Heine and Nadeau each played games for their new teams on Friday, August 16.[412] The speed with which the players found new positions suggested that they were well networked, accustomed to having to manage end-of-season financial challenges, and eager to finish out their seasons successfully.

President Farrell arrived in Waverly that same day to meet with Waverly's baseball management. Eager to continue his streak of successful NYSL seasons without a major interruption, Farrell was highly motivated to secure a resumption of Waverly's play. However, it is unlikely he had the authority, without the approval of the NYSL's collective ownership, to give Waverly a guarantee for 1902.

Ferrell spent the day in Waverly and left late in the afternoon. The official word that emerged from the meeting was that the team would finish out the season, with two new players, John Kennedy from Buffalo and Jimmy Dean from the Cortland team. McCormick was named manager, replacing Heine, and Nadeau was recalled from Binghamton. There was still no guarantee about the 1902 season, but "the reorganization carries with it a prospect of having a State league team here next year."

"Waverly gave up the ghost during the week," H. L. Fry reported in *The Sporting News*, "but it is reported in the morning papers that President Ferrell has patched up matters so that the team will finish the season under new management."[413]

As if baseball confusion was not enough, the very next day, August 17, Waverly, in its role as a busy railroad intersection, welcomed thirty-nine train carloads of western cattle being detoured from the Lehigh Valley Railroad to the Erie due to a blocked tunnel. As many villagers looked on curiously, dozens of the beasts were transferred between the railroads peacefully, but one, "a big red mooley steer," jumped the fence, escaped, and led dozens of villagers on a wild chase. "His head was down and his tail was turned up and he was out for gore," reported the *Bradford Republican*. "Pitchforks, clubs or stones made no impression." Thirty people, including ball player and umpire "Bud" Waller, failed to corral him. One group attempted to force him into a car by turning a fire hose on him, but to no avail. For his part, Waller attempted to twist the steer's tail and received a kick in the stomach for his trouble. Finally, the steer, likely tired after the chase, simply "followed a tame cow into the enclosure," thus ending the drama.[414]

Waverly's team started back up on August 19 against Rome, and Lee lost, 7-2. The result was similar the next day, as McDougal lost to Rome, 8-2.[415] Rome was on a hot streak, in part, according to Rome's hometown followers, due to Charlie Hamburg's lucky poodle. Trailing by one run in a recent game against Utica, for example, Hamburg went into the grandstand prior to the sixth inning, brought his white poodle down to the bench, and Rome's next batter led off with a base hit followed by a successful rally and a victory.[416] The poodle did not help Hamburg personally, however, as he was soon thereafter hit by a pitch and laid up for the remainder of the season with a fractured wrist.[417]

Waverly proceeded to play twelve straight games on the road, losing eleven of them. The crowd sizes on the road also tended to be barely enough to break even, with just 200, for example, in Utica on August 22, and just 100 in Schenectady on August 28. It was a brutal schedule. Lee, Ging, and McDougal were a steady rotation and kept most of the games close, but Waverly's hitting was simply not up to par. In the road trip's twelve games, Waverly scored a total of just twenty-five runs–barely two per game. The road trip brought the team's official NYSL record to 32-67, in next-to-last place, seven games ahead of Ilion.

On the bright side, Waverly welcomed twenty-year-old Charles "Heinie" Wagner onto its roster. Wagner, a veteran of several New York City semi-pro teams, including the Murray Hills Nine, appears to have batted leadoff, played right field, and had two singles in the 3-2, sixteen-inning loss on August 27. Ging once again was the game's hard-luck loser, despite pitching all sixteen innings.[418]

Charles "Heinie" Wagner during his stint with Waverly.

On August 31, Accorsini rejoined the team from Buffalo, playing the rest of the season at catcher.

On Labor Day, September 2, Waverly was swept in a doubleheader at Binghamton before crowds of 500 in the first game and 1,200 in the second. The next day, Waverly played a benefit game against Binghamton in Cortland to assist the family of injured pitcher Mickey Mullin. It was well attended, and an inspired Waverly team won 12-5 behind McDougal.[419] It was the most runs Waverly had scored since July 26, more than a month earlier.

The long season was finally winding down, and Waverly's last four games were at home. On September 4, last-place Ilion came to town for the last time. Lee pitched for Waverly and earned the win, 9-2. Wagner had two singles and two runs, and Nadeau had two doubles, pacing Waverly's uncharacteristic sixteen-hit attack.[420]

Schenectady visited next. Ging started at pitcher against Villman and gave up just seven hits over nine innings. Unfortunately, Waverly was unable to repeat its prior day's hitting, and Ging took the loss, 4-3.[421]

Troy visited the Howard Street Grounds next on Friday, September 6. Two former major leaguers were in the box for their respective teams: McDougal for the home team, and Lee Viau for the visitors.

Each team scratched a run in the first inning, and the veteran pitchers kept it close until the fifth, when Waverly scored two, and then two more in the sixth to win 5-1. Leading the Waverly hitters were Maroney with a double and a triple, and Accorsini with a double and a stolen base. Wagner scored a run, stole a base, and had a sacrifice hit.[422]

Waverly had one more game at the Howard Street Grounds on Saturday, September 7, a 7-0 loss to first-place Albany to wrap up the season. Waverly's final official NYSL record, including Cortland's record, was 36-68, good enough to keep them in second-to-last place.

Few were paying close attention to these games, however, for on Friday afternoon in Buffalo, a much more significant event took place.

CHAPTER 11

I Done My Duty

On August 30, according to the *Buffalo Evening News*, the hometown Eastern League team lost to Brockton, 11-6, before a crowd of just two hundred people. Although proudly nicknamed the "Pan-Am Baseball" team in honor of the summer-long Pan-American Exposition, Buffalo was in last place, trailing Brockton, and was so solidly entrenched "that their position is impregnable." Among the players leading the Brockton attack was former Waverly manger Bill Heine, playing second base.[423] The Brockton franchise had been in Syracuse, but moved from Syracuse in late July due to financial challenges.

The *Evening News* also reported that there was tremendous anticipation for President McKinley's upcoming visit to the Exposition. "Details for President McKinley's entertainment, the programme for President's Day [the day the President was visiting the Exposition; not a holiday] and every arrangement for the President's visit were completed at a meeting of the ceremonies committee held at the Saturn Club last evening," the *News* stated. "Assurances have been received that President's Day will be honored with the attendance of many members of the Cabinet, the diplomatic corps and the bench of the United States Supreme Court." The Marine Band of Washington and multiple police, military, and honor escorts were also slated to participate. "Great honors will be shown" and "great crowds are expected," the *News* assured its readers.

Buffalo and Brockton followed up their August 30 contest with a double-header the next day. Buffalo won both contests, perhaps portending better times ahead. Heine went zero for six that day, and his friend Jack Barnett took the loss in the nightcap, 5-3.

The Pan-Am team went on to play at Toronto while the President was at the Exposition, losing 9-3 on September 5 and 9-7 on September 6. Meanwhile, Heine and Brockton went eleven innings in Hartford on September 6, only to settle for a 2-2 tie due to darkness.

That same afternoon, September 6, at approximately four o'clock, as the out-of-town ball games were underway, a long line of well-wishers greeted the president at the Temple of Music. An organist played Bach while President McKinley greeted one person after another.

After several days of stalking the president at the Exposition, twenty-eight-year-old Leon Czolgosz made his way through the line with a handgun hidden under a handkerchief in his right hand. When Czolgosz reached the president, McKinley noticed the handkerchief and reached for Czolgosz's left hand. Czolgosz shot him twice in the abdomen before being overpowered and pummeled by witnesses and taken into custody. "I done my duty," Czolgosz was heard to have said as he was taken away.[424] The gunshots were not immediately fatal, and McKinley was rushed from the scene for treatment.

News of the shooting was fast and furious. Umpire Francis "Silk" O'Loughlin somberly interrupted the Brockton-Hartford game to read a telegram with the news to the 200 spectators on hand, a scene undoubtedly repeated throughout the country.[425] Many of these early reports were also full of confusing and inaccurate information. The *Waverly Free Press* edition of Saturday, September 7, for instance, reported that McKinley had already died from the shots and that the "assassin" was a man named "Numan": "The assassin was promptly arrested and it was with difficulty that the police prevented the crowd from lynching him," the *Free Press* said. "He is a young man named Numan from Detroit, Michigan, and admits that he is an anarchist."

In fact, "Nieman" was an alias Czolgosz used frequently, including with Emma Goldman and her associates, and the president was not yet dead. So hungry were Americans for news that the media rushed its stories, and a flurry of corrections and updates were constantly required.

Upon interviewing Czolgosz, police ascertained his connection with Emma Goldman, and a nationwide search for Goldman ensued. Conspiracy theories about anarchists and possible additional terrorist activities spread around the country like wildfire and further fueled the hunt for Goldman and other possible conspirators. "I don't regret my act," Czolgosz told police, "because I was doing what I could for the great cause."[426]

On September 14, one week after the *Free Press*'s premature report of McKinley's death, it ran a story from Buffalo that declared the President would recover: "The condition of the President continues favorable and nothing has occurred to shake the faith the attending surgeons and physicians have expressed that he will recover," the *Free Press* reported on its front page, the entirety of which was devoted to details of the incident:

> Nieman was detained in a side room in the Temple of Music while the president was removed to the hospital. Then, under escort of police, with a guard of soldiers to fight back the enraged throng in the Esplande, Nieman was placed in a carriage and driven at a gallop down Delaware avenue, past the home where the invalid wife of the president was waiting for her husband, to police headquarters, where he was locked up. The thousands who waited about the Temple of Music surged forward when he appeared, tearing down the barrier ropes, fighting with the officers and the soldiers and shouting: "Lynch him – lynch him – hang him – kill him." Some

clutched at the horses, others at the wheels of the carriage. The police and soldiers fought back the crowd and the carriage galloped away.

Sadly, notwithstanding the optimistic news report, President McKinley, the old Civil War soldier, died in Buffalo on September 14, the very day the *Free Press* reported otherwise, and Vice President Roosevelt, the Hero of San Juan Hill, was sworn in to replace him. At that moment, Roosevelt was the youngest President in the nation's history.

This desire for swift vengeance was not limited to the crowds in Buffalo. "I could not conceive how a man who had perhaps fewer enemies than any President we ever had would be singled out for punishment," Senator Thomas Platt said. "I recall, however, that when there came the astounding, distressing, sickening message from Buffalo describing how Anarchist Czolgosz had put a pistol to the President's heart, I exclaimed: 'Had I been there, I should have forgotten there is a law against lynching.' I really could not control myself. Had there been a rope handy I should have helped to hand the brute to the nearest lamppost."[427]

On September 11, as the nation was still praying for President McKinley to survive, the anti-saloon activist Carrie Nation, "vendor of hatchets and autographs," arrived in Waverly as part of her Eastern tour, apparently more bent on raising money than on smashing saloons.

The Waverly Free Press reported:

> She came in on a late train, went direct to the Norwood, where she registered as "Carrie Nation, Your Home Defender, Kansas," and to her room for the night. Next morning she was up betimes, and after an early breakfast seated herself at a front window, with an open Bible before her, and in full view of a crowd of early risers, began writing and selling autograph cards. They sold readily at ten cents each, but her baby hatchets did not

go at all. Spotting a youth smoking a "nasty cigarette" she asked, "ain't you got nothing else to do?" The bad youth reformed at once. She made no attempt to do her more or less popular act of "bar-room smashing," and soon paid her bill and took the 7:08 car for wicked Sayre, a more congenial field.[428]

While Sayre had a busier railroad yard than Waverly, it did not have a necessarily more "wicked" reputation, so the comment was likely a friendly jab at its nearby rival. Meanwhile, it remained unclear at the time whether Carrie Nation intended to visit the Exposition in the wake of the McKinley tragedy.

Like other leagues, the NYSL, including the Waverly franchise, passed a resolution honoring President McKinley. The resolution read, in part, "resolved that we, in recognition of the foul blow of a demoniacal assassin, an anarchist, be it resolved that we, in recognition of the lovable characteristics and devotion to duty of our late lamented President, make public the sense of this meeting in respect to his memory and our profound sorrow in his sad death." [429]

The 1901 NYSL season ended with Albany in first, Binghamton in second, and Utica in third. Rome, Schenectady, Troy, Waverly and Ilion rounded out the standings in that order. "The minor league season has been successful beyond expectations," opined *The Sporting News,* pointing out how ten of the eleven organized minor leagues, including the NYSL, had competitive pennant races with multiple financially healthy franchises.[430]

It was an opportune time for the minor leagues to form their own professional association in an effort to unite their interests in dealing with the American and National Leagues, and proactively deter the Leagues from poaching minor league players without compensation. With this primary goal in mind, the minor league leaders met on September 5th in Chicago and created the National Association of Professional Baseball Leagues (NAPBL), an association formed to protect the rights of minor league franchises.

NYSL President John H. Farrell, fresh from saving the Waverly franchise and maintaining his streak of successful seasons, was named the new organization's inaugural Secretary-Treasurer, and its headquarters was established in Farrell's hometown, Auburn.[431]

The home of the new NAPBL, Auburn, was founded in 1793 by a veteran of the Revolution's Sullivan-Clinton campaign, John Hardenburgh, and was renamed from Hardenburgh Corners to Auburn in 1805. Just a short distance from the Erie Canal, Auburn served as a way station for shipping goods, and it was given a station on the South Central Railroad in 1871. In 1900, Auburn's population was 30,345, just under one-third the size of Syracuse or Scranton. Yet despite its small size, Auburn had the honor of becoming the new home of organized minor league baseball.

It was also the home of one of the state's most important prisons, and, likely unaware of and unconcerned with the NAPBL news, Fred Krist remained in his death row cell in the middle of town, working with advocates on his appeal.

At the same time, also likely unbeknownst to Krist, his old Waverly Hall & Lyon co-worker Earl Burgess came to Auburn in the first week of September with his orchestra and vaudeville troupe on behalf of the Bennett and Moulton Company. Burgess's company offered six straight days and nights of singing, dancing, and plays at the Burtis Opera House, not far from the prison.

Burgess's show had just spent consecutive weeks at Saratoga and Watertown to rave reviews and was scheduled to head to Schenectady and Troy immediately afterwards, followed by several months of weeklong stints in various towns and cities throughout New York, Pennsylvania, and New Jersey. It was a very busy schedule, but in the days before cinema and recorded music, it was the only professional entertainment most local townspeople ever experienced.

Amidst coverage of McKinley's assassination and the subsequent arrest and investigation of Emma Goldman, who would remain in custody for two weeks before being released, the

Auburn Bulletin declared the Burgess shows and "specialties" to be well attended, excellent, enjoyable, and "well worth the admission price" of ten-to-thirty cents. "This is a good company, who act well, are well gowned and have good scenery."[432]

Baseball, Krist, and vaudeville were not the town's only centers of attention in 1901. Auburn would also soon welcome an even more prominent guest. The world's most infamous criminal anarchist at the time, Leon Czolgosz, was quickly tried for the murder of President McKinley in Buffalo. The public expected Czolgosz's attorneys to mount an insanity defense, similar to Krist's, but Czolgosz refused to cooperate, and his behavior did not seem consistent with such a defense. "Except for one brief episode of denial, Czolgosz had always been lucid, conversant, and more than willing to take responsibility for the murder," wrote historian Scott Miller. "The only odd behavior [medical examiners] could name was his extreme fastidiousness about his clothing, which hardly qualified him as mentally deficient."[433] As a result, Czolgosz's legal team called no witnesses and mounted only a token defense.

Not even his own family would defend him. "None of us had a great liking for Leon," said his father, Paul.

His brother Jacob added, "If Leon did it, I hope he swings for it."[434]

Czolgosz was convicted on September 24, and early in the morning of September 26, he was taken by train from Buffalo to the Auburn State Prison, which sat in the middle of town, directly across the street from the train station.

Auburn State Prison

In contrast to Krist's quiet arrival to the prison almost a year earlier, Czolgosz's was loud and dangerous.

> Several hundred people were there waiting for him, all apparently anxious to cheat the electric chair of its victim. Chanting and cursing, the mob was determined to grab Czolgosz before the police could get him within the safety of the prison.
>
> Surrounded by a phalanx of guards, Czolgosz was pushed, pulled, and dragged the fifty yards that separated the railway platform and the front gates of the prison. Ordering Czolgosz to remain close to him, his police escort absorbed repeated blows that were meant for the convict. Another guard tried unsuccessfully to restrain the crowd by brandishing his pistol. The mob was so rough that at one point it knocked Czolgosz to his knees. Picking up their charge "like a bag of salt," the guards carried him to the gates of the prison, where the crowd very nearly got its prey. One blow fell heavily on

Czolgosz's neck. Someone managed to grab his shoulder. When the group finally reached the penitentiary gates, guard John Martin, a giant of a man, grabbed him and "with a mighty heave tossed him through."[435]

Once Czolgosz was inside the prison, he joined the others on death row, including Waverly's Fred Krist.

Safely inside the prison, Czolgosz awaited his fate on death row.

As the days in prison went on, the outside media clamor continued. The general public, many of whom still thirsted for revenge against Czolgosz, Goldman, and other declared and suspected anarchists, was eager to hear how things were going for Czolgosz within Auburn's death row block, and local newspapers issued daily statements on how the prisoners were supposedly getting along. These widely circulated reports stated that the prisoners gave Czolgosz a hard time, frequently mocking and insulting him. The reports thrilled the public, which was all too eager to see Czolgosz suffer.

Waverly residents reading these reports were no doubt intrigued that their former fellow townsman, the "jovial, pleasant and good natured" Krist, now shared death row with the world's most hated man, with ample opportunity to abuse and persecute him on behalf of a vengeful public.

Krist and the other death row inmates reportedly harassed him. Clarence Egnor, who murdered an Auburn prison guard during an escape attempt in January 1901, occupied a adjacent cell and according to news reports placed a picture of McKinley, decorated in black crape, within Czolgosz's sight. Krist, meanwhile, was reported to have taunted Czolgosz, telling him "You will go through there and you'll never come back…If you listen, you'll hear us cheer as you go."[436]

The news and speculation of even worse unprintable treatment was intriguing, and helped satisfy the public's thirst for retribution.

There was just one problem.

According to less widely distributed reports, Krist said that all these tales of abuse were false. Instead of sitting on death row in the midst of intense persecution, Krist said, Czolgosz sat quietly in his cell all day like the rest of death row's inmates.

In fact, Krist's spiritual advisor, Father Hendrick, was said to be interested in ministering to Czolgosz as well as to Krist, but Czolgosz rebuffed his efforts. Based on his limited observations when visiting Krist, Hendrick questioned the accuracy of the reports that the death row inmates taunted each other, and he asked Krist to provide a statement. He may have felt that the stories hurt Krist's chances for a pardon or acquittal. In any event, Krist sent him a letter on October 7 that was subsequently circulated in some local papers:[437]

Rev. Thomas A. Hendrick,

My Dear Friend: -- I just this moment received your letter and will without delay answer it. The newspaper articles that you refer to, I have read them also and am proud to say that every word therein is a bold, brazen lie. There is not one man in the condemned cells that has spoken one word to him (meaning Czolgosz); neither has he spoken one word to us. Neither have any of us made a remark for him to hear. I have not as yet heard him speak one word since he has been here. Just write to Warden [J. Warren] Mead of this prison and ask him if there is even one word of truth to these articles that you refer to.

I have troubles enough of my own without making insulting remarks to him. I will close again saying even more emphatically than ever, that there had not one man among us even said one word to Czolgosz.

Very truly yours,
FRED KRIST

P.S. – The guard in the condemned cell makes a written report every day of what takes place here in the condemned cells and this report is given to Warden Mead.

Given the discrepancies in newspaper accounts, it's up to speculation whether any words, pleasantries or insults were actually exchanged among the prisoners. Notwithstanding the speculation, on October 29, Father Hendrick visited Krist as Czolgosz was taken to the electric chair and executed. According to news accounts, Czolgosz was unrepentant, and he "refused to heed the words of the priests who came to urge spiritual preparation for death, and declined to either re-embrace Roman Catholicism or renounce anarchy." He was reportedly "sullen and indifferent."

"I killed the President because he was the enemy of the good people, the good working people," Czolgosz reportedly said immediately prior to his death.[438]

Four days later, on November 2, Krist received word that his execution, scheduled for November 4, had been postponed yet again as his appeals moved through the court system–yet another respite. Krist reportedly "seemed pleased at the news but manifested no unusual emotion."

Krist's parents in Ithaca, immigrants from Germany, did not read English newspapers and were unaware of each postponement until others told them. When the August date was postponed to November, for instance, a local *Elmira Gazette* reporter told them. According to the reporter, Krist's mother at the time "expressed much joy over the news and spoke enthusiastically of her renewed hopes that her son's sentence would ultimately be changed from death in the electric chair, to life imprisonment. She said that she had always entertained hopes that such might be the case." She also "expressed the greatest sympathy and love for her erring son."[439]

Buffalo's Pan-American Exposition closed on November 4, as a financial success. The Exposition had attracted eight million visitors, and daily attendance averaged over forty thousand between August and closing day.

As a Republican running for Buffalo City Attorney, PPA Counsel Taylor certainly followed the assassination events with at least as much intensity as the rest of the country. With respect to the baseball business, the PPA was very interested in having good relations with the new minor league organization, the NAPBL. His organization also continued to stress that its relationship with both the National and American Leagues was "on an entirely harmonious footing."[440]

Based on attendance figures for its inaugural season, the American League (AL) successfully competed with the National League (NL) for the public's attention and favor. Although the NL outdrew the AL overall, the AL outdrew the NL in two (Boston and Chicago) of the three cities where both leagues had teams (Philadelphia being the third). Moreover, while the NL's St. Louis club had the largest attendance (379,988), the AL's Chicago club had the second largest (354,350). In 1902, the AL's overall attendance exceeded the NL's.[441] The AL's success stimulated rivalries and increased the public's interest in baseball as a whole.

Chicago won the 1901 American League championship with a record of 83-53, four games ahead of Boston. Pittsburgh won the National League championship with a record of 90-49, seven and one-half games ahead of Hughie Jennings' Philadelphia club.

Waverly finished the 1901 NYSL season in second-to-last place, ahead of Ilion, with a record of 36-68. Albany won the championship with a record of 72-43. Taking into consideration Cortland's record of 21-34—which Waverly inherited—their net official NYSL record was 15-34. When taking the independent portion of its schedule into consideration, Waverly's combined 1901 record was a respectable 38-38-1.

More importantly, Waverly demonstrated it was a much stronger NYSL team at home (8-11) than on the road (7-23), and having 61 percent (30 of 49) of its NYSL games on the road was a distinct disadvantage. This was due to having to inherit Cortland's imbalanced remaining NYSL schedule rather than starting fresh.

Even with this disadvantage, combining Waverly's 1900 and 1901 records yielded a much more impressive 78-54-1, and throwing in 1896 brought the total record to 102-75-1. Waverly's independent record during the three-season period was 87-41, a .679 winning percentage. This was cause for continued optimism among Waverly's baseball fans.

With a fresh 1902 start in mind, the team scheduled its second annual four-day Baseball Fair for mid-December at the Opera House. Other cities were vying for a league franchise, but Waverly felt that it was still in good position. A successful baseball fair would only present additional cause for optimism.

Optimism was especially high in the major leagues. The attendance figures for the NL and AL were comparable, and both structures were stable. For the Americans, Ban Johnson planned to move two franchises to solidify the league and directly compete directly with the Nationals: 1901's last-place Milwaukee would move to St. Louis for the 1902 season and 1902's last-place Baltimore would move to New York for 1903. These would be the last franchise moves either league would make until the NL moved Boston to Milwaukee in 1953 and the AL moved St. Louis to Baltimore in 1954. These sixteen franchises remained stable within the two leagues for over fifty years—a tremendous record of stability after so many turbulent years. This stability helped secure many generations of lifelong fans. By comparison, in the twenty-five seasons from the birth of the NL to 1901, there had been thirty-one major league franchises in twenty-four different cities.

"The bitter struggle between the American and National Leagues turned out to be beneficial to baseball," explained historian Harold Seymour. "The business end of the game reached a new maturity, and the foundation was laid down on which Organized Baseball has rested ever since."[442]

For Harry Taylor, this foundation marked the end of his enormous influence on major league baseball–an influence marked by precision, "courtesy and tact."[443] The PPA that he and other old Orioles so enthusiastically promoted gradually declined in influence and by 1903 was defunct. Fortunately, the notoriety of his baseball activities during the PPA's heyday helped him build a prosperous legal practice in Buffalo. He briefly served as the president of the Eastern League, but he otherwise focused on his law practice, his Republican activities in Buffalo, and his service as a Cornell trustee. In 1906, he began his career as a judge for the New York State judiciary, earning plaudits for his learned impartiality.

"If he is as good a judge as he was a first baseman and hitter," wrote former teammate John McGraw at the time, "they won't get away with many inside legal plays on him."[444]

Taylor was appointed Erie County Judge in 1906, and served in that capacity through 1913. In 1913, he was elected as a Republican to be a Justice of the New York State Supreme Court for the Eighth District, a post he held through 1936, after which time he acted as an Official Referee until 1944. Upon retirement, he settled in Buffalo until passing away on July 12, 1955. "Even in his 80s," the *Buffalo Evening News* reported, "his memory was keen on baseball, and he loved to discuss it with old friends, including Joe McCarthy, former manager of the New York Yankees."[445] He lived with his sister and never married. He is buried with his family in the Halsey Valley Cemetery, just a stone's throw from two of the author's paternal great grandparents.

The stable system Taylor helped create provided an important degree of justice to white ball players, but would not be well balanced so long as baseball was divided by a "separate but equal" color line. Fortunately, stability in white baseball at both the major and minor league levels helped lead to a proliferation of African-American teams after 1901, prompting creation in 1906 of the International League of Independent Base Ball Clubs, which featured two white teams and four non-barnstorming African-American teams. This league lasted just the full 1906 season, but, according to player Sol White, featured for the first time a championship contest played before 10,000 spectators in a major league stadium,[446] thus confirming the game's commercial viability. As the number of "colored" teams continued to increase in ensuring years, more attempts were made to organize a league, culminating in 1920 with the creation of the first sustained African-American league, the National Association of Colored Professional Base Ball Clubs, also known as the Negro National League (NNL). The NNL and its eventual fellow circuit, the Negro American League, would last until just a few years after Jackie Robinson broke the major league color barrier in 1947, sixty years after Bud Fowler and Frank Grant last battled one another in integrated minor league games.

Beyond the baseball diamond, there was initially some cause for optimism in 1901 that racial tensions and segregation pressures in broader American society would ease with the more progressive Roosevelt in the White House. As evidence of this potential thaw, in late September just weeks after taking office, Roosevelt met secretly with African-American writer and activist Booker T. Washington at the White House to discuss Roosevelt's idea for a new approach to patronage where African-Americans would be nominated to government positions in both north and south on a more balanced basis, regardless of political party. Washington was receptive to the idea, and Roosevelt began to follow through on it, despite angering Mark Hanna and other Republican elites, who expected only Republicans to be nominated. In the country at-large praise for Roosevelt's approach was "loud and bi-partisan." [447]

Emboldened by what he perceived to be the public's reaction, Roosevelt on October 16, openly invited Washington to the

White House for dinner, ostensibly to celebrate Washington's new book, *Up From Slavery*.

The dinner proceeded well without incident, but once it was widely publicized, the public exploded in a much different reaction than Roosevelt anticipated, with many of both races heralding the event, and others deriding it. Even the African-American community was split on the dinner's significance, with many feeling it was a token gesture in the face of widespread legal segregation. Meanwhile, white Southerners were overtly hostile and angry, with Mississippi Senator James K. Vardaman complaining that the White House was now "so saturated with the odor of nigger that the rats had taken refuge in the stable," and the *Memphis Scimitar* calling it "the most damnable outrage which has ever been perpetrated by any citizen of the United States." Other southern journals and citizens expressed similarly crass and abrasive contempt.

Roosevelt was surprised and melancholy about the intensity of the negative reactions. Even Samuel Clemens told Roosevelt that as President he was not as free as others to invite whomever he liked to dinner, noting privately that Roosevelt should "refrain from offending the nation merely to advertise himself and make a noise."[448]

For his part, although Roosevelt continued to stay in contact with Washington, he did not again invite him or any other African-American to the White House for dinner.

Clearly, a stable race environment was not in place in society as a whole, just as it was not for professional baseball, and many more years of racial discord and injustice lay ahead.

CHAPTER 12

The Last Out

Despite the best efforts of his advisors, family, friends, and attorneys, Fred Krist's appeals were eventually exhausted.

Krist spent the night of Tuesday, November 19 in prayer, "fully resigned to his fate," according to the *Auburn Democrat-Argus*. He had that afternoon received a visit from his older sister Josephine, a nun (Sister Evarista of the Sisters of St. Joseph) who was a teacher in Steuben County. She was the last member of his family to see him alive. He then made a confession to his long-time priest, Reverend J. W. E. Kelly, assistant pastor of Holy Family Church, "who had known the prisoner as a boy in Ithaca."[449]

At five a.m. on Wednesday, November 20, Reverend Kelly returned to the prison, accompanied by Reverend A.J. Evans of Ithaca. They were taken to Krist's cell, where "the condemned man greeted them cordially." Krist received communion and prayed until called to the execution chamber.

Once in the chamber, Krist, "clad in a sack coat and trousers of dark material, soft shirt and shoes," walked to the chair carrying a crucifix in his clasped hands.

> He was pale but his eye was bright and his demeanor indicated entire resignation. He seated himself in

the chair after a glance about the room. Father Kelly dropped to his knees on the rubber mat on which the chair is located, and Father Evans stood directly in front of the chair. Krist's face lighted up, he proffered the crucifix so Father Evans, who stepped forward to take it, and, as the keepers picked up the straps to bind him in the chair he uttered these words: "I give my heart and soul to God. I am heartily sorry for all my sins."[450]

As the electrodes were being adjusted, Father Evans stepped forward and pressed the crucifix to Krist's lips, and Krist kissed it. Father Evans repeated this action twice more, and each time Krist kissed it "with fervor."

At 6:34 a.m., Warden Mead gave the signal to the electrician, and an electrical current of 1,740 volts was "shot into the body." After several seconds of varying the current's strength, it was shut off, and attending physicians confirmed that Krist was dead. Once an autopsy was completed, the body was turned over to Krist's two brothers, who buried him in Ithaca.

"Governor Odell declined to interfere himself to save the man from the penalty of his crime," the *Auburn Democrat-Argus* summarized, "but he afforded Krist's attorneys every chance to save him through the courts, if they could make a case. Their efforts were futile and the law executed the fixed penalty, despite all the influences brought to bear on the Governor."[451]

Following the execution, Krist's parents and brothers continued to live in Ithaca, and his sister continued to serve as a nun in the Rochester diocese. Krist's parents share their son Fred's gravestone in Ithaca's Calvary Cemetery. Krist's widow, Josephine, moved away from the area and eventually remarried. She passed away in 1954 and is buried near her parents in St. James Cemetery in Waverly.

Katie Tobin's parents and siblings continued to live and work in the Waverly area. Most are buried in the Tobin family plot, not far from Josephine Krist. Katie's father, James, died in 1919, and her mother, Mary, in 1921.

Katie's sister, Lizzie, the heroic woman who tried to save her from Krist, became a highly successful local businesswoman, marrying coal dealer Michael Nunan and assuming leadership of his coal company following his premature death in 1921. At a time when female business leaders were uncommon, she was enterprising and firm in her business dealings, taking customers and suppliers to court when necessary to protect her company's rights. She was also a reliable, civic-minded patron, serving as one of the founding board members of the Waverly Free Library. She passed away in 1943, but her daughter, Bette, carried on the family tradition of public service, graduating from Marymount College and serving as the Tioga County Supervisor for the National Youth Administration at the height of the New Deal in the 1930s. She was also a leader of the local Democratic Party and served with the Catholic Charities office in Binghamton for a time before passing away in 1966.

Lizzie and Katie's older sister, Mary, never married. She was a successful businesswoman in her own right, listing her vocation as "sales lady" in the 1930 census. She also passed away in 1966.

Their younger brother, Harold, moved to Ithaca and worked on the Lehigh Valley Railroad, living only a couple blocks from Krist's parents, near the local Catholic church. His daughter, Marjorie, also graduated from college–in her case, Cornell–and worked on the staff of the American Agriculturalist Magazine. Like the Krists, she is buried in Ithaca's Calvary Cemetery.

For so many independent, well-educated, successful, and civic-minded women to emerge from the same family at the time was unusual. As of 1940, only 3.8 percent of U.S. adult females had four or more years of college.[452] Their record of success speaks well of the family, and it is likely that Katie would have been similarly successful in her life, had it not ended so early and so tragically.

Civic-minded leaders and citizens throughout the region pondered what sort of new commercial and sporting landscape would emerge following 1901's structural changes to organized baseball. Several large cities in upstate New York had trouble holding onto their baseball franchises in 1900 and 1901. Over that two-year period, Elmira and Syracuse each lost franchises to other towns: Elmira to Rome and Syracuse to Brockton. Now that the minor leagues were becoming formally organized, the notion that large rather than small towns should control minor league franchises gained increased popularity.

In addition, some of the larger cities that previously hosted higher-level minor league teams—such as teams in the Eastern or International Leagues—were now vying for franchises in the lower minors, like the NYSL, thinking that they would be easier to win and maintain and would probably still draw just as large a crowd. Therefore, as the smallest town in the new minor league organization, Waverly was fighting for its life against much larger competition.

As early as late August 1901, with their Eastern League team barely departed for Brockton, Syracuse investors led by saloon and pool parlor owner George N. Kuntzsch were already scheming to obtain the NYSL franchise in Rome as a replacement. President Farrell was reported to have also been interested in securing the Syracuse team for the NYSL, as it would have been financially beneficial for the league to be there, but the Syracuse initial offer price for Rome was too low. As a result, the Waverly franchise remained as a possible target.

Waverly's baseball fair was held December 17 through 20, 1901, and it was highly successful in raising money for and interest in the team. As with the fair in March, events were held each night at the Waverly Opera House, featuring games, raffles, door prizes, and entrainment. *The Waverly Free Press* issued "The Daily Diamond" each day to publicize the event and give the advertisers exposure.

Door prizes included a piano, a violin, a bedroom set, and other similar items. Bill Ging and Jack Barnett each made an appearance to greet the crowds. As with the March fair, entertainers included the R.A. Packer Band and McGuffie's Orchestra. The team netted $750 as a result of the fair, to go with the thousands investors had reportedly compiled ahead of the 1902 season.

While Waverly compiled the required money, paid its franchise fee, and planned to continue being an official league member, discussions about the future of the NYSL proceeded among the NYSL's directors. The consensus among news reports was that when Farrell gave the Cortland franchise to Waverly, he did so for just the remainder of the season, after which the franchise would be returned to the NYSL for the directors to dispose of as they see fit. Waverly's baseball investors, however, insisted that their payment, and the NYSL's acceptance, of annual league franchise dues confirmed Waverly's retention of the franchise.

In January, Rome's ownership confirmed that prospective investor Kuntzsch still wanted its franchise for Syracuse and did not want the Waverly franchise. Rome continued to insist, however, that it would be in the league with a strong team, and that its investors already had enough money "and are willing to put in more." They also confirmed that Syracuse made an offer for the franchise, but "it was not high enough."[453]

Outside of Waverly, local media continued to push the idea that either Rome's or Waverly's team moving to Syracuse would be an improvement for the league, but Kuntzsch was adamant. He told the *Syracuse Herald*:

> "I won't stand for the Waverly team. They can give me the Waverly franchise and the Rome team if they want to but they can't give me a no-good team like Waverly and expect me to either build it up, or to release all the players and get an entirely new team in its place.
>
> "In justice to Syracuse as well as to myself, I will not stand for any such deal. Syracuse must have a good

team, or it won't have any. There is no time to build up a pennant-winning nine now and Syracuse will not stand for a team of losers, if it stands for a State League team at all."[454]

The Syracuse Herald in mid-January attempted to obtain a response from President Farrell or at least a comment on his plans for the league, but was unable to do so.

Farrell's primary interest was in keeping the league as strong and viable as possible, and that meant securing franchises that had the greatest likelihood of financial success. In an interview several days later with the *Rome Citizen*, Farrell predicted that the league would be comprised of Albany, Troy, Schenectady, Utica, Syracuse, Ilion, Binghamton, and Rome–leaving out Waverly. This cast further doubt on the team's fate within the league.[455]

"Waverly is anxious to remain in the league, and has raised several thousand dollars to sustain a team the coming season," the *Syracuse Journal* reported regarding the upcoming league meeting at the end of January. The *Journal's* reporters were supremely confident that tiny Waverly would be no match for Syracuse. "The representatives of that town will ask for the franchise under which they operated the latter half of last season, but their application will undoubtedly be denied."[456]

"The circuit committee of the New York State base ball league to which was left the matter of the makeup of the league for next season met and failing to come to a decision adjourned to meet to-day," the *Waverly Free Press* reported on February 8, 1902. "In regard to Waverly's chances for a franchise it seems to be conceded that if Syracuse wants a team Waverly will be out of it. President Farrell has said, however, that Waverly should have preference over the other applicants for admission and as he is a member of the circuit committee Waverly may yet have [a] chance."[457]

Syracuse remained eager for a franchise, and Rome's management was ultimately unable to raise the three thousand dollars required to retain its franchise. As a result, on March 12, after weeks of speculation, Farrell engineered a deal in which the Rome franchise went to Syracuse, guided by Kuntzsch and his veteran manager Sandy Griffin. Several of the Rome players, including George Wheeler, Jim McGuire, and Charlie Hamburg, reportedly did not want to play for Syracuse, and they pursued options with other teams.

As part of the deal, the NYSL directors transferred ownership of the Waverly franchise to Charles H. Ball, manager of amusement attractions for the Fonda, Johnstown, and Gloversville Railroad. Ball in turn planned to move the team from Waverly to the Johnstown-Amsterdam-Gloversville area, not far from Rome.[458] The Railroad would be a reliable investor for the team, and in return, the team would help the Railroad promote its large amusement facility at Sacandaga Park across the river from Northville. In 1901, the Railroad had built "a huge midway, roller coaster, carousels and even a kinescope theater in a railroad car with genuine rocking motion and moving scenery." The park also included a large island in the middle of the river with a picnic area, a baseball diamond, a grandstand, and a miniature train to transport visitors to and from the island over a bridge. The new owners believed NYSL ball games there were sure to be a big hit with local fans.[459]

It was a huge blow to Waverly's baseball supporters, who pledged to appeal the decision, but were already resigned to futility in the face of Syracuse's resources and the ambitious President Farrell's power, not only over the NYSL, but also over the new national minor league organization.

"As Waverly is not to have a state league ball team this season, the suggestion is made that the $750 receipts of the fair held last fall be given to the Sunshine club to use in their charitable work, or that it be divided between that society and the Y.M.C.A.," reported the *Waverly Free Press*. "Probably something of the kind will be done with the funds that were so generously given by the public."[460]

It was a particularly bitter time for Waverly, as in the first week of March, due to a combination of winter run-off and heavy rain, the town and its neighbors experienced some of the worst flooding the region had seen since 1865, washing out many farms and businesses and causing "havoc with the railroads."[461] "The streams in this vicinity went on a tearing rampage," the *Free Press* reported, "flooded the lowlands around the village, caused a money loss of thousands of dollars and untold trouble and inconvenience."[462]

The national sports media was hardly sympathetic to the village's plight. To the skeptical writer H. L. Fry, Waverly had never emerged from beneath the postage stamp, and he assumed the town's demise was a fait accompli as early as January, noting in *The Sporting News*: "Another milestone has been passed in the onward march of the New York State League. It was definitely announced during the past week that Syracuse would have a team in the state league and that Mr. George M. Kuntzsch would be the guiding spirit and chief owner, Waverly having died a natural death from cholera…or some other infantile disorder."[463]

It was an abrupt and soggy end to Waverly's life as a professional baseball town.

CHAPTER 13

Waverly's Baseball Legacy

Waverly's professional season in 1901 coincided with the founding of the American League and the National Association of Professional Baseball Leagues (NAPBL), two organizations that were indispensable to the growth and stability of professional baseball and still operate today. The impact of these organizations was not only evident at the major league level, but in the Southern Tier minor leagues. Prior to 1901, for example, there were many seasons where no professional baseball existed in the Southern Tier. Since 1901, professional baseball has been played in Elmira, Binghamton or both every season but three (1920-1922), up through and including 2019's Binghamton Rumble Ponies in the Eastern League.

At the major league level, the impact was clear right away, but particularly over the first twenty years following Waverly's last professional season. Major league baseball by 1921 had evolved from a single eight-team league with average attendance not much more than Waverly's, to a mature enterprise with consistent teams, large world-class stadiums, and much larger attendance numbers. Higher attendance prompted major-league cities to build larger stadiums. By 1915, fourteen of the sixteen major league franchises had new stadiums.

In fact, the early twentieth century was a heyday for stadium building; between 1901 and 1921, many of the game's most iconic stadiums were built, including Shibe Park in Philadelphia (1909), Ebbets Field in Brooklyn (1913), Fenway Park (1912) and Braves Stadium (1915) in Boston, Navin Field in Detroit (1912), White Sox Park (1910) and Weeghman Park (1914) in Chicago, Redland Field in Cincinnati (1912), National Park in Washington (1911), and the final Polo Grounds in New York (1911). Most of these were initially built with capacities around fifteen thousand, but were expanded to over thirty thousand as the decades wore on and the game's popularity continued to grow.[464] Yankee Stadium, barely in the planning stages in 1921, would be finished in 1923 with a capacity of fifty-eight thousand.

Baseball in New York City by 1921 had already grown into a huge entertainment enterprise, luring more spectators than ever. In 1920, for example, the Yankees, sharing the Polo Grounds with their cross-town rivals the Giants, became the first team to draw over one million fans in a season–a far cry from the paltry average major league crowds in the final years of the nineteenth century.

This trend mirrored the nation's demographics, as increasing numbers of people moved into cities from rural areas. In 1920, half of the U.S. population lived in cities, versus just forty percent twenty years earlier. [465]

Baseball also got busier and more stable at the minor league level, with John H. Farrell, serving as the Secretary-Treasurer of the NAPBL, essentially the minor league's chief administrator. He remained in that role for the next thirty-six years. During that time, he was commonly known as "the busiest man in baseball," rendering "90 percent of all decisions in organized baseball controversies," having jurisdiction over seven thousand players in thirty-five minor leagues, which received over forty million admissions per year. At the time of his retirement, he is said to have conveyed the records of over fifty-five thousand players to his successor. "Farrell in Auburn built up the largest sports organization the world has ever seen," an Auburn historian wrote.[466] His 1945 obituary described him as "a virtual czar of the minor league baseball world," noting that his "wonderfully remarkable system, his constructive ability and clean-cut business methods worked wonders for the National Association's owners and players."[467]

FOLLOWING THE WAVERLY FRANCHISE'S MOVE TO JOHNstown-Amsterdam-Gloversville, in 1902, several Waverly players continued to play for the team, settling in with the Johnstown-Amsterdam-Gloversville "JAGs" and enjoying a measure of success. Among these were Bill Ging, Tom Dwyer, Jim McCormick, and Sandy McDougal.

The Waverly squad had many fine pitchers over the years, but Ging and McDougal stood out for the length of time and number of games they pitched for the team. Each had a brief stint in the National League before joining Waverly, and each also had stints in the high minors (the Eastern League) before, during and after their time in Waverly, thus demonstrating their on-going ability to be noticed and recalled.

In 1902, they both started with the JAGs and faced plenty of good competitive hitters in the NYSL. One such competitor was Syracuse's Frank "Wildfire" Schulte, a former Waverly player himself. Another was Troy's Johnny "Crab" Evers. Both Ging and McDougal faced Schulte and Evers multiple times with mixed success.

Ging, at twenty-nine, and McDougal, at twenty-eight, were crafty baseball veterans by 1902, while Schulte and Evers were each just twenty years old. "To see 'Bill' mix 'em up and toss 'em over, one would imagine he was playing ping-pong at a swell evening party," the *Gloversville Daily Leader* wrote. "His smile was childlike and bland, but he was a gay deceiver with the sphere."[468]

Schulte, who earned the nickname "Wildfire" after giving the name to one of his favorite ponies in honor of a Lillian Russell play, was known as a power hitter who gripped the bat low around the knob and took a "long, forceful swing."[469] He used an unusually thin-handled bat made of ash and broke an estimated fifty bats per year.[470] He was also notoriously superstitious, regularly searching the street for dropped hairpins for good luck, believing, "The bigger the pin, the bigger the hits."[471]

Frank "Wildfire" Schulte played for Waverly and Lestershire, and later played for fifteen seasons in the major leagues, helping the Cubs win four pennants and two World Series. Portrait from the Library of Congress.

McDougal faced Syracuse at Johnstown on May 13, 1902, and Schulte, playing left field and batting third in the order, hit a double and scored two runs off him in five trips to the plate. McDougal, himself an excellent hitter, landed two singles and a triple, but gave up ten hits and took the 10-8 loss.[472]

Ging faced Syracuse next, on July 8, and held Schulte hitless in earning the 9-2 victory.[473] Just over a week later, on July 16, McDougal faced them again and won 13-2, this time holding Schulte to one hit. For his part, McDougal cracked a home run, a triple, and two singles, leading the team's nineteen-hit attack.[474]

Ging would meet Schulte many more times before their minor league careers were over. In 1903, Ging started against Schulte in at least three games, and Schulte gradually caught up to him, going five for fourteen in 1903. By 1904, Schulte had the fifth-highest batting average in the league, at .307, and was sent to the major leagues for outfield duty with the Chicago Cubs in time to help propel them to World Series championships in 1907 and 1908.

One of Schulte's teammates for those Cubs championships, Johnny Evers of "Tinker-to-Evers-to-Chance" fame[475], played for Troy in 1902 and finished his season with them with a .285 batting average. A talented infielder, Evers reached the Cubs after just one season in the NYSL. This was plenty of time for him to get a good taste of Ging and McDougal. Unlike the hard-swinging, right-handed Schulte, Evers was an excellent bunter and a "pesky left-handed hitter"[476] with a good batting eye, which made him less likely to be fooled by "crafty" pitches.

In his first game against Ging on June 25, 1902, Evers tagged Ging for a double and two singles. Hamburg batted behind him in the cleanup spot and smacked two more hits, but Ging held on for an 11-10 victory.[477]

McDougal had slightly better luck against Evers on July 1, holding him to a double in four trips to the plate and earning a 13-2 win.[478] Four weeks later, however, Evers tagged McDougal for a home run and a single, leading Troy to a 6-5 victory.[479] Evers returned the favor for Ging at their next meeting on August 23, cracking a triple and two singles.[480] The future Hall-of-Famer clearly feasted on Ging's and McDougal's pitching.

The two pitchers also had a number of opportunities to face each other during their years in the NYSL. On August 18, 1903, for instance, Ging pitched for the JAGs and faced McDougal, pitching for Schenectady.

The umpire that day was twenty-nine-year old Bill Klem, who was in the midst of a miserable year for umpires in the NYSL. Umpires were so routinely harassed by players and fans that most left the league before the season was over. In Klem's case, he was in perpetual battle with fans and players, resorting to whatever means he could to keep the peace. On June 25th, for example, he fined Binghamton outfielder Harry Croft five dollars for laughing at one of his decisions. On July 10th, Binghamton fans were so annoyed by his calls that they locked him out of the ballpark. On several other occasions, police protection was required to keep crowds from mobbing him. Klem repeatedly threw fans and players out of games for abusive language. He was unwelcome in Syracuse, Utica, Binghamton, and a host of other towns. "His tenacity and courage were tested on an almost daily basis in a league, which refused to hire more than one umpire for a game."[481]

On August 18th, both hurlers "pitched fine ball" against one another, and Schenectady won 3-0. McDougal had five strikeouts to Ging's two, and McDougal helped himself to a single and scored a run. The game lasted just one hour and twenty minutes, and appeared to be free of incident, which must have suited the young Klem just fine.[482] He would eventually go on to umpire in the major leagues from 1905 until 1941, and be elected to the National Baseball Hall of Fame.

"Bill Ging with the Wonderful Wing," as local crowds knew him, never did return to the major leagues, despite his legendary victory over the New York Giants in 1899, but continued to pitch in the minors until his arm stopped "working properly" in 1905.[483] In the meantime, he "had all the curves in the book and remarkable control."[484] After a successful outing against Ilion in '03, the *Gloversville Leader* remarked, "The way [Ging] treated the Ilion crowd was like refusing children a ride on a merry-go-round. They wanted to hit the ball and William knew it. He had all the change in his pocket–and kept it there."[485]

Ging continued to be an active Democrat in Elmira politics, serving as city sealer in 1906, the position in charge of the city's weights and measures. He worked in Elmira for the next forty-four years as a bartender, clerk, and watchman. He never married or had children. His grand nephew, Jerry Coffey, recalled that Ging was an invalid and chain smoker in his later years, who, contrary to his pitching reputation, always gave his nephews pocket change to use to buy candy.[486] Upon Ging's death in Elmira in 1950, multiple newspapers in the state mentioned both his five-hit victory against New York and his "iron man stint" against Albany.[487]

Ging's love of baseball was passed onto his niece Gladys. Gladys in turn shared this love of baseball with her husband John, a graduate of St. Bonaventure. They frequently attended minor league games at Elmira's Dunn Field, the same Maple Avenue location where "Uncle Will" once pitched, and traveled to New York City several times to watch the World Series. By the late 1940s, the two were Brooklyn Dodgers fans on account of Jackie Robinson.

Just a little more than a year following Ging's death, Gladys and John left their five children with a sitter and took the DL&W train from Elmira to New York City to catch the World Series. The Yankees had already clinched the American League pennant, and the National League pennant was up for grabs between the Dodgers and Giants.

So, prior to the World Series, on October 3, 1951, was the third of a best-of-three playoff series between the two pennant contenders. It was to be held at the Polo Grounds, the same spot "Uncle Will" had spun his complete game victory over the Giants fifty-two years and eight days earlier.

Not to miss such an occasion, Gladys and John were there at the Polo Grounds that auspicious day to witness the Giants' revenge. It was the first ever nationally televised baseball contest and arguably the century's most dramatic game, as the Giants defeated the Dodgers 5-4 on Bobby Thomson's ninth inning walk-off home run, known by fans as baseball's "Shot Heard 'Round the World," akin to Ralph Waldo Emerson's reference to the first shot of the American Revolution in his poem "Concord Hymn."[488]

Sandy McDougal would return to the major leagues briefly in 1905, taking the opportunity as a pitcher for St. Louis on September 25 to fire a pitch "straight at" the mouth of veteran John Titus in an effort to knock Titus's famed lucky toothpick "down his throat." McDougal missed the toothpick, but it fell out of Titus's mouth, and he called time and went down on all fours for four minutes "frantically" searching for it. Eventually, the umpire demanded he return to the batter's box and resume his at-bat. "At that point," wrote historians Bruce Nash and Allan Zullo, "Titus knew he was a doomed man. He slowly trudged back to the plate…and struck out."[489]

McDougal had earned his only major league victory a few days earlier on September 17, in Chicago against the Cubs. Former Waverly teammate Frank Schulte batted cleanup and played left field for the Cubs that day.[490]

A year after his major league victory, McDougal found himself back in the minors, playing with Cristall, Roth, and Archibald "Moonlight" Graham of *Field of Dreams* fame and winning a New York State League championship for Scranton. Moonlight Graham played outfield for three years in Scranton after his famous one-game 1905 appearance with the New York Giants.

McDougal unfortunately lived just a few years beyond his professional baseball career, passing away in Buffalo in 1910 of typhoid fever at the age of 36.[491]

"Moonlight" Graham had connections to other Waverly players as well. Before joining McDougal in Scranton in '06, for example, "Moonlight" played a partial season in Memphis with the Southern Association, where he teamed up with another ex-Waverly player, Phil Nadeau.

After leaving Waverly, Nadeau played in Binghamton for the 1902 season and then traveled to Portland in the Pacific Coast League for two seasons, before heading back to the Southern League in 1906 and 1907. His stints included a portion of the 1909 season in the South Atlantic League, where his opponents included a young "Shoeless Joe" Jackson. Nadeau eventually returned to the Pacific Northwest for many more years. The breadth of his baseball travels could have been due to his on-going late-summer hay fever and perhaps the changes in climate did him good. Nadeau continued to play in organized baseball until 1914—when he was forty-two—a career that spanned twenty-one years. According to SABR, he collected at least 1,906 base hits during his career, but never made it to the major leagues. He passed away in Seattle on March 20, 1958.

George "Knotty" Lee went to Concord in the New England League in 1902 and remained in the New England or Canadian Leagues for the next several years as a player, and then for many more as a manager, scout, and league organizer. Lee helped create the Canadian-American League in 1936. His pioneering work on behalf of Canadian baseball earned him a place in the Canadian Baseball Hall of Fame in 1998.[492]

Vic Accorsini, who played much of 1901 under the name "Andrews," went directly from Waverly to Memphis in the Southern League before the '01 season was over. He then remained in the Southern League for most of the next five seasons, rotating among Memphis, Nashville, New Orleans, and Little Rock, before playing his final three seasons in the Connecticut State League. All told, according to SABR, Accorsini played ten seasons in the minor leagues and had over 471 hits. Like Nadeau and Lee, he never made it to the major leagues, although he consistently had a strong on-field reputation. Accorsini eventually worked in a variety of jobs, including as a collector for a clothing store and a factory foreman.[493] He worked for Union Carbide in Niagara Falls for many years, playing on industrial league teams in the area and visiting his friends in Waverly on occasion.[494] Accorsini passed away on October 30, 1962, in his hometown of Lynchburg.

*Waverly's Vic Accorsini in catcher's gear.
Portrait by Joseph Mastrantuono.*

Mickey Mullin, despite his enormous potential, did not return to organized baseball after his leap from the fourth floor of the Binghamton hotel. He eventually became a railroad investigator, a deputy sheriff, and was an active Republican who served as coroner in Philadelphia at the time of his death in 1933. Mullin's obituaries indicate he played major league baseball for Detroit's American League club and that he also scouted for the team for several years. While there is no official SABR record of his playing with Detroit, he may have pitched for the club on a trial basis during the 1901 exhibition season, prior to joining Waverly.

Despite the injuries he sustained from his leaping incident, he continued to be involved in baseball, and his son Michael Junior was signed to a Yankees trial contract as a pitcher in 1933. Two of the elder Mullin's obituaries noted that immediately prior to his death he suffered a stroke while listening to the last game of the 1933 World Series on the radio.[495]

Matt Broderick never joined the Waverly team, as he did not move with the Cortland franchise in '01. Just before the 1902 baseball season began, his young brother Charles was killed in a mining accident. "The young man was employed at the bottom of the main slope as a hitcher, and had been at work only a short while when a mass of top rock fell upon him without warning and crushed out his life."[496] It was yet another reminder of what many of these ball players' lives would have been, had they not the talent and opportunity to escape the mines and factories and play ball professionally.

Following the tragedy, Broderick signed with Ned Hanlon's Brooklyn club for the '03 season as a backup infielder and appeared in two major league games, the first on May 1 against Boston, and second on May 16 against "Iron Man" McGinnity and the New York Giants. In his first game, Broderick substituted for Tim Flood at second base and had no hits in one trip to the plate.[497] In his last game, he pinch-hit for the pitcher and did not reach base.[498] He was released soon thereafter and played several seasons in the Tri-State and Ohio-Pennsylvania Leagues.

Broderick's Anthracite region pal Barney McFadden went 3-4 with Cincinnati in 1901 and then played for St. Joseph, Missouri, in the Western League in 1902 to refine his skills. Among the stars he faced there was twenty-six-year-old, right-hander Mordecai Brown, nicknamed "Three Finger" due to having lost most of his right index finger in a childhood farming accident. Brown, who would go 27-15 during the 1902 season as Omaha's ace, squared off against McFadden on May 15, in a classic pitcher's duel, besting him, 1-0. McFadden gave up just three hits to Brown's seven, but Brown deftly kept the hits separated, and a controversial run in the second inning by Omaha was all the scoring Brown needed.[499] McFadden received a call-up at season's end to Philadelphia, but his "miserable pitching" against the same Boston club Broderick faced led to a 13-3 loss. He never pitched in organized baseball again.[500]

"Three Finger" Brown would go on to join "Crab" Evers and "Wildfire" Schulte on the Chicago Cubs' 1907 and 1908 championship teams, and, with Evers, eventually be elected to the National Baseball Hall of Fame.

Waverly native Owen Dunham played for both the 1896 and 1900 Waverly teams, and remained a strong baseball supporter in the town after the 1901 season, periodically coaching the Waverly High School team while continuing to work as a sign painter. Upon one such coaching stint, the local media lauded Dunham as "a player of ability having been a member of several of Waverly's best independent teams."[501] Upon his premature death in 1916 of peritonitis, the *Elmira Telegram* described him as "genial, kind hearted" and "one of Waverly's best known young men."[502]

Dunham's good friend Fred Tucker did not join the JAGs or immediately continue in organized baseball, but rather resumed his cigar store duties in Waverly. In June 1902, at his trial in Owego, the jury acquitted him of the manslaughter charges for punching or shoving Frank W. Preston and contributing to his death the previous summer. Providing Tucker's defense were high-priced attorneys Frederick E. Hawkes, who had assisted with the Krist prosecution in 1900, and unsuccessful 1900 gubernatorial candidate John Stanchfield. Former baseball teammates Bud Waller and Sandy McDougal were among those who testified at the trial.

Upon the announcement of the jury's "not guilty" decision, "a burst of applause sounded through the court room," according to the *Tioga County Record*. "Judge Mead vigorously used his gavel" and unsuccessfully attempted to determine who had been responsible for the outburst. The judge said, "Not in all his experience upon the bench had his court been so grievously outraged." After court was dismissed, "Tucker's friends at once surrounded him and extended hearty congratulations."[503]

In 1907, Tucker briefly played for the Flint Vehicles in the Southern Michigan League. *The Waverly Free Press* reported that he had gone to Michigan to manage the team in Tecumseh, but local game accounts only list him as a player for Flint. It was his last documented foray into professional baseball–twenty-two years after his first. He returned to Waverly soon after the season, discontinued his cigar manufacturing business—inexpensive cigarettes had by then snuffed out most cigar-making profits—and became an auditor for the Lehigh Valley Railroad (LVRR), working at the railroad's major repair center in Sayre, a site that covered 70 acres and included 21 buildings, the largest of which, at 740 feet long and 336 feet wide, was the third largest in the country. The Sayre LVRR shops turned out 200 locomotives during its lifetime. The overall facility at its height employed up to 2,000 workers, a truly significant operation.[504]

Tucker remained a well-regarded citizen, chairing the athletics committee for Waverly's giant 1910 Old Home Week celebration, serving in 1923 as the first president of the Lehigh Valley Sayre System Shops Welfare and Athletic association,[505] and continuing to be active in athletic and community events, coaching numerous local baseball and football teams and competing in golf tournaments at Waverly's Shepard Hills Country Club. Upon his death in Waverly in 1943, *The Evening Times* pronounced him "one of the greatest baseball players ever turned out in the Valley."[506]

As for Tucker's mentor, John F. Doran, the last definitive reference the author could locate in the news media was related to his April 1901 incarceration in Owego for intoxication. According to the 1900 census, he worked as a blacksmith and lived with his father and sisters, Helen and Mary, at 110 Willow Street in Athens. By 1910, his younger brother, Michael, lived there instead, and John was no longer in the area. He may have passed away during the decade or moved. His mother had passed away in

1898, and his father would follow in 1917. Both of them, along with most of John's siblings, are buried in Sayre's Epiphany Roman Catholic Cemetery, but John's final resting place has yet to be located.

Bill Heine's professional career in organized baseball began in 1888 as John Doran and Harry Taylor's teammate in Elmira. He had played competitively for over a decade with some of the best players of the era, ranging from John McGraw, Jimmy Collins, and Willie Keeler to Honus Wagner and Napoleon Lajoie, but never got a shot at the highest stage himself. Following his 1901 season with Waverly, he settled with his young family in Addison, New York, ran a successful company, and played and coached semi-pro and amateur teams in the area. Among the young players Heine coached at Addison were many who later played in the major leagues, including Bill Mack, a lefty pitcher born in Elmira who appeared briefly for the Chicago Cubs in 1908; Lew Groh, an infielder from Rochester who played for the Philadelphia Athletics in 1919; and John Joseph "Red" Murray, a hard-hitting smooth-fielding outfielder who played eleven years for the Cardinals, Giants and Cubs.

Heine's Addison team during this 1904-1905 period was in the Southern Tier League, where players were generally paid $75 "per month," which according to players at the time, meant "perhaps" they got the pay and "perhaps" they did not.[507]

Outfielder John Joseph "Red" Murray was an excellent local player who went from playing for Bill Heine in Addison, New York, to playing many seasons for Heine's former teammate John McGraw in New York City. Portrait from the Library of Congress.

Before joining Heine in Addison, Murray, Mack and many other young Elmira players got their start with the Father Mathew Society team, and several then went on to play college ball, playing semi-pro with Southern Tier League teams in the summers. One of Murray's teammates and best friends on the Father Mathew teams of the early 1900s, for instance, was another future major leaguer, Joe "Dode" Birmingham. Murray and Birmingham each played college sports (Murray for Lock Haven and Birmingham for Cornell) before enrolling at Notre Dame together in 1905. While Birmingham dropped out after one semester due to malaria,[508] and spent an extra season in the NYSL with the JAGS before sticking with Cleveland for nine seasons, Murray played two seasons for the Irish and immediately went to the majors to stay in the 1906 season, playing three seasons for the Cardinals before playing over six seasons (and four World Series) for John McGraw's New York Giants.

During their major league playing careers, each outfielder had the reputation for having his league's best throwing arm – Birmingham for the American League and Murray for the National.

Birmingham was one of the American League's top outfielders in Cleveland, known to have the ability to throw strikes over home plate from center field,[509] and consistently ranking among the league leaders in outfield assists. He succeeded Napoleon Lajoie as the team's player-manager in 1912, and eventually managed in the minor leagues, persuading Murray to join him in Toronto for the 1916 season. He stayed active in baseball as a scout and umpire after his retirement, and passed away in 1946 while working as an umpire in the Mexican Baseball League.[510]

Murray was also known as an excellent fielder, and, while with the Giants, was "rated with Mel Ott as one of the two finest right-fielders in New York Giant history."[511] After his playing career, Murray settled in Elmira and spent over three decades running youth sports in the city, eventually serving as Elmira's recreation director. He passed away in Sayre in 1958.

Among Murray's teammates in St. Louis was Waverly native Tom O'Hara, who had played with Waverly under Heine in 1901. O'Hara hit a solid .252 in 1906 and 1907 for the Cardinals before returning to the minor leagues and playing in Lancaster, Williamsport and Albany through 1911. He eventually became a scout for at three different major league teams (Yankees, Cubs and Cardinals) and moved to Kansas City where he worked as an auto salesman for Pierce-Arrow through the early 1940s. He passed away in Denver, Colorado, in 1954.[512]

Waverly native Tom "Snibs" O'Hara played for Waverly and Manhattanville College before embarking on a multi-year professional career as an outfielder and scout, including stints with the Cardinals, Cubs and Yankees. Portrait by Gary Cieradkowski.

Heine's influence over young baseball stars was not limited to his professional coaching experiences. His own son, William Henry, known as "Bud," was born in 1900, just as Heine finished his first season at Waverly. Under his father's tutelage,

Bud wound up pursuing a baseball career, playing baseball for St. Bonaventure College. Bud also captained the basketball team at St. Bonaventure before graduating in 1921.

Upon graduation, Bud had a choice among professional baseball offers, and his father persuaded him to disregard an offer from Detroit in lieu of waiting on a potential offer from his longtime personal friend John McGraw, who had been manager of the New York Giants since 1902.

McGraw was originally a big proponent of the new American League, and managed the League's Baltimore Orioles franchise in 1901. However, when American League President Ban Johnson moved the Baltimore franchise to New York the following year, McGraw took the opportunity to move to New York as well, but to the National League. His bitter relations with Johnson–sowed in Ithaca in the spring of 1901 when Johnson misrepresented McGraw's situation to Hughie Jennings–had passed the breaking point.

McGraw teamed up with Christy Mathewson, former Heine mentee Red Murray, former John Doran opponent Joe McGinnity, and other stars to create a powerful National League team in New York, reminiscent of his 1890s dynasty in Baltimore. McGraw's New York Giants continued to personify the same "scientific" or "inside" baseball that he and his teammates had pursued in Baltimore.

Mathewson, who had struggled so mightily for Taunton in 1899, was McGraw's dominant pitcher for over a decade. He retired from playing in 1916 and managed the Cincinnati Reds for three years before volunteering to serve in the Army's Chemical Warfare Division during World War I. During the war, he was exposed to mustard gas. Upon his return, he grew increasingly sick with tuberculosis, and his baseball activities declined. Before passing away from the disease in 1925, he enjoyed opportunities to stay in touch with McGraw and his old teammates throughout this period.

For all the criticism he took for being a tough guy, McGraw was known to be very loyal to his friends. He regularly brought his old Truxton coach and mentor, Albert Kenney, to Giants games, especially when the Giants were in the World Series. McGraw was also known to favor college baseball players and frequently gave them opportunities to play, especially at the end of seasons.

"The difference is simply this," McGraw explained, "the college boy, or anyone with even a partially trained mind, immediately tries to find his faults; the unschooled fellow usually tries to hide his. The moment a man locates his faults he can quickly correct them. The man who thinks he is keeping his mistakes under cover will never advance a single step until he sees the light."[513]

Since McGraw had a warm, longstanding friendship with his old teammate Bill Heine,[514] and Bill's son Bud was looking for a major league shot, McGraw included the young Heine on his list of collegiate prospects and signed him to a Giants contract. He also signed prospects from Swarthmore, Dartmouth, and Columbia. It served his best interests to give young college stars an opportunity to play on the game's greatest stage and, in this case, it also benefited an old friend and teammate.

In 1921, McGraw's team was at the top of the National League standings for the seventh time in his twenty years at the helm, and Hughie Jennings, after 14 years of managing the Tigers, joined him in the dugout as a coach.

Truxton native John McGraw was a former Baltimore Oriole, a longtime manager of the New York Giants, and a longtime friend of Bill Heine. Portrait from the Library of Congress.

After following Harry Taylor to study law at Cornell, Jennings remained in baseball for many years, most notably as a manager of Bill Donovan's and Ty Cobb's repeat-pennant-winning Detroit Tigers, where he earned fame for his enthusiastic two-handed dancing "Ee-Yah" coaching. Jennings would continue to coach for the Giants through 1925, but suffered a nervous breakdown near the season's end that prevented him from rejoining the team in 1926. He spent the next two years recuperating in the Pocono Mountains and at his home in Scranton, where he passed away from meningitis in 1928.

Meanwhile, the franchise McGraw left after 1901–the American League New York club–was also atop the standings in 1921. Despite fielding such Hall-of-Fame stars as Willie Keeler, Jack Chesbro, and Frank "Home Run" Baker, they had faced years of mediocrity. Yet now, the team nicknamed "the Yankees" was on the verge of breaking new ground and winning games with a new type of slugging, swing-from-the-heels baseball that was taking the sport by storm.

Chief among these hard-hitting Yankees was the baby who had nursed near his father's Eutaw Street saloon in the midst of Baltimore baseball's halcyon days: George Herman "Babe" Ruth. As a twenty-four-year-old with Boston in 1919, his first full season as a regular outfielder, Ruth swatted twenty-nine home runs, utterly obliterating former Lancaster star and Charlie Hamburg teammate Socks Seybold's major league season home run record of sixteen, set in 1902. In 1920 and 1921, Ruth progressively broke his own records, hitting fifty-four and fifty-nine home runs, respectively–unheard of numbers at the time. There was talk that the baseballs themselves were "juiced" and more prone to travelling long distances than previously, but, nevertheless, Ruth's power was unique and unprecedented.

Jennings observed Ruth closely during 1921 and even went moose hunting with him on one occasion, and he said he "never saw a hitter like him and never expect to see another."[515] This was high praise coming from a man who had managed Ty Cobb for years in Detroit. Regrettably, Jennings thought Ruth's prowess and success meant the death of "scientific baseball" since he figured all young players will now swing from the heels to hit home runs rather than work hard for little things like singles, walks, stolen bases. Still, Ruth's exciting home runs were revitalizing a sport that was still suffering from World War I and from the infamous "Black Sox" gambling scandal, where a number of White Sox players were accused of throwing the 1919 World Series to the Cincinnati Reds. This was no time for McGraw and Jennings to simply cling to their old ways at the expense of the new.

It was against this backdrop that on Saturday, October 1, 1921, McGraw's Giants met the Phillies, managed by Irvin "Kaiser" Wilhelm, for a doubleheader. The Giants had already clinched the National League pennant and were playing out the season. They had one last game scheduled back in Brooklyn for October 2 and would then play the World Series against the cross-town Yankees.

The games were held in Philadelphia's old Baker Bowl at the corner of North 15th and West Huntingdon Streets, one of only two major league stadiums—with Robison Field in St. Louis being the other—to predate the 1901 season.

Heine was with the Giants, and had been working out with Jennings, who spoke very highly of his abilities, especially his fielding. However, Heine had not yet gotten into a game. This doubleheader might be his last chance. He was understandably eager to impress McGraw as well as the fans and the New York sportswriters.

Another recent Giants acquisition on the bench, outfielder Casey Stengel, was likely even more eager to impress.

Whereas Heine was a raw rookie, Stengel, recently acquired from bottom-dwelling Philadelphia, was a veteran with a mixed reputation. He hated losing, but had been buried on losing teams nearly his entire career, earning a bigger reputation as a clown than as a competitor. After misplaying a ball in the Philadelphia outfield once, for example, he claimed to fans that he committed the error because he lacked nourishment and that the team was not paying him well enough to eat. Being on McGraw's team was a huge wake-up call. Stengel had previously played in Brooklyn, and he recognized what a great opportunity he had on a big-city winner. He planned to milk it for all it was worth.

Outfielder Casey Stengel joined the New York Giants in mid-season 1921, and was desperate to impress manager John McGraw, who would eventually become his mentor. Portrait courtesy of the National Baseball Hall of Fame.

Despite the opportunity, both Stengel and Heine sat on the bench in the first game, as McGraw started Phil Douglas on the mound, Mike Gonzalez behind the plate, George "High Pockets" Kelly at first, Johnny Rawlings at second, Dave Bancroft at short, Frankie Frisch at third and "Silent George" Burns, Ross Youngs and Irish Meusel in the outfield. Philadelphia started Lee Meadows at pitcher, Butch Henline at catcher, Ed Konetchy at first, John Monroe at second, Don Rader at short, Goldie Rapp at third, and an outfield of Russ Wrightstone, Cy Williams, and Cliff Lee.

On paper, the lineups were very lop-sided in the Giants' favor: three of the Giants (Bancroft, Frisch, and Youngs) were future Hall of Famers, whereas none of the Phillies were close to that category.

Stengel and Heine watched from the bench as the Giants scored three runs in the first inning to take a 3-0 lead. Maybe a big lead would give McGraw enough comfort to put in substitutes. Unfortunately, the Phillies scored once in the fourth and twice in the sixth to tie the game. Stengel and Heine continued to watch helplessly as the teams went back and forth for the last three innings, with the Phillies ultimately scoring twice in the ninth to win, 10-9.

For the second game, Philadelphia retained the same line-up, just swapping in John Peters at catcher and Jimmy Ring at pitcher.

Stengel and Heine were undoubtedly restless, wondering whether they would get a shot in the second game. Stengel likely found creative ways to remind McGraw of his availability, perhaps mentioning something slyly to Jennings, with a joke.

Not surprisingly, McGraw did not want to risk injuries to his regulars prior to the World Series, so changed his line-up for the second game. He went with Red Causey on the mound, Alex Gaston at catcher, Gonzalez at first, Hank Schrieber at second, Bancroft at short, Frisch at third, and rookies Joe Connolly and Bill Cunningham in two of the three outfield spots.

To Stengel's delight, McGraw penciled him in the third outfield spot, replacing Youngs. This was Stengel's big opportunity.

Heine was still on the bench.

The Giants took an early 2-0 lead in the second inning, and pitcher Red Causey appeared to have the Phillies well in hand, just allowing scattered singles.

Given the circumstances at this point of the game, McGraw and the coaching staff pondered their best options, and decided to remove future Hall-of-Famer Dave Bancroft to rest him along with many of the other starters. They then moved Schreiber to shortstop and looked down the bench for a substitute at second base.

Bud Heine got the call.

Heine raced out to take his spot at second base. He was now a major leaguer, something his father strived to reach for over a decade but never achieved.

Infielder Bud Heine, son of Bill Heine, was born in Elmira the first summer his father played for Waverly, and followed in his father's footsteps as a professional ball player. McGraw gave him a major league shot with the Giants in 1921, and he was eager to take advantage of it.

The Giants took a 3-0 lead in the fifth and held onto it, cruising to a 3-0 victory. Just as he had intended, Stengel wound up being the game's hitting hero, with a double and two singles to go with one run scored It was the breakout game he had been hoping for.

A lefty hitter, Bud Heine went up to bat twice without a hit. In the field, he had two assists, a putout at second, and no errors.

The Giants went on to defeat Ruth and the Yankees in the 1921 World Series, McGraw's first World Series victory since 1905. The entire series was played in the new Polo Grounds, contiguous to Coogan's Bluff in upper Manhattan. It would continue to be the home field for both the Giants and the Yankees until Yankee Stadium was built in 1923.

Stengel went on to play for the Giants for two more seasons, and eventually became a McGraw disciple, spending many hours with McGraw, asking him questions and listening to his stories and advice, not too dissimilar from how Billy Martin would eventually pester Stengel for the same advice when Stengel was his manager years later in Oakland and New York.

"Billy watched every move that Casey made," noted teammate Gil McDougald, "and questioned every move in his own mind."[516] Undoubtedly, Martin was pulling from the same reservoir of inside baseball as Stengel, nurtured by McGraw on the fields and sandlots of the Southern Tier, and perfected over decades in Baltimore and New York. It was a reservoir of fundamentals that Martin's Hall-of-Fame mentee Rod Carew characterized simply as "aggressiveness," just as McGraw had done decades earlier.

"He wanted an aggressive club," Carew said of Martin. "We never stopped at second base. Make them make mistakes. Force them to make mistakes."[517]

According to McGraw's wife, Blanche, Stengel frequently spent the night at their house and did more than his fair share of cooking. "Casey liked to cook bacon and scrambled eggs, which he did two or three times a night," she said, "and John liked to eat them."[518]

"They talked through countless nights in the kitchen," she recalled. "What on earth they gabbed about I never learned.

Each blamed the other. John confided that Casey could talk your head off. In the morning Casey would pay tribute to John's old baseball stories, and how he couldn't get a word in edgeways."[519]

Heine joined the Giants for spring training the next year in San Antonio, and was sold before the regular season started to Indianapolis in the "Three I" League (Indiana, Illinois, and Iowa), where McGraw and Jennings could "keep a string on him," slang for being part of the Giants' minor league farm "system." Heine never made it back to the major leagues. He played in the Piedmont League for three seasons, earning a respectable lifetime batting average of .287, and then played several years for semi-pro and company teams. He also played professional basketball for a time. Among his last stops on the industrial baseball circuit was a stint in 1927 with the Sayre Lehigh Valley Railroad (LVRR) Shops team, nicknamed in local newspapers as the "Engine Builders," on account of Sayre's role as an engine manufacturer for the LVRR system. Heine worked for the Shops and played before large crowds at Coleman Field in Sayre throughout the summer of 1927, just a couple miles south of the Howard Street Grounds where his Dad played in Waverly almost three decades earlier.

Among Heine's teammates in Sayre was twenty-nine-year-old World War I veteran Davey Claire, a speedy shortstop who haled from Michigan and played three major league games with Detroit in 1920. The two ex-major leaguers led Sayre to a phenomenal 1927 season, coming within a game of winning the LVRR system championship.

Following the season, Claire decided to return to the Kellogg's factory team back home in Battle Creek, Michigan, and persuaded Heine to join him. Both players joined Kellogg's for the 1928 season, and became long-time players and employees. Heine eventually became a factory foreman and executive, and, following retirement, passed away in Fort Lauderdale, Florida, in 1976.

According to an October 4, 1977, letter to a baseball researcher at the National Baseball Library, his widow claimed, "'Bud' was always proud of his baseball career, short-lived as it was."

"Anyway," she added proudly. "He loved the game."[520]

Bud Heine's father, Bill, "an affable, genial man," died in 1929, following years of being a tobacco merchant and superintendent of the local tobacco company plant in Addison, New York, and being "entrusted with public offices on many occasions," including the positions of mayor and trustee. As recently as June 1928, he was a Steuben County Democratic Party Committeeman.[521]

Among the baseball milestones noted by the *Corning Evening Leader* upon Bill Heine's death were his days in Olean with McGraw, his 1892 championship season in Binghamton, and his "well known" captaincy of the Addison Nine in the Southern Tier League following his professional career.[522]

The mourners at "one of the largest funerals in recent years" included his old Binghamton, Brockton, and Waverly teammate and fellow Elmira native, Doctor John F. Barnett, a popular local dentist.[523] Barnett passed away several years later, in 1954.

FEW PLAYERS IN THE EARLY PART OF THE TWENTIETH CENTURY were more respected than "Wild Bill" Donovan, who played outfield and pitched for Waverly's 1896 squad.

After he left Waverly, Donovan pitched in the minors for Waterbury, Hartford, and Richmond and had a brief stint with Washington before landing with the 1900 Brooklyn National League club run by old Oriole Hall-of-Famers Ned Hanlon, Hughie Jennings, Willie Keeler, Joe Kelley, and Joe McGinnity. The next year, at the age of twenty-four, he led the National League in wins with twenty-five. Two years later, he moved to Ed Barrow's Detroit Tigers, where he would star for the next ten years before winding up his career with the Yankees in New York. Over his eighteen-year major league career, Donovan was 185-139, and among his best seasons were those for the '07-'09 pennant winners in Detroit under manager Hughie Jennings.

The 1907 American League champion Detroit Tigers featured, among others, former Waverly pitcher "Wild Bill" Donovan (top row fourth from left), outfielder Ty Cobb (middle row, third from left), and manager Hughie Jennings (front row, third from left with dog). Photograph courtesy of the National Baseball Hall of Fame.

The Tigers of that period were a brawling bunch, most notably due to fiery and moody outfielder Ty Cobb. Donovan was a mentor for the young Cobb, becoming, at times, Cobb's only confidant on the team.

Even before he arrived in Detroit, Cobb had had some serious run-ins with his teammates. One of the most notable was in Augusta in 1905, when Cobb was just eighteen. His manager was none other than thirty-one-year-old catcher Andy Roth–the same Roth who had roomed with Charlie Hamburg and played against Waverly when the two played for Rome in 1901. According to one Cobb biographer, Cobb's imperious attitude "didn't work with the veteran Roth," who challenged Cobb to a fight after the fresh-faced Cobb told him to "Go to Hell."[524]

The fight was anything goes. Feelings had festered so long that the Tourist players saw no reason to break it up. Cobb went berserk, punching anywhere he could reach Roth, from jaw to crotch. Roth applied a choke hold and cutting off his wind until Ty bit Roth's ear and wrenched on it like a bulldog. Blood was lost by both. Roth tore loose to batter Cobb's eye, closing it. He headbutted Cobb to the ground. Cobb kicked Roth while he was down and a moment later had Roth on his back. It went on to a no-decision when some of the Tourists finally intervened. Each was helped away, exhausted and needing bandaging. Cobb ranked this one as among the dozen or so dirtiest brawls he ever engaged in. It effectively eliminated Roth as a leading team factor.[525]

Cobb's irascibility only continued when he was promoted to the Tigers at age twenty. He was tremendously competitive on the field, but had significant trouble getting along with teammates off the field. At one point, Donovan stepped in to stop a fight between Cobb and thirty-two-year-old pitcher Ed Siever. In doing so, Donovan explained to the young Cobb, "These guys hate you. They'll do anything to hurt you,"[526] and he encouraged Cobb to make more of an effort to get along with his teammates. Ultimately, Cobb got along well enough—thanks to the early personal coaching of both Donovan and manager Jennings—to remain with the Tigers for twenty-two seasons, during which time, Cobb became arguably the game's most brilliant player.

Following his playing career, Donovan became a manager, first for Providence in the International League—where he mentored a young Babe Ruth—then for the Yankees from 1915 to 1917, then for Jersey City in the International League, and then for the Philadelphia Phillies in early 1921.

Donovan was one of the very few players and managers to have had a significant influence on both a young Ty Cobb and a young Babe Ruth.

As mentioned earlier, the year 1921 was when the infamous "Black Sox" scandal of 1919—in which eight players on Kid Gleason's Chicago White Sox team were accused of throwing the 1919 World Series—fully erupted. Unfortunately, although Donovan was not accused in the scandal, he testified as part of its proceedings due to his familiarity with the game's players and processes, and the implications of even being named as a witness prompted Philadelphia to fire him from his manager position before the season was over.

It was then that George Weiss of the Eastern League's New Haven franchise contacted Donovan. For years, Weiss had done phenomenal work as a semi-pro baseball organizer in New Haven, attracting some of the game's biggest major league stars to play exhibition games in New Haven on Sundays when laws in neighboring jurisdictions did not allow Sunday baseball. He paid high stipends for these appearances, and among the most grateful for such opportunities was Donovan's old Tigers teammate, Ty Cobb. Cobb recommended Donovan to Weiss, and the two quickly became partners, with Donovan managing the New Haven club in 1922 and 1923.

On December 9, 1923, as Weiss and Donovan were traveling by train to Chicago for the winter baseball meetings, the two argued over who should take the more comfortable lower berth in the sleeping car versus the less comfortable upper berth. As the younger of the two, Weiss insisted on taking the upper berth so Donovan could sleep more easily. That night, in far western New York near the Pennsylvania border, the train crashed. Tragically, Donovan and all the others in the car who were sleeping in lower berths perished instantly. Weiss suffered serious injuries, but survived.

Weiss, already a good friend of Casey Stengel's, would eventually bring Stengel to New York, where he would be the architect of the great Yankee teams of the 1950s. Had Donovan refused Weiss's insistence that he sleep in the lower berth, baseball history would have been very different.

CHARLES "HEINIE" WAGNER PLAYED WITH WAVERLY DURING the 1901 season. The next season, he went on to briefly play for the New York Giants and then spent several years on the Eastern League's Newark team before eventually becoming a player, captain, coach, and manager of the Boston Red Sox.

The 1916 World Series champion Boston Red Sox featured, among others, former Waverly player Charles "Heinie" Wagner (top row, second from left) and pitcher Babe Ruth (front row, fourth from left). Photograph from the Library of Congress.

Wagner was a solid and dependable player and a well-respected member of the Red Sox family for many years. In his twelve-year major league career, he collected 834 hits and had a batting average of .250. According to a baseball guide from the time, Wagner was the "backbone" of the Red Sox team, "owing to his ability and his brains." Later, as a coach, Wagner was credited with developing a young Everett Scott, one of baseball's greatest shortstops.[527]

As a reliable team leader, one of Wagner's assignments was to keep an eye on Babe Ruth during Ruth's wild early years following his acquisition from the Baltimore Orioles in 1914. Ruth was just starting out in pro baseball after growing up in and first developing his phenomenal pitching skills at St. Mary's Industrial School for Boys.

At 6'2", the nineteen-year-old Ruth towered over most of his teammates, including the 5'9" Wagner, and his behavior off the field was similarly over the top. "His loud, breezy, carefree ways irritated the regulars, many of whom were veterans of Boston's World Championship team of 1912," wrote biographer Robert Creamer.[528]

He was an overgrown "creature of impulse" in need of constant management. "Ruth's presence in the Red Sox clubhouse was impossible to ignore," wrote biographer Kal Wagenheim. "He loved to yell, play practical jokes, and wrestle around with the younger players." According to former teammate Waite Hoyt, Ruth was unaware of the "sensation he was causing" with his behavior. He routinely ate in the dugout during games–hot dogs, peanuts, ice cream–and even occasionally had the ushers bring food for him. He "cussed so much," said Harry Hooper, that he and his teammates were regularly kicked off golf courses. "He had no idea whatsoever of money," Boston manager Bill Carrigan said of him. "You've got to remember his background–that orphan asylum and all–and this was his first big job." Meanwhile, his driving was so bad—at one point, his license was suspended—that the *Boston Herald* reported, "He has struck pedestrians while going at a speedy clip."[529]

Carrigan sent the young pitcher down to Providence for a short time in mid-August 1914, where manager Bill Donovan took the prodigy under his wing and taught him "much about the art of pitching."[530] Then, upon Ruth's return to the majors, Carrigan arranged for Ruth to room with Wagner, by this time a player-coach, in an effort to keep him under better control. Consequently, two of Waverly baseball's most important alumni, Donovan and Wagner, played key roles in Ruth's development.

Wagner was unable to keep Ruth completely under control, but they developed a good rapport. Each admired the other, and Ruth's career with the Red Sox blossomed.

Ruth was primarily a pitcher in his first few seasons–one of the finest in the game, in fact–but by 1918, his hitting prowess was also prominent. Wagner, Hooper, and others tried to convince new manager Ed Barrow that Ruth should play the outfield more regularly, but Barrow did not want to risk it; to him, Ruth was too valuable as a pitcher. This is the same Ed Barrow who had managed a young Honus Wagner, so he knew talent. The tension over this decision, layered with Ruth's continued misbehavior—and Barrow's relative intolerance of it compared to Carrigan—came to a head on July 1st, when Ruth ignored Barrow's instruction to take a pitch, leading to a $500 fine, which prompted Ruth to leave the team and head to his father's home in Baltimore.[531]

Upon reaching Baltimore, Ruth contacted the Chester Shipyards team in the Delaware River Shipbuilding League and agreed to play for them on July 4.

It looked possible that one of baseball's biggest stars, a player whom fans came to see whether as a pitcher or a hitter, would be leaving the major leagues to play for the semi-pros. Incensed, Barrow threatened both Ruth and the Chester team with litigation to prevent Ruth from breaking his Boston contract.

There was very little time to break the impasse. On the evening of July 3, just one day before the big Chester Shipyards game, Barrow summoned perhaps the only person with enough loyalty to both the team and to Ruth to convince the big slugger to return to Boston: Heinie Wagner.

Wagner took the train to Baltimore, convinced Ruth to return, and calmed both Ruth and Barrow down when the two almost came to blows again on July 4. Eventually, the fine was rescinded, Ruth returned to pitching, and, thanks to urging of Wagner and others, Ruth also played more outfield, which resulted in more home runs, more excitement, and eventually, a revolutionized game.

Not everyone was pleased with the change. "Purists in that era were forever frowning on home runs and deploring their increasing prevalence as a sign the game was degenerating," explained Creamer,[532] but it was also undeniable that the home run was bringing in more fans.

The Red Sox went on to win the pennant and the World Series in 1918–the last Boston would win until 2004.

Ruth became the game's most celebrated slugger.

Wagner spent many more years in baseball following his days with Ruth, including a stint as the Red Sox manager. He died in New Rochelle, New York, in 1943 at the age of sixty-two.

ON MAY 26, 1937, JUST EIGHT YEARS AFTER BILL HEINE'S passing and six years prior to Heinie Wagner's, the greatest player to have ever played professionally on Waverly's Howard Street Grounds, Frank Grant of the Cuban Giants, died in obscurity in New York City.[533]

Grant's strong hitting in Waverly in 1901 represented one his last productive professional days. Twin Tier baseball fans had seen him thrive on local diamonds from the time he was a young speedster and "combusticator" for Buffalo in '86 through his last veteran Cuban Giants seasons in the early 1900s.

Following his baseball career, Grant worked for many years as a waiter, porter, and laborer while living in Greenwich Village. He had no known heirs, and fellow black baseball pioneers Sol White, Smokey Joe Williams, and Nux James served as pallbearers at his funeral. Grant's grave in Clifton, New Jersey, remained unmarked until 2011.

Grant labored brilliantly in professional baseball's shadows for many years, even as his brand of speedy, smart, tough, and exciting baseball—the same winning scientific baseball of Jack Chapman and Dickey Pearce's Atlantics, McGraw's Orioles and Giants, Jennings' Tigers, and Stengel and Martin's Yankees–

ignited the passions of white and black baseball players alike. They had all seen him play or heard about his play. Some, like Jennings, had played alongside him as a teammate. They all knew what he could do.

However, instead of playing in the big cities of the major leagues, Grant played in the small towns and hamlets of the minor and amateur leagues.

In 1936, the five initial inductees into the National Baseball Hall of Fame in Cooperstown were selected: Babe Ruth, Ty Cobb, Honus Wagner, Walter Johnson, and Christy Mathewson. McGraw joined them the following year, Lajoie in 1939, Keeler in 1939, Jennings and Collins in 1945, and Chesbro in 1946. Stengel joined them in 1966, Weiss in 1971, and Vic Willis in 1995. John Farrell, Bill Donovan, and Billy Martin may yet be asked to join. Dozens of others have been inducted in the meantime.

Frank Grant, "a slick fielder with a strong arm, who hit for average and had surprising power," had to wait longer than the others, but justice was served in 2006 when he and Sol White took their places among the game's immortals, enshrined alongside them in the National Baseball Hall of Fame.

Grant was emblematic of many who found both success and failure as hard-working, courageous young ballplayers on small town diamonds at the end of the nineteenth century. It was a time of tremendous economic, political, demographic, and technological changes, not unlike those we continue to experience today.

Frank Grant's Hall of Fame plaque. Courtesy of the National Baseball Hall of Fame.

Waverly may not have had another professional team after its 1901 season, but skilled baseball continued to be played in the immediate Waverly area.

Waverly's Howard Street Grounds continued to be used for baseball and football until sometime about 1920 when a large manufacturing plant was built on the site, first used as a silk mill by the Frank and Dugan Company, then as a toy factory by Manoil Manufacturing Company and later by a variety of companies up to its most current use by Rynone Industries, a furniture manufacturer that also uses the old Hall & Lyon building.

By 1920, Waverly's amateur teams were playing baseball on a field on Lincoln Street, roughly one mile northwest of the old Howard Street Grounds.

The identity of baseball as a workingman's game became increasingly clear as industrial teams and leagues grew in popularity during the early twentieth century. They were a natural evolution from the semi-pro town teams Waverly played in 1896, 1900 and 1901. Athens and Sayre, for example, had successful teams sponsored by Ingersoll-Rand (I-R) and, as mentioned earlier, the Lehigh Valley Railroad (LVRR) Shops, respectively.

They played similarly sponsored teams throughout the region and drew large enthusiastic crowds. In 1918 alone, for example, the I-R's and LVRR's opponents included the American Bridge Company and Willys-Morrow (manufacturer of cars and trucks) from Elmira, Thomas-Morse Aircraft from Ithaca, Corona Typewriter from Groton, Keyser Valley Shops from Scranton, Corning Glass Works, Curtiss Aeroplane and Motor Company from Hammondsport, and Symington-Anderson Company from Rochester. Teams like these flourished in the century's early decades.

Teams sponsored by YMCAs and other community, religious or ethnic organizations also competed. In the early 1920s, for example, Waverly had a successful team sponsored by the local Baraca club, and even called the Lincoln Street baseball field "Baraca Field" for a time. Like the YMCA, Baraca clubs were Christian ecumenical groups intended to promote chaste activities for young men, of which athletics was a primary one. Among the Waverly Baracas' 1920-1921 opponents were the I-R, American LaFrance (a fire engine manufacturer in Elmira), other religious groups like the Elmira Disciples Club and Elmira's St. Peter and Paul Club, and Elmira's Polathec Club, a Polish-American Athletic Club that eventually folded into today's White Eagle Club. [534]

Amateur company, town and neighborhood baseball teams in the area continued to play one another throughout the decades, drawing loyal and devoted fans. In more recent years, adult softball leagues were popular in Waverly and neighboring towns.

As in most communities, youth baseball was also popular, and remains so today. Little League Baseball, for example, founded in 1939 eighty miles south of Waverly in Williamsport (where a young Fred Talada once pitched) came to Waverly soon thereafter, in 1949, and has built a proud tradition ever since. Its own Lincoln Street field, featuring bleachers, a concession stand, dugouts, press box and an outfield fence adorned with local business advertisements, stands today as a fitting testament to its highly skilled professional forebears.

The Waverly area's close connection to major league baseball's labor history did not end with Harry Taylor's advocacy of player rights at the dawn of the American League or with Waverly's 1901 season. Nearly seventy years later, in 1969, baseball's free agent era began when St. Louis outfielder Curt Flood refused to accept a trade to Philadelphia. Echoing Taylor's earlier arguments, Flood asserted he was "not a slave," and sued major league baseball over the sport's reserve rule. Like Taylor, Flood eventually lost his case in the courts, but in the process persuaded major league owners to concede some control to the players. In the midst of Flood's case, the owners for the first time allowed the use of arbitration to decide player contract disputes, and this soon opened the door to free agency for Andy Messersmith, Jim "Catfish" Hunter, and others, launching a new era that led the average major league salary to skyrocket from $44,576 in 1975 to $1,998,034 in 2000.

In 1970, after Flood refused to accept his trade from St. Louis, but before the Supreme Court decided his case, Philadelphia traded his rights to Washington for several players, one of whom was later returned to Washington as the deal's "player to be named later," essentially being one of those very rare instances where a player was traded for himself. That player, pitcher Jeff Terpko,[535] was the son of a Sayre railroad man. Young Terpko grew up dominating the diamonds in the Sayre area, graduated from Sayre High School in 1968, and played in the major leagues from 1974 through 1977, appearing in 48 games for Texas and Montreal. While with Texas, Terpko played for the baseball descendent of John McGraw and Casey Stengel, the ultimate workingman's player and manager, Billy Martin.

"We were always playing something," Terpko said of his boyhood in Sayre. "There were a lot of kids there, so we never had a problem getting a game going."

And in a nod to the same sort of scrappy play that Martin experienced as a youngster in California, Terpko noted the kids in his particular eastside Sayre neighborhood of Milltown were as "tough as nails."

"We would play football in the street," he recalled. "You would come home every night bleeding, that's just the way it was."[536]

Yet another local star, 1974 Athens graduate Jim Farr, born in Waverly, went on to pitch for Penn State before pitching in five games as a major leaguer for the Rangers in 1982 and then coaching and managing for many years at the collegiate level, winning a school record 373 games in thirteen seasons as William and Mary's head coach. Like Martin and McGraw, Farr had a reputation not only for toughness, but intelligence. "If you have athletic ability, make sure you buckle down and hit the books," he told Athens sports banquet attendees in 1986. "Don't put all your time into athletics at the expense of your grades. You will eventually need them no matter what you accomplish on the athletic field."[537]

For the very few like Terpko and Farr, as with Taylor, Doran, McGraw, Jennings, Ging and other local stars before them, that smart and skilled toughness, in the midst of humble small town beginnings, led to the very pinnacle of athletic success, and was directly connected to, and a case study for, baseball's evolution as a true workingman's game.

Summary of Waverly's Professional Seasons

1887 Independent
Documented Record: 6 wins 5 losses

1896 Independent
Documented Record: 24 wins 22 losses

1900 Independent
Documented Record: 42 wins 18 losses
(Home: 27-11; Road: 15-7)

1901 Independent
Documented Record: 23 wins 4 losses 1 tie
(Home: 15-1-1; Road: 8-3)

1901 New York State League
Documented Record: 15 wins 34 losses
(Home: 8-11; Road: 7-23)

Overall Record
Independent: 95 wins 49 losses 1 tie
NYSL: 15 wins 34 losses
Total: 110 wins 83 losses 1 tie

1901 NEW YORK STATE LEAGUE BATTING STATISTICS

Waverly Batters as Listed in the 1902 Spalding Guide
(includes 1901 NYSL statistics with Waverly plus
with any other NYSL teams)

NAME	GAMES	AT BATS	RUNS	HITS	TOTAL BASES	BATTING AVERAGE	NYSL BA RANK
Nadeau	105	424	57	143	157	.337	5
Accorsini	34	119	17	37	51	.310	20
Hill	49	209	26	64	81	.306	21
Heine	30	118	20	36	48	.305	23
Dwyer	46	192	15	55	70	.286	40
Lee	43	146	14	39	49	.267	58
Kennedy	32	112	19	28	62	.250	71
Wagner	43	158	22	39	46	.240	80
Maroney	37	142	16	32	40	.225	87
O'Neil	44	173	20	39	41	.225	88
Hanna	28	107	13	24	28	.224	89
Mullin	26	68	7	15	18	.220	93
McCormick	93	368	37	80	111	.217	95
Ging	16	52	2	11	13	.211	99
McDougal	20	65	8	13	17	.200	103
Dean	91	353	32	70	96	.198	104

Top Ten 1901 NYSL Hitters

NAME	TEAM(S)	GAMES	AT BATS	RUNS	HITS	TOTAL BASES	BATTING AVERAGE
Hearne	Troy	92	389	102	148	189	.380
Lumley	Rome	91	351	68	123	165	.350
Cooper	Schenectady	33	112	16	39	40	.348
Coulter	Rome	107	442	100	151	193	.341
Nadeau	Cort/Bing/Wav	105	424	57	143	157	.337
Kelly	Troy	54	233	37	78	106	.334
Smink	Ilion	18	72	8	24	32	.333
Wheeler	Rome	75	265	55	88	111	.332
Jones	Albany	113	464	88	154	177	.331
Kihm	Troy	78	299	54	99	109	.331

Prominent 1901 Waverly Opponents

NAME	TEAM	GAMES	AT BATS	RUNS	HITS	TOTAL BASES	BATTING AVERAGE	NYSL BA RANK
Pickett	Utica	109	401	67	131	176	.326	13
Campau	Binghamton	112	420	67	128	158	.304	24
Hamburg	Rome	91	368	43	110	116	.298	27
Simon	Albany	113	438	69	120	150	.273	53
Shinnick	Ilion	13	50	5	9	10	.180	108
Viau	Troy	42	139	17	24	28	.172	109

WAVERLY'S PROFESSIONAL BASEBALL PLAYERS

Indicates Documented Major League Experience

LAST	FIRST	'87	'96	'00	'01	POSITION(S)	BORN	DIED
Accorsini	Victor A. "Vic"			X	X	C	10/8/1878	10/1962
Ayers			X			C, OF		
Barnett	John Francis "Jack"			X	X	P, OF, 1B	11/17/1872	6/14/1954
Beam	Isaac		X			P	7/1875	
Bennett				X		C, OF, 1B		
Brewster	Irving Washington, Jr.		X			OF	11/1870	5/21/1910
Bryan			X			3B		
Callahan	"Reddy"			X		3B		
Campbell	Will		X			OF		
Carnochan	John M		X			SS, 1B	2/1873	12/12/1928
*Clapp	John Edgar	X				C	7/15/1851	12/18/1904
Chamberlain			X			C		
Clark	George F.		X				4/1875	
Cole	Archie Burton	X				3B	12/1863	7/5/1948
Connelly	Tim			X		C		
Corbett	James J.			X		1B	9/1/1866	2/18/1933
Daniels	John "Bucky"	X				OF		
Dean	Jimmy			X	X	2B, SS, 3B	1/31/1872	9/2/1918
Dewey				X		OF		
Dodge	W.M.		X			1B		
*Donovan	William "Wild Bill"		X			P, OF	10/13/1876	12/9/1923
Dorsett	Ernest		X			OF	3/9/1874	6/4/1944
Driscoll					X			
Dunham	Owen Spaulding		X	X		SS, OF	6/12/1876	4/15/1916
*Dunkle	Edward "Davey"		X			P, OF	8/30/1872	11/19/1941

Summary of Waverly's Professional Seasons

LAST	FIRST	'87	'96	'00	'01	POSITION(S)	BORN	DIED
Dunn	Mike		X					
Dwyer	Tom			X	X	1B	11/1870	
Ferris			X			C		
Flynn			X			OF		
Ford	A.N.		X			OF		
Frost	Frank "Jack"				X			
Garey				X		P		
Garrison	W		X			OF		
*Gatins	Frank		X			3B	3/6/1871	11/1/1911
Gillan	Theodore "Tosh"		X			1B	1/7/1879	11/11/1956
*Ging	William J.			X	X	P, OF	11/7/1872	9/14/1950
Graffius	William J.		X				1/1874	7/31/1930
Grant	George W.			X		3B	10/14/1874	3/25/1936
Haley	I.F.				X			
Hall	Charles L. "Harry"	X				2B	1866	
Hamilton				X		SS		
Hanna	Timothy F. "Tim"			X	X	3B		
Harris			X					
Heine	William Charles "Bill"			X	X	2B	1/1868	2/13/1929
Herrick			X			P		
Hill	Eddie		X		X	OF		
Hughes	William "Dell"			X	X	OF	1/1877	
Kackle			X			P		
Kennedy	Edward A. "Kick"	X				OF	1860	
Kennedy	Frank P.		X			C, SS	3/1872	
Kennedy	John				X	2B, C		
Koehl	George		X			OF, P		

LAST	FIRST	'87	'96	'00	'01	POSITION(S)	BORN	DIED
Kutzner	Charles		X			OF	12/15/1875	11/22/1924
Lang	Percy Lyford	X				SS	6/8/1861	4/8/1926
LeBaron	Frank James			X		OF	4/28/1876	6/27/1959
Lee	Eddie		X			C, 2B		
Lee	George				X	P, OF	6/5/1876	9/5/1962
Lee	Jack				X	P, OF		
Leonard	H. M.		X			OF		
Lowman	Nathan Bristol "Nat"	X				P	2/11/1864	1936
Maroney	Stephen "Dad"			X	X	OF	11/16/1876	5/28/1960
*McCormick	James Ambrose			X		3B	11/2/1868	2/1/1948
*McDougal	John Auchanbolt "Sandy"			X	X	P, OF	5/21/1874	10/2/1910
*McGlynn	U. S. Grant "Stoney"			X		C	5/26/1872	8/26/1941
McKee	Joe		X			C, OF		
*McMackin	Sam			X		P	11/24/1872	2/11/1903
Mix	Ervin A.		X			C, 3B	1/9/1875	6/1923
Moore	Thomas J.	X				1B		
Mullin	Michael J. "Mickey"				X	P	9/1876	10/8/1933
Murtaugh	John F.		X				1875	
Nadeau	Phil				X	OF	6/4/1872	3/20/1958
Normile	*Frank L.*		X			P	1876	3/28/1953
*O'Brien	Pete				X		6/17/1877	1/31/1917
*O'Hara	Thomas Francis "Snibs"			X	X	OF	7/13/1880	6/8/1954
O'Neil	James J. "Jimmy"			X	X	SS	*8/29/1877*	After 1940
Pearce	Harvey D. "Doc"		X			3B	12/5/1873	6/19/1936

Summary of Waverly's Professional Seasons

LAST	FIRST	'87	'96	'00	'01	POSITION(S)	BORN	DIED
*Pickett	Dave			X		OF	5/26/1874	4/22/1950
Plunkett	Thomas F "Henry"				X	OF	3/2/1880	7/20/1941
Polhamus				X		P		
Poorman			X			SS		
Quick			X			P		
Retsiger	George				X			
Ross	George "Red"		X			2B		
Ryan	Dennis		X			3B, P	10/1872	
*Schulte	Frank M. "Wildfire"			X		OF	9/17/1882	10/2/1949
Seavers	Clinton "Goldie"		X			P, OF	11/1871	4/25/1951
Sheahan	Patrick J.	X				1B	5/1860	
Siegmund			X			P, SS		
Singer	J.A.		X			SS		
Skelton	F.W.		X			OF, 2B		
Smith	Clarence		X			P, OF		
Smith	Johnny	X				OF	1/1866	
*Taylor	Harry Leonard	X				2B	4/4/1866	7/12/1955
Touhey			X					
Tucker	Fred Fremont (Talada)		X	X	X	P, C, OF	3/26/1874	5/23/1943
Vaughn			X			C, 1B		
Vought	William A.				X	3B	1872	1940
*Wagner	Charles "Heinie"				X	OF	9/23/1880	3/20/1943
Wagner	*Johnny*				X	OF		
*Wall	Joe				X	OF	7/24/1873	7/17/1936
Waller	John "Bud"		X			2B, 3B	1/1875	

PROMINENT WAVERLY OPPONENTS

Indicates Documented Major League Experience
Bold = Member of the National Baseball Hall of Fame

LAST	FIRST	'87	'96	'00	'01	POSITION(S)	BORN	DIED
Buckheart	Jacob		X			1B	1870	1/18/1945
*Campau	Charles C. "Count"			X		1B/Mgr	10/17/1863	4/3/1938
*Doran	John F.	X				P	8/1861	
Grant	**Frank**		X		X	2B	**8/1/1865**	**5/27/1937**
Green	Guy Wilder		X			P	6/11/1873	2/11/1947
*Hamburg	Charlie			X	X	1B	11/27/1866	5/18/1931
*Lumley	Harry			X	X	OF	9/29/1880	5/22/1938
Salene	Daniel "The Terrible Swede"		X			P	12/1/1872	2/20/1943
Setley	William W. "Wild Bill"		X			P	8/28/1859	8/12/1956
*Shinnick	Tim			X			11/6/1867	5/18/1944
*Simon	Henry J. "Hank"			X		OF	8/25/1862	1/1/1925
Smith	William T. "Big Bill"		X				1869	
*Viau	Lee				X	P	7/5/1866	12/17/1947
Watkins	John M. "Pop"	X	X	X		1B	5/18/1857	2/22/1924
White	**King Solomon "Sol"**	X					**6/12/1868**	**8/26/1955**
Williams	Clarence		X	X		C	1/27/1866	9/23/1934

Names compiled from game accounts, roster references and box scores. First names, birth dates and/or death dates in italics mean the identity is based on limited or contradictory evidence. Sources for birth and death dates: Baseball-Reference.com, U.S. and State Census Records & Obituaries

WAVERLY'S PROFESSIONAL BASEBALL GAMES

Games on and after 7/12/1901 were in the New York State League

YEAR	DATE	DAY	OPPONENT	LOCATION	W/L	SCORE
1887	5/24	Tue	Sayre		PPD	
1887	5/28	Sat	Elmira	Waverly		
1887	5/30	Mon	Painted Post	Waverly	W	25-5
1887	6/3	Fri	Elmira	Elmira	L	8-4
1887	6/4	Sat	Elmira	Waverly	W	6-5
1887	6/10	Fri	Elmira	Elmira	L	8-4
1887	6/11	Sat	Bradford	Waverly	L	13-4
1887	6/15	Wed	Owego	Waverly	W	23-7
1887	6/18	Sat	Susquehanna	Waverly	W	34-7
1887	6/21	Tue	Owego	Owego	L	10-8
1887	6/30	Thu	*Lockports*	Waverly	W	11-10
1887	7/4	Mon	Elmira	Elmira		
1887	7/9	Sat	Watkins Glen	Watkins Glen	PPD	
1887	7/12	Tue	Elmira	Elmira	L	11-5
1887	7/13	Wed	Elmira	Waverly	W	3-2
1896	5/30	Sat	Corning	Waverly	L	9-6
1896	6/6	Sat	Towanda	Waverly	W	16-5
1896	6/13	Sat	Sayre	Sayre	L	11-3
1896	6/20	Sat	Binghamton YMCA	Waverly	L	13-11
1896	6/26	Fri	Sayre	Waverly	L	9-3
1896	6/27	Sat	Troy, PA	Waverly	W	8-6
1896	6/30	Tue	Binghamton AA	Binghamton	L	15-4
1896	7/1	Wed	Binghamton	Waverly	W	9-6
1896	7/4	Sat 1	Corning	Waverly	W	9-2
1896	7/4	Sat 2	Corning	Waverly	W	14-6
1896	7/7	Tue	Troy, PA	Troy, PA	L	16-9
1896	7/9	Thu	Bainbridge	Waverly	L	6-3

YEAR	DATE	DAY	OPPONENT	LOCATION	W/L	SCORE
1896	7/16	Thu	Binghamton AA	Waverly	W	17-3
1896	7/18	Sat	Troy, PA	Waverly	W	7-5
1896	7/23	Thu	Binghamton AA	Binghamton	W	19-15
1896	7/25	Sat	Bainbridge			
1896	7/27	Mon	Oxford			
1896	7/28	Tue	Binghamton YMCA	Binghamton	W	17-3
1896	7/30	Thu	Sidney	Waverly	L	5-4
1896	8/1	Sat	Bainbridge	Waverly	L	12-1
1896	8/13	Thu	Athens	Athens	L	15-6
1896	8/15	Sat	Sayre	Sayre	W	11-1
1896	8/19	Wed	Sayre	Waverly	W	15-3
1896	8/20	Thu	Corning	Waverly	L	16-5
1896	8/21	Fri	Towanda	Towanda	W	8-3
1896	8/22	Sat	Towanda	Waverly	L	9-7
1896	8/24	Mon	Troy, PA	Troy, PA	W	13-12
1896	8/27	Thu	Troy, PA	Waverly	W	19-11
1896	8/28	Fri	Towanda	Towanda	W	7-3
1896	8/29	Sat	Sayre	Sayre	W	17-11
1896	8/31	Mon	Towanda	Towanda	L	7-3
1896	9/5	Sat	Sayre	Sayre	L	16-4
1896	9/7	Mon	Corning	Waverly	W	8-4
1896	9/8	Tue	Towanda	Waverly	W	19-2
1896	9/9	Wed	Troy, PA	Troy, PA	W	16-8
1896	9/10	Thu	Hornell	Waverly	W	17-10
1896	9/11	Fri 1	Towanda	Towanda	L	18-10
1896	9/11	Fri 2	Towanda	Towanda	L	13-0
1896	9/12	Sat	Sayre	Sayre	L	8-1
1896	9/14	Mon	Towanda	Waverly	W	8-6
1896	9/15	Tue	Towanda	Towanda	W	15-7
1896	9/16	Wed	Sayre	Sayre	L	9-5
1896	9/17	Thu	Wilkes-Barre	Wilkes-Barre	L	13-6
1896	9/18	Fri	Cuban Giants	Waverly	L	7-1
1896	9/23	Wed	Towanda	Towanda	L	15-7

Summary of Waverly's Professional Seasons

YEAR	DATE	DAY	OPPONENT	LOCATION	W/L	SCORE
1896	9/24	Thu	Towanda	Waverly	W	8-6
1896	9/26	Sat	Sayre	Sayre	W	8-6
1896	10/1	Thu	Sayre		L	12-4
1900	5/30	Wed 1	Athens	Waverly	W	6-0
1900	5/30	Wed 2	Athens	Athens	L	2-0
1900	6/2	Sat	Corning	Waverly	L	9-5
1900	6/4	Mon	Elmira	Waverly	L	11-7
1900	6/9	Sat	Corning	Waverly	W	5-0
1900	6/9	Sat	Hammondsport	Waverly	L	8-4
1900	6/11	Mon	Elmira	Waverly	L	11-7
1900	6/12	Tue	Reading	Waverly	W	10-7
1900	6/13	Wed	Reading	Waverly	W	7-2
1900	6/14	Thu	Canisteo	Canisteo	W	11-4
1900	6/15	Fri	Canisteo	Waverly	W	16-8
1900	6/16	Sat	Hammondsport	Hammondsport	W	17-7
1900	6/20	Wed	Lestershire	Waverly	W	13-5
1900	6/23	Sat	Corning	Waverly	W	27-4
1900	6/25	Mon	Lestershire	Lestershire	W	18-17
1900	6/27	Wed	Hammondsport	Waverly	W	14-0
1900	6/28	Thu	Hammondsport	Hammondsport	W	7-4
1900	6/30	Sat	Moravia	Waverly	W	13-0
1900	7/4	Wed 1	Athens	Athens	W	4-2
1900	7/4	Wed 2	Athens	Waverly	W	4-2
1900	7/7	Sat	Athens	Athens	W	5-3
1900	7/10	Tue	Weedsport	Waverly	W	9-3
1900	7/11	Wed	Weedsport	Waverly	W	10-7
1900	7/12	Thu	Moravia	Moravia	W	5-4
1900	7/13	Fri	Weedsport	Weedsport	L	9-3
1900	7/14	Sat	Athens	Waverly	W	5-2
1900	7/17	Tue	Lestershire	Lestershire	L	15-12
1900	7/19	Thu	Walton	Waverly	W	9-3
1900	7/20	Fri	Hammondsport	Bath	W	9-5
1900	7/21	Sat	Athens	Athens	W	4-2

YEAR	DATE	DAY	OPPONENT	LOCATION	W/L	SCORE
1900	7/24	Tue	Lestershire	Waverly	W	7-4
1900	7/26	Thu	Cuban Giants	Waverly	L	5-4
1900	7/27	Fri	Hammondsport	Elmira	W	10-7
1900	7/28	Sat	Athens	Waverly	W	11-5
1900	8/2	Thu	Athens	Waverly	W	11-2
1900	8/3	Fri	Moravia	Waverly	L	6-5
1900	8/4	Sat	Athens	Waverly	W	16-6
1900	8/8	Wed	Athens	Waverly	W	5-2
1900	8/9	Thu	Hammondsport	Hammondsport	W	10-4
1900	8/11	Sat	Athens	Elmira	W	17-10
1900	8/16	Thu	Moravia	Waverly	W	11-2
1900	8/18	Sat	Susquehanna	Waverly	W	6-4
1900	8/20	Mon	Hammondsport	*Bath*	W	14-4
1900	8/21	Tue	Hammondsport	Bath	L	5-4
1900	8/24	Fri	Lestershire	Waverly	W	14-6
1900	8/25	Sat	Hammondsport	Waverly	L	14-7
1900	8/29	Wed	Lestershire	Newark Valley	L	6-4
1900	8/31	Fri	Lestershire	Owego	W	9-2
1900	9/1	Sat	Lestershire	Lestershire	L	10-9
1900	9/3	Mon 1	Nebraska Indians	Waverly	W	9-4
1900	9/3	Mon 2	Nebraska Indians	Waverly	W	6-5
1900	9/4	Tue	Susquehanna	Susquehanna	W	9-7
1900	9/6	Thu	Moravia	Moravia	L	5-2
1900	9/7	Fri	Susquehanna	Waverly	W	13-3
1900	9/11	Tue	Rome	Waverly	L	3-2
1900	9/12	Wed	Binghamton	Waverly	W	4-3
1900	9/15	Sat 1	Rome	Waverly	L	9-8
1900	9/15	Sat 2	Rome	Waverly	W	3-2
1900	9/24	Mon	Cuban X Giants	Waverly	L	3-2
1900	9/25	Tue	Cuban X Giants	Waverly	L	6-5
1901	4/29	Mon	Syracuse Shamrocks	Waverly	W	28-8
1901	4/30	Tue	Syracuse Shamrocks	Waverly	W	10-8

Summary of Waverly's Professional Seasons

YEAR	DATE	DAY	OPPONENT	LOCATION	W/L	SCORE
1901	5/4	Sat	Ithaca H.S.	Waverly	W	18-0
1901	5/6	Mon	Binghamton	Waverly	W	10-3
1901	5/7	Tue	Binghamton	Binghamton	W	10-3
1901	5/11	Sat	Wyoming Seminary	Waverly	W	12-2
1901	5/14	Tue	Syracuse Eastern Lge	Waverly	L	4-1
1901	5/18	Sat	St Bonaventure	Waverly	W	7-4
1901	5/20	Mon	St Bonaventure	St Bonaventure	W	7-4
1901	5/23	Thu	Jamestown	Waverly	W	11-6
1901	5/27	Mon	Binghamton	Waverly	W	16-3
1901	5/30	Thu	Syracuse Univ	Waverly	W	10-1
1901	5/30	Thu	Syracuse Univ	Waverly	T	6-6
1901	6/1	Sat	Corning	Waverly	W	22-2
1901	6/8	Sat 1	Syracuse Univ	Waverly	W	22-2
1901	6/8	Sat 2	Syracuse Univ	Waverly	W	25-0
1901	6/12	Wed	Brownson AC	Wilmington, DE	W	8-6
1901	6/13	Thu	Brownson AC	Wilmington, DE	L	8-5
1901	6/14	Fri	Chester	Chester	L	6-5
1901	6/15	Sat	Chester	Chester	L	7-6
1901	6/17	Mon	Cuban Giants	Owego	W	20-6
1901	6/18	Tue	Cuban Giants	Waverly	W	10-1
1901	6/19	Wed	Cuban Giants	Waverly	W	24-10
1901	6/23	Sun	Syracuse Shamrocks	Syracuse	W	14-0
1901	7/4	Thu 1	Lestershire	Lestershire	W	4-1
1901	7/4	Thu 2	Lestershire	Waverly	W	7-5
1901	7/6	Sat	Lestershire	Lestershire	W	5-3
1901	7/10	Wed	Father Mathew	Elmira	W	20-1
1901	7/12	Fri	Ilion	Waverly	W	7-4
1901	7/13	Sat	Ilion	Waverly	L	3-2
1901	7/15	Mon	Rome	Waverly	W	2-1
1901	7/17	Wed	Utica	Waverly	W	15-11
1901	7/18	Thu	Utica	Waverly	L	5-4
1901	7/19	Fri	Rome	Rome	L	4-3

YEAR	DATE	DAY	OPPONENT	LOCATION	W/L	SCORE
1901	7/20	Sat	Rome	Rome	L	3-1
1901	7/21	Sun	Rome	Rome	L	3-2
1901	7/22	Mon	Utica	Utica	L	5-2
1901	7/23	Tue	Utica	Utica	L	5-2
1901	7/24	Wed	Schenectady	Schenectady	W	6-3
1901	7/25	Thu	Schenectady	Schenectady	L	10-4
1901	7/26	Fri	Ilion	Ilion	W	16-12
1901	7/27	Sat 1	Ilion	Ilion	L	7-2
1901	7/27	Sat 1	Ilion	Ilion	W	9-5
1901	7/29	Mon	Albany	Waverly	L	11-6
1901	7/30	Tue	Albany	Waverly	W	8-6
1901	7/31	Wed	Troy, NY	Waverly	L	4-3
1901	8/1	Thu	Troy, NY	Waverly	L	6-5
1901	8/2	Fri	Binghamton	Binghamton	L	6-4
1901	8/3	Sat 1	Binghamton	Waverly	W	3-0
1901	8/3	Sat 2	Binghamton	Waverly	L	10-1
1901	8/5	Mon 1	Binghamton	Binghamton	L	4-3
1901	8/5	Mon 2	Binghamton	Binghamton	L	8-5
1901	8/7	Wed	Troy, NY	Troy, NY	L	11-1
1901	8/9	Fri 1	Albany	Albany	W	3-1
1901	8/9	Fri 2	Albany	Albany	W	2-0
1901	8/10	Sat	Albany	Albany	L	2-0
1901	8/12	Mon	Ilion	Waverly	L	8-4
1901	8/13	Tue	Ilion	Waverly	W	12-6
1901	8/19	Mon	Rome	Waverly	L	7-2
1901	8/20	Tue	Rome	Waverly	L	8-2
1901	8/21	Wed	Utica	Utica	L	7-1
1901	8/23	Fri	Rome	Rome	L	6-3
1901	8/24	Sat	Rome	Rome	L	16-3
1901	8/25	Sun	Rome	Rome	L	6-1
1901	8/26	Mon	Ilion	Ilion	W	4-3
1901	8/27	Tue	Schenectady	Schenectady	L	3-2
1901	8/28	Wed	Albany	Albany	L	12-4
1901	8/29	Thu	Troy, NY	Troy, NY	L	3-1

Summary of Waverly's Professional Seasons

YEAR	DATE	DAY	OPPONENT	LOCATION	W/L	SCORE
1901	8/30	Fri	Binghamton	Binghamton	L	1-0
1901	8/31	Sat	Binghamton	Binghamton	L	12-2
1901	9/2	Mon 1	Binghamton	Binghamton	L	7-2
1901	9/2	Mon 2	Binghamton	Binghamton	L	4-2
1901	9/3	Tue	Binghamton	Cortland	W	12-5
1901	9/4	Wed	Ilion	Waverly	W	9-2
1901	9/5	Thu	Schenectady	Waverly	L	4-3
1901	9/6	Fri	Troy, NY	Waverly	W	5-1
1901	9/7	Sat	Albany	Waverly	L	7-0

Acknowledgements

I am grateful for the help of many in the research and writing of this book, especially my parents who from the very beginning nurtured my curiosity. I also thank my many teachers and coaches who built on this foundation.

I am indebted to the staff of the National Baseball Hall of Fame and Library in Cooperstown, most notably Chris Docter, who tirelessly and without complaint fulfilled multiple information requests during my initial visit, and photograph guru John Horne. I also thank the staffs and volunteers of the Waverly Free Library, the Sayre Public Library, the Spaulding Memorial Library, the Susquehanna River Archaeological Center, the Sayre Historical Society, the Chemung Valley Museum, the Tioga County Historical Society and the Waverly Historical Society. Many at each of these institutions were helpful and encouraging, but especially Chris Brewster, Deb Twigg, Rachel Dworkin, Barb Koehn and Don Merrill.

A special thanks is due to the descendants and relatives of characters in the book, with whom I was able to communicate by phone and email, especially William O'Shaughnessy, grandson of Fred Tucker, Jerome Coffey, grandnephew of Bill Ging, and Maureen Kravec, grandniece of Katie Tobin. I hope my work does justice to our conversations and to the characters and times described to me. I encourage other relatives, descendants and friends of characters in this book to contact me, whether with questions or additional information. This aspect of the work is for me especially rewarding.

Thanks also to my fellow Society of American Baseball Research members, whose work continues to shine light on baseball's past, and without whom much of the context of this book would have been impossible to discover. In particular, thanks to baseball historian Tony Kissel, who provided insights and answered many of my questions about the nineteenth century game.

Thanks to my longtime friend Joe Mastrantuono for his artwork, and to Gary Joseph Cieradkowski for the cover design and numerous portraits he created for the book. More of Gary's excellent work can be found at studiogaryc.com.

Thanks to my editor Elisabeth Chretien for her excellent work and feedback. Any errors remaining following her work are mine alone.

Significant thanks to Patricia, Kim, Melissa, Nina and the rest of the team at Luminare Press for their time and expertise in pulling this final product together.

Finally, thanks to my wife Maria for her proof-reading, advice, encouragement and patience, and to other friends and family members who read (or listened to) portions of the manuscript, whether they wanted to or not, and provided constructive feedback, especially my children Angie, Sam and Abby, my brothers Chris and Nate, my son-in-law Ryan, my daughter-in-law Allie, and my father Howard, to whom this book is dedicated.

Notes

1. Kevin Baker, "Backtalk; The Day it Rained Candy Bars," New York Times, April 12, 1998, Section 8, 11.
2. Al Mari, "A sweet 'rain' for Yankee hero," The Journal News, April 14, 1978, 21.
3. George Sweet Gibb, *The Whitesmiths of Taunton*, (Cambridge, MA: Harvard University Press, 1943), 281.
4. Boston Globe, April 27, 1897, 5.
5. Letter dated 4/20/1981, from McDougal's daughter Charlotte in his Hall of Fame player file, described McDougal as having "reddish" hair and standing about 5'10"; "lanky and graceful on the mound"; "known as a warm-weather pitcher"; "Grandma & Grandpa McDougal were dead set against his playing professionally. Guess it was almost a sin in their eyes."
6. "Owns Taunton," Boston Globe, May 31, 1898, 10.
7. "Baseball Notes," Boston Globe, May 20, 1898, 9.
8. "Baseball Notes," Boston Globe, August 13, 1898, 3.
9. "In Full Swing," Boston Globe, April 24, 1899, 4.
10. "Baseball Notes," Boston Globe, May 18, 1899, 9.
11. "Baseball Notes," Boston Globe, July 21, 1899, 5.
12. "Baseball Notes," Boston Globe, June 21, 1899, 5.
13. Sol White, *Sol White's History of Colored Base Ball*. (Lincoln, NE: University of Nebraska Press, 1995), 38.
14. Wayne County Herald, June 29, 1899, 3.

15 "Honesdale," The (Scranton) Tribune, June 26, 1899, 6.

16 "Honesdale," The (Scranton) Tribune, June 26, 1899, 6.

17 Wayne County Herald, June 29, 1899, 3.

18 More information about McGraw's and Lawson's 1891 Cuban trip is in *The Workingman's Game*, 137-138.

19 Christy Mathewson, "My Life So Far," Baseball Magazine, December 1914, 55.

20 Boston Globe, August 3, 1899, 4.

21 "Close Games to Finish," Boston Globe, August 4, 1899, 4.

22 Mathewson, 55.

23 Mathewson, 62.

24 Mathewson, 55.

25 "In Favor of Newport," Boston Globe, September 6, 1899, 5.

26 Mathewson, 55.

27 "Baseball Notes," Boston Globe, September 20, 1899, 5.

28 "Jack Doran Again," Elmira Telegram, March 5, 1899.

29 Elmira Daily Gazette and Free Press, July 29, 1897.

30 "Kinney's Kids," Sporting Life, July 2, 1898, 6.

31 Sporting Life, July 30, 1898, 13.

32 Sporting Life, August 20, 1898, 19.

33 Attendance figures from Baseball-Reference.com. Population ranking from 1900 U.S. Census.

34 "Connecticut Lease," Sporting Life, May 20, 1899, 7.

35 "Notes of the Game," Hartford Courant, August 23, 1899, 2.

36 Sporting News, September 30, 1899, 5.

37 William Nack, "Collision at Home" with special reporting by Mike Donovan. Sports Illustrated, June 4, 2001.

38 Brian McKenna, SABR Biography of Marty Bergen.

39 William Nack, "Collision at Home" with special reporting by Mike Donovan. Sports Illustrated, June 4, 2001.

40 "News and Gossip," Sporting Life, January 27, 1900.

41 "Bergen's Queer Ways," Rochester Democrat and Chronicle, January 30, 1900.

42 "The Boston Players," Sporting Life, October 21, 1899

43 New York City's borough consolidation was led by Tom "Boss" Platt from Owego.

44 "Wind Smashes Bridge Lights," New York Times, September 26, 1899.

45 "Echoes of the Game," Boston Globe, September 26, 1899, 5.

46 *National Baseball Hall of Fame Almanac, 2014 Edition*, 128.

47 "Hub Happenings," Sporting Life, October 7, 1899

48 Dan Lindner, SABR Biography of Kid Gleason.

49 In a popular 1988 movie about the 1919 World Series, "Eight Men Out," veteran actor John Mahoney played Gleason.

50 "Hub Happenings," Sporting Life, October 7, 1899

51 "Boston 2: New York 1," New York Sun, September 26, 1899, 8.

52 Sporting Life, September 30, 1899, 3.

53 "Hub Happenings," Sporting Life, October 7, 1899

54 "Hub Happenings," Sporting Life, October 7, 1899

55 Sporting Life, December 9, 1899, 4. The reference to "Class Z" was likely a tongue-in-cheek reference to a very low (i.e. the lowest) salary available in the National League's classification system.

56 "Hub Happenings," Sporting Life, September 30, 1899

57 Sporting Life, January 6, 1900.

58 "Bergen Kills Self and Family," New York Herald, January 20, 1900.

59 Ibid.

60 "Bergen's Awful Deed," Buffalo Express, January 21, 1900.

61 "Case of Catcher Bergen," New York World, February 18, 1900.

62 "Bergen's Crime," Sporting Life, February 17, 1900, 2.

63 "Reserve Rule All Wrong," Rochester Democrat and Chronicle, January 30, 1900.

64 Solomon, 123-124.

65 "Terribly Injured," Elmira Daily Gazette and Free Press, July 19, 1900, 8.

66 "Surplus Players," The Sporting News, March 31, 1900, 3.

67 "Players Organize," Sporting Life, June 16, 1900, 4.

68 Warren N. Wilbert, *The Arrival of the American League*, (Jefferson, NC: McFarland, 2007), 27.

69 Ibid.

70 Ibid.

71 Attendance figures from Baseball-Reference.com.

72 "The Players' Union," Sporting Life, July 14, 1900, 1.

73 Ibid.

74 "Tips to Players," The Sporting News, August 11, 1900, 5.

75 Ibid.

76 "Dying of Dry Rot," The Sporting News, August 18, 1900, 5.

77 "May Join Forces," The Sporting News, September 1, 1900, 1.

78 *People v. Krist*, 168 N.Y. 19, 59 (1901).

79 *People v. Krist*, 60 N.E. 1057, 1058 (N.Y. 1901).

80 "'Bud' Waller," Owego Daily Record, April 7, 1900.

81 Waverly Free Press, April 7, 1900.
82 Ibid.
83 Waverly Free Press, April 7, 1900, p 6.
84 *People v. Krist*, 60 N.E., 1057, 1058 (N.Y. 1901).
85 *People v. Krist*, 168 N.Y. 19, 44 (1901).
86 *People v. Krist*, 168 N.Y. 19, 53-54 (1901).
87 "Woman Murdered," Waverly Advocate, April 10, 1900, 1.
88 "Witnesses Being Sworn," Elmira Daily Gazette and Free Press, April 11, 1900, 8.
89 "Is Under Guard," Elmira Daily Gazette and Free Press, April 11, 1900, 8.
90 Waverly Free Press, April 14, 1900, 4.
91 "Deliberate Murder!" Waverly Free Press, April 14, 1900, 3.
92 Ibid.
93 "Krist's Victim Buried," Owego Daily Record, April 11, 1900.
94 Waverly Free Press, April 14, 1900, 5.
95 "Jennings Instructs in Bunting," Cornell Daily Sun, February 7, 1900, 1.
96 "Binghamton By One Run," Elmira Daily Gazette and Free Press, April 24, 1900, 2.
97 Ibid.
98 "Binghamton Victorious," Elmira Daily Gazette and Free Press, April 25, 1900, 2.
99 Ibid.
100 "Elmira Was the Winner," Elmira Daily Gazette and Free Press, April 26, 1900, 2.
101 "Binghamton Won the Game," Elmira Daily Gazette and Free Press, April 27, 1900, 8.

102 "Binghamton Was So Easy," Elmira Daily Gazette and Free Press, April 28, 1900, 2.

103 Sporting Life, March 3, 1900, 7.

104 Sporting Life, May 5, 1900, 6.

105 "Oswego After Ging," Elmira Daily Gazette and Free Press, May 10, 1900, 6.

106 "Veteran of Veterans," Sporting Life, June 16, 1900, 1.

107 Charles DeMotte, Bat, Ball & Bible: Baseball and Sunday Observance in New York. (Washington, DC: Potomac, 2013), 4-5.

108 Steven A. Riess, Sport in Industrial America 1850-1920. (Wheeling, IL: Harlan-Davidson, 1995), 71.

109 "Our Nations," Wilkes-Barre Times, May 1, 1899, 3.

110 "Will There be Sunday Ball?" Elmira Daily Gazette and Free Press, April 28, 1900.

111 "Sunday Baseball," Elmira Daily Gazette and Free Press, April 30, 1900.

112 "Stopped by the Sheriff," Oswego Daily Palladium, June 18, 1900.

113 DeMotte, 155.

114 "Wilkes-Barre Was Downed," Elmira Daily Gazette and Free Press, May 3, 1900, 6.

115 "Crushed to Death," Elmira Daily Gazette and Free Press, May 15, 1900, 6.

116 "Farmers Strike," Elmira Daily Gazette and Free Press, May 15, 1900, 6.

117 "Report Erroneous," Scranton Tribune, May 30, 1900, 1.

118 "Baseball for Waverly," Waverly Free Press, May 19, 1900, 1.

119 "Base Ball," Waverly Advocate, May 18, 1900, 1.

120 Ibid.

121 According to U.S. Census Records, Layton Sickler was a Great Uncle of Nelson Sickler, a popular area trumpeter and music teacher whose son Robert was one of the author's first music teachers.

122 "Two Games," Waverly Advocate, June 1, 1900, 1.

123 "Happenings Hereabout," Waverly Free Press, June 2, 1900.

124 The author was unable to confirm a first name in the local newspapers for McGlynn, but several pieces of evidence point to him being "Stoney" McGlynn, a player for a semi-pro team in Harrisburg, who later played in the major leagues. In a local Harrisburg story at the time ("Sport Potpourri," Harrisburg Telegraph, April 24, 1900, 2.) "Stoney" McGlynn is said to have been a catcher and pitcher, "one of the best all-round players in this city," and to have received "a number of offers to play with amateur teams." His age was appropriate for a relatively short stint in Waverly, plus Tucker and Heine were each likely well acquainted with him due to their mutual connections in Harrisburg and Easton, respectively. Tucker and McGlynn may even have been teammates briefly in Harrisburg in 1895.

125 "Baseball This Week," Waverly Free Press, June 9, 1900, 1.

126 The school was called both Allegany College and St. Bonaventure during the 1890s. A classmate of McGraw's and Jennings's, John Murtagh, for example, was said in "The Buffalo Times" on December 2, 1918, to have graduated from "Allegany College" in 1896; and in "The Elmira Gazette" from that same day to have graduated from "St. Bonaventure College at Allegany." Both newspapers said "Allegany College" granted him an honorary LL.D. in 1909.

127 "Baseball This Week," Waverly Free Press, June 9, 1900, 1.

128 Ibid.

129 Ibid.

130 William Brewster, *The Workingman's Game*, (Eugene, OR: Luminare Press, 2019), 49 and 220.

131 "From Waverly," Elmira Daily Gazette and Free Press, July 20, 1893.

132 "Baseball This Week," Waverly Free Press, June 9, 1900, 1.

133 Ibid.

134 "Judgment Granted," Elmira Daily Gazette and Free Press, June 19, 1900, 3.

135 "Baseball This Week," Waverly Free Press, June 16, 1900, 1.

136 Ibid.

137 Ibid.

138 "Fred Krist Makes a Statement," Waverly Free Press, June 16, 1900, 2.

139 "Baseball This Week," Waverly Free Press, June 23, 1900, 1. The term "kodak fiend" was most likely referring to the prevalence of individual cameras, due to Corbett's appearance. Per the Kodak.com website, George Eastman began manufacturing the inexpensive "Kodak Brownie" camera in 1900, bringing "photography within financial reach of consumers."

140 Elmira Daily Gazette and Free Press, June 23, 1900.

141 Multiple secondary sources refer to Schulte having played for Waverly, including some written following his major league career, but the author failed to locate any box scores that included his name in Waverly's line-up. His name does appear in some Athens' line-ups, so, like Ging, he may have played for Athens as well as Waverly. Moreover, there were not box scores published for every game.

142 "Corbett was in the Game," Elmira Daily Gazette and Free Press, June 16, 1900, 8.

143 "Sayre Strike at an End," The Plain Speaker, July 3, 1900, 4.
144 Waverly Free Press, July 7, 1900, 2.
145 "Wind Causes Damage," Elmira Daily Gazette and Free Press, July 6, 1900.
146 "Waverly Doings," Elmira Daily Gazette and Free Press, July 6, 1900.
147 "Baseball This Week," Waverly Free Press, July 14, 1900.
148 Ibid.
149 "Waverly's First 'Mobile," Waverly Free Press, July 14, 1900, 1.
150 "Waverly Won," Elmira Daily Gazette and Free Press, July 16, 1900.
151 "Notes," Waverly Free Press, July 21, 1900, 1.
152 "Waverly Beat Hammondsport," Rochester Democrat and Chronicle, July 21, 1900.
153 Waverly Advocate, July 27, 1900, 1.
154 Ed Aswad & Suzanne M. Meredith, *Images of America: Endicott-Johnson*. (Charleston, SC: Arcadia, 2003), 86.
155 "Elmira Team Playing Well," Elmira Daily Gazette and Free Press, August 1, 1900.
156 "Baseball This Week," Waverly Free Press, August 4, 1900
157 "Elmira Team Playing Well," Elmira Daily Gazette and Free Press, August 1, 1900.
158 "Teams Broke Even," Elmira Daily Gazette and Free Press, August 3, 1900.
159 "And Still Another," Elmira Telegram, August 2, 1900.
160 "Baseball This Week," Waverly Free Press, August 4, 1900
161 Waverly Free Press, August 4, 1900, 5.
162 "Local News," Hammondsport Herald, August 15, 1900, 2.
163 "Baseball Season Closes," Waverly Free Press, August 11, 1900.

164 Ibid.

165 The author's research of newspaper accounts reflects a record of 31-9 at this point of the season, which somewhat splits the difference between the Waverly and Elmira newspapers. It's very possible that some games were considered "exhibitions" and not counted by certain parties, while other games were possibly not formally documented in the newspapers.

166 Ibid.

167 "In Waverly," *Elmira Daily Gazette and Free Press*, September 4, 1900, 8.

168 "Both Teams Disband," *Elmira Daily Gazette and Free Press*, August 13, 1900.

169 *Waverly Free Press*, August 25, 1900.

170 Ibid.

171 "McDougal Back Again," *Waverly Free Press*, September 1, 1900.

172 Ibid.

173 "Nebraska Indians Roster," *Waverly Free Press*, September 8, 1900.

174 "Ging Pitched Well," *Elmira Daily Gazette and Free Press*, September 1, 1900, 6.

175 "News and Comment," *Sporting Life*, February 17, 1900, 4.

176 Guy W. Green, *The Nebraska Indians and Fun and Frolic with an Indian Ball Team. Edited by Jeff P. Beck.* (Jefferson, NC: McFarland, 2010), xv.

177 "Red Men Against Colored Men," *Chicago Tribune*, June 4, 1900, 2.

178 "Indian Team in New York," *Nebraska State Journal*, August 31, 1900, 2.

179 "Indians Beat Clifton Springs," Rochester Democrat and Chronicle, September 2, 1900, 18.

180 "Nebraska Indians Baseball" Waverly Free Press, September 8, 1900.

181 Ibid.

182 "Nebraska Indians Baseball," Waverly Free Press, September 8, 1900, and "Waverly Won Two," Elmira Daily Gazette and Free Press, September 4, 1900,

183 Green, 61.

184 U.S. Census Records.

185 Waverly Free Press, September 8, 1900.

186 "Won Out in Ninth," Cortland Evening Standard, September 8, 1900.

187 Ibid.

188 "Baseball Season Nearly Over," Waverly Free Press, September 15, 1900.

189 Ibid.

190 Ibid.

191 Ibid.

192 "Baseball This Week," Waverly Free Press, September 22, 1900.

193 Ibid.

194 "Notes," Waverly Free Press, September 29, 1900.

195 "Three Days' Sport," The Wellsboro Gazette, October 3, 1900, 1.

196 "Baseball Season Closes," Waverly Free Press, September 29, 1900.

197 Ibid.

198 "Notes," Waverly Free Press, September 29, 1900.

199 "Benefit Game," Waverly Advocate, September 18, 1900, 1.

200 "An Excellent Record," Elmira Daily Gazette and Free Press, September 26, 1900.

201 Standings according to Baseball-Reference.com.

202 John J. McGraw, *My Thirty Years in Baseball*, (New York: Boni and Liveright, 1923), 128.

203 "Stand Together," The Sporting News, October 27, 1900, 1.

204 Doris Kearns Goodwin, *The Bully Pulpit*, (New York: Simon & Schuster, 2013), 77.

205 Goodwin, 248.

206 Steffens, Lincoln, "Governor Roosevelt—As an Experiment," McClure's Magazine, June 1900.

207 Goodwin, 292.

208 Louis J. Lang, ed., *The Autobiography of Thomas Collier Platt*, (New York: B.W. Dodge, 1910), 396.

209 Goodwin, 262.

210 Brewster, 29-49

211 Lang, 390-392

212 Jon Grinspan, "How to Run During a Pandemic," Sunday Review, New York Times, May 3, 2020, 6.

213 Brewster, 145.

214 Grinspan.

215 Goodwin, 272.

216 Gordon, 271.

217 "Free Silver, Trusts, and the Philippines," TR speech dated September 7, 1900.

218 Brewster, 242.

219 Mary Harris Jones, *Autobiography of Mother Jones*, (Chicago, Illinois: Charles H. Kerr and Company, 1925), 51-52.

220 The timeframe for the incident is estimated based on

descriptions of the general strike situation in contemporary newspaper accounts, for example: "Miner's Convention," The Scranton Times, October 9, 1900, 1.

221   Jones, 52.

222   The conclusion of Bryan's "Cross of Gold" speech (July 9, 1896): "Having behind us the producing masses of this nation and the world, supported by the commercial interests, and the toilers everywhere, we will answer their demand for a gold standard by saying to them: 'You shall not press down upon the brow of labor this crown of thorns; you shall not crucify mankind upon a cross of gold.'"

223   Melvyn Dubofsky, *Industrialism and the American Worker 1865-1920*, (Arlington Heights, IL: Harlan Davidson, 1975), 70.

224   See "Official List of Nominations," Elmira Daily Gazette and Free Press, February 27, 1894, for one example. Billy Ging's big brother John is also listed as an Election Inspector Nominee for the Fifth Ward.

225   "Outside Opinions," Elmira Telegram, November 19, 1893, 2.

226   "Official List of Nominations," Elmira Daily Gazette and Free Press, February 27, 1894.

227   "Bryan's Third Day Begins at Elmira," Buffalo Courier, October 21, 1900, 3.

228   Elmira Daily Gazette and Free Press, September 24, 1900.

229   "Bryan's Third Day Begins at Elmira," Buffalo Courier, October 21, 1900, 3.

230   "Mr. Bryan's Welcome the Greatest Demonstration in Buffalo's History," Buffalo Courier, October 21, 1900, 1.

231   Ibid.

232   "Roosevelt in Waverly!" Waverly Free Press, October 14, 1899, 1.

233 Ibid.
234 "Roosevelt Mobbed by Hoodlum Gang in Stanchfield's Home," New York Weekly Press, October 31, 1900.
235 Ibid.
236 Ibid.
237 "Bryanism Breeds Rowdyism," New York Tribune, October 30, 1900, 6.
238 "Summary of the News," Williamsport (PA) Sun-Gazette, October 31, 1900, 1.
239 "The Disgrace of Elmira," Rochester Democrat and Chronicle, November 3, 1900, 6.
240 "Result of a Plot," Cortland Evening News, November 1, 1900.
241 Ibid.
242 Ibid.
243 Brewster, 99.
244 "In Police Circles," Elmira Daily Gazette and Free Press, October 8, 1900.
245 Elmira Daily Gazette and Free Press, January 3, 1900.
246 "Result of a Plot," Cortland Evening News, November 1, 1900.
247 Ibid.
248 "And in the Sun," Elmira Daily Gazette and Free Press, November 1, 1900.
249 Ibid.
250 "Corning Boys Fared Badly," Elmira Daily Gazette and Free Press, October 30, 1900, 7.
251 "Made a Record," Indianapolis Journal, November 3, 1900.
252 Ibid.

253 Ibid.

254 Lang, 396-397

255 "Murder Trial," Elmira Daily Gazette and Free Press, November 20, 1900.

256 "Fred Krist Has Sympathy," Elmira Daily Gazette and Free Press, April 10, 1900.

257 "Murder Trial," Elmira Daily Gazette and Free Press, November 20, 1900.

258 *People v. Krist*, 60 N.E., 1057, 1062 (N.Y. 1901).

259 "Murder in the First Degree is the Verdict," Buffalo Courier, November 24, 1900.

260 "Murder in the First Degree," Tioga County Record, November 29, 1900.

261 "Murder in the First Degree is the Verdict," Buffalo Courier, November 24, 1900.

262 *People v. Krist*, 168 N.Y. 19, 162 (1901).

263 Ibid.

264 "Fred A. Krist Sentenced," Waverly Free Press, December 1, 1900.

265 "Ithaca Recovers From Rain Storm," Ithaca Daily News, November 27, 1900.

266 "Lehigh Wreck," Elmira Daily Gazette and Free Press, November 27, 1900.

267 "Sheriff Thurston Hurt," Tioga County Record, November 29, 1900.

268 "Saved Sheriff's Life," Auburn Journal, March 29, 1907.

269 The facts regarding Krist's momentary freedom and his decision to rescue Thurston rather than escape were not reported until six years later. According to the Auburn Journal of March 29, 1907: "That Fred Krist saved the

life of former Sheriff Abe Thurston of Tioga County, while the latter was taking the murderer to Auburn to be electrocuted several years ago has never been made public and the fact was not generally known until Mr. Thurston of Owego recovered $1,800 from the Lehigh Valley Railroad company for injuries received in that wreck."

270 "Krist in Prison," Owego Daily Record, November 28, 1900.

271 "Murderer Krist Writes a Letter," Ithaca Daily News, December 5, 1900.

272 Ibid.

273 "Players Present Petition," The Sporting News, December 15, 1900, 1.

274 Krister Swanson, *Baseball's Power Shift*, (Lincoln, NE: University of Nebraska Press, 2016), 45.

275 "Players Present Petition," The Sporting News, December 15, 1900, 1.

276 Lee Lowenfish, *The Imperfect Diamond*, (Lincoln, NE: University of Nebraska Press, 1980), 63.

277 "To Placate the Players," The Sporting News, February 9, 1901, 1.

278 "Strong Letter to Players," Buffalo Express, January 9, 1901, 10.

279 U.S. Bureau of Labor Statistics. https://www.bls.gov/opub/uscs/1901.pdf

280 "Player's Association," Sporting Life, January 19, 1901.

281 "Gossip of the Players," The Sporting News, March 2, 1901, 2.

282 "Advice to Ball Players," The Sporting News, February 16, 1901, 5.

283 "The Conference," Sporting Life, February 9, 1901, 3.

284 "Magnates are Weakening," Buffalo Express, February 9, 1901, 10.

285 "Victory for the Players," Buffalo Express, February 28, 1901, 12.

286 Francis C. Richter, "Players' Progress," Sporting Life, March 9, 1901, 6.

287 "Taylor's Tips," Sporting Life, February 16, 1901.

288 "Tips to Players," The Sporting News, March 9, 1901, 2.

289 "Forced to Yield," The Sporting News, March 9, 1901, 3.

290 "Amounts to Nothing," The Sporting News, March 16, 1901, 4.

291 McGuffie's Orchestra, according to newspaper accounts, appears to have been based in the Valley, likely Waverly or Sayre. Most of the events they were reported to have played at were in Waverly, particularly high school graduations.

292 Waverly Advocate, March 19, 1901, 1.

293 "Players' Friend," The Sporting News, May 18, 1901, 6.

294 Waverly Advocate, March 22, 1901, 1.

295 Waverly Advocate, April 12, 1901, 1.

296 "Still Another League," Elmira Gazette and Free Press, March 27, 1901, 8.

297 "Jack, He Breaks Stones," Owego Daily Record, April 13, 1901.

298 Harold Seymour, *Baseball: The Early Years,* (New York: Oxford University Press, 1960), 314.

299 Marty Appel, "Retroactive Rewards," Memories and Dreams, Fall 2016. Per SABR analysis, Billy Sullivan earned the NL award for 1900 and Harry Lumley for 1904. Also available via: http://www.appelpr.com/?page_id=3320

300 John Thorn, *Baseball in the Garden of Eden,* (New York: Simon & Schuster, 2011), 251-252.

301 Jack Smiles, *"Ee-Yah,"* (Jefferson, NC: McFarland, 2005), 98.

302 Appel, "Retroactive Rewards," Memories and Dreams, Fall 2016. Per SABR analysis, Chesbro earned the NL award for 1902, Mathewson for 1903, and McGinnity for 1900 and 1904. Chesbro earned the AL award for 1904 while Cy Young earned the same for 1901-1903. Also available via: http://www.appelpr.com/?page_id=3320

303 Smiles, 101.

304 "Strange But True," The Sporting News, June 1, 1901, 5.

305 "Has the Foundation," The Sporting News, September 22, 1900, 1.

306 U.S. Census records for 1900 and 1910

307 Bob Mayer, "The Asylum Base Ball Club," *The National Pastime* (Phoenix, AZ: SABR, 2017), 52.

308 Brewster, 238.

309 Cappy Gagnon, from Robert Tiemann and Mark Rucker, eds., *Nineteenth Century Stars, 2012 Edition*, 48.

310 Robert C. Kennedy, "On This Day," HARP Week, NY Times on the Web, June 8, 2001. http://www.nytimes.com/learning/generl/onthisday/harp/0608.html

311 Waverly Advocate, May 3, 1901, 1.

312 "Editors at the Pan American," Hammondsport Herald, June 19, 1901.

313 "Baseball Notes," Waverly Free Press, April 27, 1901.

314 "Baseball Season to Open Soon," Waverly Free Press, April 20, 1901, 1.

315 "Baseball Notes," Waverly Free Press, April 27, 1901.

316 Waverly Advocate, April 30, 1901, 1.

317 "Baseball Rooter Dead," Owego Record, January 14, 1902. and "Charles Boggs," Waverly Free Press, January 18, 1902.

318 Waverly Advocate, April 30, 1901, 1.

319 "A Game of Errors," Waverly Advocate, May 3, 1901, 1.

320 "Waverly Plays Ball," Waverly Free Press, May 11, 1901, 1.

321 "Strange But True," The Sporting News, June 1, 1901, 5.

322 "Players' Friend," The Sporting News, May 18, 1901, 6.

323 "Waverly Plays Ball," Waverly Free Press, May 11, 1901, 1.

324 Ibid.

325 Ibid.

326 "Beaten by Syracuse," Waverly Free Press, May 18, 1901, 1.

327 Waverly Advocate, May 14, 1901, 1.

328 Seymour, 327.

329 Oswego Daily Times, May 16, 1901.

330 "Continue to Win," Elmira Daily Gazette and Free Press, May 20, 1901

331 "Did the Blow Cause Death?" Waverly Free Press, May 25, 1901, 1.

332 One sample story in the series – "A Story with Many Morals," Waverly Free Press, May 25, 1901, 1.

333 "Waverly's Luck," Elmira Daily Gazette and Free Press, May 24, 1901.

334 Auburn Bulletin, July 26, 1901, 6.

335 Penn Yan Democrat, August 23, 1901, 8.

336 "Tie at Ten Innings," Waverly Free Press, June 1, 1901, 1.

337 Waverly Free Press, June 8, 1901.

338 "Corning Done Up," Waverly Free Press, June 8, 1901.

339 Jamestown Evening Journal, June 27, 1901.

340 Hammondsport Herald, August 7, 1901.

341 Lockport Daily Journal, August 1, 1901.

342 Waverly Free Press, June 22, 1901.

343 "Another Victory," Elmira Daily Gazette and Free Press, June 19, 1901.

344 "The Waverly Baseball Team Trims the Dark Nine," Waverly Advocate, June 21, 1901, 1.

345 Waverly Free Press, June 22, 1901.

346 "Large Barns Burned," Ontario Repository-Messenger, August 22, 1901, 8.

347 Waverly Free Press, June 22, 1901.

348 "The Waverly Baseball Team Trims the Dark Nine," Waverly Advocate, June 21, 1901, p 1.

349 Ibid.

350 "New York League Stars," Sporting News, July 13, 1901, 4.

351 "Game was Played," Syracuse Evening Telegram, June 24, 1901.

352 Thorn, 99.

353 "Designs on the Saloons," Cortland Evening Standard, August 13, 1901.

354 "Pick Ups," Waverly Free Press, June 1, 1901, 1.

355 Endicott Johnson undated pamphlet "Labor and Capital Honor Themselves," 13.

356 Jim Maggiore and Michael J. McCann, *Celebrating 100 Years of Baseball in Greater Binghamton*, (Vestal, NY: Superior Print on Demand, 2014), 11.

357 Press and Sun Bulletin, September 6, 1906, 29.

358 New York Times, August 16, 1901. The Groton plant was bought back from American Bridge in 1902, but it never regained its previous size or market, and was sold back to American Bridge in 1920.

359 Scott Miller, *The President and the Assassin*, (New York: Random House, 2011), 287-288.

360 Miller, 273.

361 "The Spectre Rises," The Sporting Life, June 9, 1900, 5.

362 Ibid.

363 Robert Burk, *Never Just a Game: Players, Owners, and American Baseball to 1920*, (Chapel Hill, NC: University of North Carolina Press, 1994), 147.

364 "Ithaca's Frog Pest," Elmira Daily Gazette and Free Press, July 8, 1901, 8.

365 "Cortland Out," Sporting Life, July 20, 1901.

366 "We Join the State League," Waverly Free Press, July 13, 1901, 1.

367 McCormick, Nadeau, Lee and Mullin are identified in a Cortland Evening Standard story on July 9, 1901, as passing from Waverly to Rome through Cortland by train and "being greeted by many friends while the train was standing at the station." Not specifically identified is whether "Lee" was George "Knotty" Lee or John M. "Jack" Lee. Baseball Reference opts for Jack, and several newspapers mention that George Lee was playing for a team in Gananoque, Ontario, in 1901. On the other hand, there are later secondary references to George Lee playing "for such stops as Binghamton, Utica, Cortland and Waverly" and it's possible that George pitched for multiple teams in 1901. Both George and Jack were associated with New York State League teams during the time, and neither is credited with any major league experience.

368 "Gaining in Schenectady," The Sporting News, July 20, 1901, 1.

369 "Cause of Trouble," The Sporting News, July 27, 1901, 5.

370 "Waverly Plays Great Ball," Waverly Free Press, July 20, 1901, 1.

371 Ibid.

372 Ibid.

373 Ibid.

374 "Base Hits," Waverly Free Press, July 20, 1901, 1.

375 "Waverly Plays Great Ball," Waverly Free Press, July 20, 1901, 1.

376 Brewster, 85-87.

377 Sporting Life, August 10, 1901.

378 "Base Ball," Waverly Free Press, August 3, 1901, 1.

379 "Colored People Celebrate," Waverly Free Press, August 3, 1901, 1.

380 Frederick Douglas, *Two Speeches,* (Rochester, NY: C.P. Dewey, 1857), 8.

381 "Colored People Celebrate," Waverly Free Press, August 3, 1901, 1.

382 Ibid.

383 Ibid.

384 Ibid.

385 "Base Ball," Waverly Free Press, August 3, 1901, 1.

386 "State League," Elmira Daily Gazette and Free Press, August 2, 1901, 6.

387 "Base Ball for the Week," Waverly Free Press, August 10, 1901, 1.

388 "Syracuse Situation," The Sporting News, August 10, 1901, 7.

389 "Base Ball for the Week," Waverly Free Press, August 10, 1901, 1.

390 "Lead New York League," The Sporting News, July 27, 1901, 1.

391 "Mullen Got a Fall," Waverly Advocate

392 "Base Hits," Waverly Free Press, August 10, 1901, 1.

393 Ibid.
394 "The Game of His Life," Elmira Daily Gazette and Free Press, August 8, 1901, 6.
395 "Wilson is a Wonder," The Sporting News, August 17, 1901, 1.
396 "Base Hits," Waverly Free Press, August 10, 1901, 1.
397 "Plays and Players," Albany Evening Journal, August 9, 1901, 6.
398 "Albany Lost Two to Waverly," Albany Evening Journal, August 10, 1901, 6.
399 Ibid.
400 "Waverly Wallops the Senators," Cortland Evening Standard, August 10, 1901, 7.
401 "Albany Lost Two to Waverly," Albany Evening Journal, August 10, 1901, 6.
402 "Wilson is a Wonder," The Sporting News, August 17, 1901, 1.
403 Waverly Free Press, August 17, 1901, 1.
404 "News Notes," Sporting Life, August 3, 1901.
405 "Baseball," Cortland Evening Standard, August 7, 1901, 7.
406 "No More Baseball," Waverly Free Press, August 17, 1901, p 1.
407 Ibid.
408 Ibid.
409 "Binghamton Gains," Cortland Evening Standard, August 6, 1901, 7.
410 "No More Baseball," Waverly Free Press, August 17, 1901, 1.
411 Sporting Life, August 31, 1901.
412 Ibid.
413 "Utica in First Place," The Sporting News, August 24, 1901, 1.

414 "Wild Steer Loose," Wilkes-Barre News, August 23, 1901, 2.

415 Sporting Life, August 31, 1901.

416 "Pop Hamburg's Poodle," Rome Sentinel, August 2, 1901, 2.

417 "News Notes," Sporting Life, August 17, 1901.

418 Sporting Life, September 7, 1901. Charles "Heinie" Wagner is listed in his SABR biography as playing for Waverly in 1901, but Baseball-Reference lists the Wagner who joined Waverly as "Johnny" Wagner (which is consistent with some *Sporting Life* references). Therefore, it's unclear whether this was in fact a different Wagner, if Heinie Wagner used an assumed name, or some other possibility. The SABR biography's reference to Wagner playing for Waverly in 1901 is corroborated by stories in the *Hartford Courant* (3/3/1916, 21 and 1/5/1917, 11), that were written while Wagner was still playing and coaching, as well as by Wagner's *New York Times* obituary (3/20/1943).

419 "Waverly Won the Game," Syracuse Post Standard, September 4, 1901.

420 Sporting Life, September 14, 1901.

421 Ibid.

422 Ibid.

423 "Just One More They Gave Away," Buffalo Evening News, August 31, 1901, 6.

424 Miller, 301.

425 "Last Game was a Tie," Hartford Courant, September 7, 1901, 9.

426 Miller, 304.

427 Lang, 400

428 Waverly Free Press, September 14, 1901.

429 "New York's League," Sporting Life, September 28, 1901.

430 The Sporting News, September 14, 1901, 4.
431 "Farrell's Force," Sporting Life, September 28, 1901.
432 "Amusements," Auburn Bulletin, September 10, 1901, 4.
433 Miller, 324.
434 Miller, 305.
435 Miller, 327-328
436 Miller, 329.
437 "They Are All Fakes," Auburn Weekly Bulletin, October 11, 1901.
438 Miller, 330.
439 "Krist's Reprieve," Elmira Daily News and Free Press, August 26, 1901, 8.
440 "Players Practice," Sporting Life, September 14, 1901.
441 Wilbert, 182.
442 Seymour, 324.
443 Seymour, 310.
444 John McGraw, 58.
445 "Judge Harry L. Taylor Dies; Jurist for Nearly 40 Years," Buffalo Evening News, July 13, 1955, 23.
446 Robert Peterson, *Only the Ball Was White*, (New York: Oxford University Press, 1970), 63.
447 Edmund Morris, *Theodore Rex*. (New York: Random House, 2001), 47-51.
448 Edmund Morris, 56.
449 "Krist was Resigned," Auburn Democrat-Argus, November 22, 1901.
450 Ibid.
451 Ibid.

452 U.S. Department of Education. *120 Years of American Education: A Statistical Portrait*. Table 4, p 18.

453 "In the Base Ball Field," Rome Daily Sentinel, January 24, 1902, 3.

454 Syracuse Herald, January 19, 1902.

455 "Must Buy Franchise," Rome Citizen, January 24, 1902.

456 "State League to Meet Next Week," Syracuse Journal, January 22, 1902.

457 Waverly Free Press, February 8, 1902.

458 "We Get League Ball," Amsterdam Evening Recorder, March 13, 1902, 5.

459 Sacandaga Park – park history. Website @ www.sacandagastation.com/sac_park.html

460 Waverly Free Press, April 15, 1902.

461 "Railroads Tied Up by the Flood," Elmira Daily Gazette and Free Press, March 3, 1902, 5.

462 "Tremendous Floods," Waverly Free Press, March 7, 1902, 1.

463 "Syracuse Succeeds Waverly," The Sporting News, January 25, 1902, 1.

464 Stadium years and capacities from Baseball-Reference.com

465 John Helyar, *Lords of the Realm*, (New York: Ballantine Books, 1994), 7.

466 Harry R. Melone, *150 Years of Progress*, (Auburn, NY: Finger Lakes Press, 1929), 282-294.

467 "John H. Farrell, 'Grand Old Man of Baseball,' Is Dead," Auburn Citizen Advertiser, May 17, 1945, 6.

468 Gloversville Evening Leader, July 16, 1902, 5.

469 Cait Murphy, *Crazy '08*, (New York: Harper Collins, 2007), 269.

470 "Schulte Swings Hard and Breaks 50 Bats Per Year," Binghamton Press, March 22, 1913, 11.

471 Murphy, 274.

472 Sporting Life, May 24, 1902, 19.

473 Sporting Life, July 19, 1902, 21.

474 Sporting Life, August 2, 1902, 6.

475 "Tinker to Evers to Chance" was the Cubs double play combination made famous by the poem "Baseball's Sad Lexicon" by Franklin P. Adams, first published in 1910 in the New York Evening Mail. The poem in its entirety: *These are the saddest of possible words: "Tinker to Evers to Chance." Trio of bear cubs, and fleeter than birds. Tinker and Evers and Chance. Ruthlessly pricking our gonfalon bubble, Making a Giant hit into a double – Words that are heavy with nothing but trouble: "Tinker to Evers to Chance."*

476 David Shiner, SABR Biography of Johnny Evers.

477 Sporting Life, July 5, 1902, 21.

478 Sporting Life, July 12, 1902, 20.

479 Sporting Life, August 16, 1902, 6.

480 Sporting Life, August 23, 1902, 6.

481 David W. Anderson, SABR Biography of Bill Klem.

482 Sporting Life, September 5, 1903, 12.

483 Sporting Life, June 17, 1905, 21.

484 "Death Serves to Recall Ging and His Work," Gloversville and Johnstown Morning Herald, September 16, 1950, 9.

485 Gloversville Daily Leader, July 24, 1903, 3.

486 Author interview with Jerry Coffey, February 22, 2018.

487 "Ex-Ball Player Billy Ging Dies," Elmira Star Gazette, September 15, 1950, 14.

488 Author interview with Jerry Coffey, February 22, 2018. In the interview, Coffey, Bill Ging's grand nephew, also shared that as a high school basketball player for Notre Dame High School, his opponents included Elmira Free Academy's Ernie Davis, who would go on to be the first African American to win the Heisman Trophy and was an "amazing athlete" in every sport he played. Coffey explained his father's special affinity for Jackie Robinson was possibly related to his own experience of discrimination as a young Irish-American, and the desire to be "fair-minded" and to judge by abilities and character rather than race.

489 Bruce Nash and Allan Zullo, *The Baseball Hall of Shame: The Best of Blooperstown*, (Guilford, CT: Lyons, 2012), 35.

490 Sporting Life, September 23, 1905, 4-5.

491 Cause of death is according to McDougal's findagrave.com entry at Memorial ID 51375825.

492 Baseballhalloffame.ca/inductees/george-lee

493 U.S. Census Records – 1910 and 1920

494 "Victor Accorsini, Old Time Catcher, Visits Waverly," Elmira Star-Gazette, August 24, 1926.

495 "Former Cortland Ball Player Dead," Cortland Standard, October 11, 1933. Also "Mike Mullin, Former NYP Player, Dies," Wilkes-Barre Evening News, October 9, 1933, p 10; and "Michael Mullin," Philadelphia Enquirer, October 9, 1933, p 23.

496 "Crushed by Fall of Rock," article posted to Charles Broderick's FindaGrave site. https://www.findagrave.com/memorial/147294413/charles-broderick

497 Sporting Life, May 9, 1903, 6.

498 Sporting Life, May 16, 1903, 6.

499 Sporting Life, May 31, 1902, 18.

500 Sporting Life, September 27, 1902, 8.

501 "Coach is Engaged for Team," Elmira Star-Gazette, March 2, 1910, 7.

502 "Owen Dunham," Elmira Telegram, April 16, 1916.

503 "Tucker Acquitted" Owego Record, June 19, 1902.

504 Richard Palmer, *The Coming of the Railroad to Sayre*, (Sayre, PA: Sayre Historical Society, 2017), 1.

505 Paul Seibel, "Lehighlights," The Evening Times, September 26, 1946, 6.

506 "Fred L. Tucker of Waverly is Taken," The Evening Times, May 22, 1943, 7.

507 "Baseball Pays Players Well," Elmira Star-Gazette, October 22, 1910, 9.

508 Cappy Gagnon, *Notre Dame Baseball Greats*, (Charleston, SC: Arcadia, 2004), 41.

509 "New International League Umpire is Former Elmiran Who Rose up From Sandlot," Elmira Star-Gazette, March 6, 1929, 10.

510 "Baseball Mourns Death of Dode Birmingham," Elmira Star-Gazette, April 26, 1946, 16.

511 "John (Red) Murray Dead," Elmira Star-Gazette, December 4, 1958, 25.

512 Tom O'Hara Obituary, Denver Post, June 10, 1954, 64.

513 John McGraw, 1-2.

514 "John McGraw Celebrates Early Start in Olean," The (Olean) Times Herald, April 28, 1925, 19.

515 Smiles, 182

516 Michael DeMarco, *Dugout Days*, (New York: American Management Association, 2001), 27.

517 DeMarco, 230.

518 Blanche McGraw, *The Real McGraw*, (New York: David McKay, 1953), 284.

519 Blanche McGraw, 283-284.

520 Letter from the National Baseball Hall of Fame Player File for William "Bud" Heine.

521 "W.C. Heine, Sr., Buried at Addison," The (Corning) Evening Leader, February 18, 1929, 1.

522 Ibid.

523 Ibid.

524 Al Stump, *Cobb – A Biography*, (Chapel Hill, NC: Algonquin, 1996), 88.

525 Ibid.

526 Stump, 132-133.

527 "Heinie Wagner Red Sox Boss Next Year," Elmira Star-Gazette, December 23, 1929, 10.

528 Robert W. Creamer, *Babe: The Legend Comes to Life*, (New York: Simon and Schuster, 1974), 90.

529 Kal Wagenheim, *Babe Ruth: His Life and Legend*. (Washington, DC: Waterfront Press, 1990), 34-36

530 Creamer, 93

531 Creamer, 162

532 Creamer, 106

533 "Frank Grant, Noted Baseball Star of Generation Ago, Dies," New York Age, June 5, 1937.

534 Multiple news articles and advertisements regarding Waverly Baracas' baseball were published in the Sayre Evening Times summer editions of the early 1920s. Among the earliest is one entitled "Two Big Games on Waverly Grounds, (May 29, 1920, p 8), which describes "Baraca field" on Lincoln Street.

535 Brad Snyder, *A Well-Paid Slave: Curt Flood's Fight for Free Agency in Professional Sports*, (New York: Penguin, 2006), 200-201.
536 Tim Birney, "Jeff Terpko (Part I): The Early Years," Valley Sports Report, August 10, 2017.
537 "Athens Athletes Saluted by Blue & White Club," The Evening Times, May 30, 1986, 11.

Sources

ARCHIVE, LIBRARY, AND GOVERNMENT COLLECTIONS

Bradford County (PA) Historical Society (Towanda, PA)
Chemung Valley (NY) Historical Society (Elmira, NY)
National Archives and Records Administration (Washington, DC)
National Baseball Hall of Fame and Library (Cooperstown, NY)
New York State Library (Albany, NY)
Sayre (PA) Historical Society
Sayre (PA) Public Library
Spalding Memorial Library (Athens, PA)
Susquehanna River Archaeological Center (Waverly, NY)
Tioga County (NY) Historical Society (Owego, NY)
Waverly (NY) Free Library
Waverly (NY) Historical Society

NEWSPAPERS AND PERIODICALS

Addison Advertiser, The (Addison, NY) 1879-1902
Albany Evening Journal (Albany, NY) 1896-1901
Albany Express, The (Albany, NY) 1888
Albany Times-Union, The (Albany, NY) 1892-1900
Allentown Leader, The (Allentown, PA) 1897
Altoona Tribune, The (Altoona, PA) 1910-11
Amsterdam Evening Recorder, The (Amsterdam, NY) 1902, 1950
Angelica Advocate, The (Angelica, NY) 1913
Athens Daily News, The (Athens, PA) 1890

Athens Gazette, The (Athens, PA) 1910
Athens Gleaner, The (Athens, PA) 1871
Auburn Bulletin, The (Auburn, NY) 1890-1902
Auburn Citizen-Advertiser, The (Auburn, NY) 1945 and 1975
Auburn Democrat, The (Auburn, NY) 1901
Auburn Democrat-Argus, The (Auburn, NY) 1901
Baseball Magazine, December 1914
Baseball Research Journal, SABR, Spring 2016
Binghamton Press, The (Binghamton, NY) 1903-1954
Bloomfield Independent Press, The (Bloomfield, NJ) 1933
Bradford Era, The (Bradford, PA) 1886
Bradford Star, The (Towanda, PA) 1895-1899
Broome Republican, The (Binghamton, NY) 1901-1902
Buffalo Courier, The (Buffalo, NY) 1887-1936
Buffalo Evening News, The (Buffalo, NY) 1881-1955
Buffalo Express, The (Buffalo, NY) 1890-94
Canaseraga Times, The (Canaseraga, NY) 1882
Canisteo Times, The (Canisteo, NY) 1900
Central News, The (Perkasie, PA) 1916
Chicago Tribune, The (Chicago, IL) 1898-1901
Cincinnati Enquirer, The (Cincinnati, OH) 1921
Citizen, The (Phelps, NY) 1904
Clifton Springs Press, The (Clifton Springs, NY) 1902
Columbia Herald, The (Columbia, PA) 1897
Cornell Daily Sun, The (Ithaca, NY) 1888-1952
Corning Journal, The (Corning, NY) 1878-1901
Corning Evening Leader, The (Corning, NY) 1942
Cortland Democrat, The (Cortland, NY) 1880-1913
Cortland Evening Standard, The (Cortland, NY) 1900-1902
Cortland News, The (Cortland, NY) 1885
Cortland Standard, The (Cortland, NY) 1900-1933
Daily Argus, The (Mount Vernon, NY) 1900
Daily Eagle, The (Brooklyn, NY) 1895-1901
Daily Eagle, The (Poughkeepsie, NY) 1902
Daily Journal, The (Lockport, NY) 1890

Daily News, The (Ithaca, NY) 1896-1902
Daily Sentinel, The (Rome, NY) 1890-1902
Daily Times, The (Oswego, NY) 1900-1903
Day, The (New London, CT) 1907
Democrat, The (Penn Yan, NY) 1901-1909
Democrat, The (Rochester, NY) 1895-1900
Democrat and Chronicle, The (Rochester, NY) 1897-1930
Denver Post, The (Denver, CO) 1954
Detroit Free Press, The (Detroit, MI) 1907
Economist, The, 1998
Elmira Daily Gazette and Free Press (Elmira, NY) 1891-1902
Elmira Star-Gazette (Elmira, NY) 1910-1955
Elmira Telegram, The (Elmira, NY) 1888-1916
Emporia Weekly News, The (Emporia, KS) 1862
Evening Herald, The (Syracuse, NY) 1900-1901
Evening News, The (Jamestown, NY) 1887
Evening Telegram, The (Herkimer, NY) 1900
Evening Telegram, The (New York, NY) 1886
Evening Times, The (Little Falls, NY) 1897
Evening Times, The (Sayre, PA) 1891-1984
Free Press, The (Montour Falls, NY) 1895
Freeland Tribune, The (Freeland, PA) 1897
Geneva Daily Times, The (Geneva, NY) 1901
Geneva Gazette, The (Geneva, NY) 1887
Glens Falls Times, The (Glens Falls, NY) 1887
Gloversville Daily Leader, The (Gloversville, NY) 1901-1903
Greenpoint Daily Star, The (Long Island City, NY) 1886
Harrisburg Independent, The (Harrisburg, PA) 1897
Harrisburg Telegraph, The (Harrisburg, PA) 1895
Hartford Courant, The (Hartford, CT) 1901
Herald, The (Hammondsport, NY) 1886-1905
Herald, The (Honesdale, PA) 1898
Homer Republican, The (Homer, NY) 1879
Independent, The (New York, NY) 1902
Ithaca Daily News, The (Ithaca, NY) 1896

Ithaca Journal, The (Ithaca, NY) 1914-1919
Johnson City – Endicott Record, The (Johnson City, NY) 1916
Journal, The (Auburn, NY) 1907
Lebanon Daily News, The (Lebanon, PA) 1897-1916
Leavenworth Times, The (Leavenworth, KS) 1870
Lewiston Daily Sun, The (Lewiston, ME) 1900
Lockport Journal, The (Lockport, NY) 1901
Los Angeles Herald, The (Los Angeles, CA) 1901
Mansfield Advertiser, The (Mansfield, PA) 1944
Mercury, The (Pottstown, PA) 1941-54
Miltonian, The (Milton, PA) 1910
Miners Journal, The (Pottsville, PA) 1897
Moravia Republican, The (Moravia, NY) 1900
Naples Record, The (Naples, NY) 1946
National Police Gazette, The (New York, NY) 1887
New York Age, The (New York, NY) 1937
New York Clipper, The (New York, NY) 1870-1885
New York Herald, The (New York, NY) 1887-1916
New York Morning Telegraph, The (New York, NY) 1901
New York Evening Post, The (New York, NY) 1901
New York Press, The (New York, NY) 1889-1902
New York Sun, The (New York, NY) 1887-90
New York Telegram, The (New York, NY) 1886-1892
New York Times, The (New York, NY) 1896-2020
New York Tribune, The (New York, NY) 1921
New York World, The (New York, NY) 1890-1898
Niagara Falls Gazette, The (Niagara Falls, NY) 1954-1968
North Adams Transcript, The (North Adams, MA) 1896
Otsego Farmer, The (Cooperstown, NY) 1892-1896
Oswego Daily Palladium, The (Oswego, NY) 1900
Oswego Times-Express, The (Oswego, NY) 1885
Ovid Gazette, The (Ovid, NY) 1901
Owego Daily Blade, The (Owego, NY) 1884-87
Owego Daily Record, The (Owego, NY) 1887-88
Palladium Times, The (Oswego, NY) 1941

People, The (New York, NY) 1897
Philadelphia Inquirer (Philadelphia, PA) 1892-1944
Pittsburgh Courier, The (Pittsburgh, PA) 1927-31
Pittsburgh Daily Post, The (Pittsburgh, PA) 1887-1911
Pittston Gazette, The (Pittston, PA) 1901
Port Jervis Gazette, The (Port Jervis, NY) 1886
Post-Standard, The (Syracuse, NY) 1900
Potsdam-St. Lawrence Herald, The (Potsdam, NY) 1900
Pottstown Mercury, The (Pottstown, PA) 1935
Pottsville Republican, The (Pottsville, PA) 1897
Poughkeepsie Eagle News, The (Poughkeepsie, NY) 1889
Public Opinion, Volume 23, 1897
Reading Times, The (Reading, PA) 1891-1901
Record, The (Johnson City & Endicott, NY) 1916-1919
Record-Argus, The (Greenville, PA) 1900
Rome Citizen, The (Rome, NY) 1901-1902
San Francisco Call, The (San Francisco, CA) 1905
Scranton Republican, The (Scranton, PA) 1896-1922
Scranton Tribune, The (Scranton, PA) 1897
Sentinel, The (Carlisle, PA) 1890
Shamokin Dispatch, The (Shamokin, PA) 1924
Sporting Life (Philadelphia, PA) 1885-1908
Sporting News (St. Louis, MO) 1886-1902
Sports Illustrated, 2001-2012
Star, The (Long Island, NY) 1886-1898
Syracuse Evening Telegram, The (Syracuse, NY) 1900-1901
Syracuse Herald, The (Syracuse, NY) 1900-1902
Syracuse Journal, The (Syracuse, NY) 1897-1905
Syracuse Post-Standard, The (Syracuse, NY) 1901-1904
Syracuse Standard, The (Syracuse, NY) 1886-1887
Times, The (Philadelphia, PA) 1896-00
Times-Herald, The (Olean, NY) 1921-31
Times-Picayune, The (New Orleans, LA) 1895-96
Tioga County Record, The (Owego, NY) 1887-1905
Tribune, The (Bismarck, ND) 1890-1914

Troy Daily Times, The (Troy, NY) 1900-1901
Tyrone Herald, The (Tyrone, PA) 1897
Utica Daily Press, The (Utica, NY) 1902
Utica Herald, The (Utica, NY) 1896
Utica Journal, The (Utica, NY) 1901
Valley Sports Report (Sayre, PA) 2017
Washington Evening Star, The (Washington, DC) 1888
Washington Post, The (Washington, DC) 1891
Watkins Express, The (Watkins Glen, NY) 1880
Waverly Advocate, The (Waverly, NY) 1879-1901
Waverly Free Press, The (Waverly, NY) 1886-1914
Wayne County Herald, The (Wayne County, NY) 1898-1904
Weekly Bulletin, The (Auburn, NY) 1901
Weekly Tribune, The (Hornellsville, NY) 1893-1896
Wellsboro Gazette, The (Wellsboro, PA) 1897-1900
Wilkes-Barre Record, The (Wilkes-Barre, PA) 1896-97
Wilkes-Barre Times (Wilkes-Barre, PA) 1899
Wilkes-Barre Times Leader, The (Wilkes-Barre, PA) 1890-1910
Williamsport Sun-Gazette (Williamsport, PA) 1900-12

BOOKS AND JOURNAL ARTICLES

Albertson, Capt. Charles L. *History of Waverly, NY, and Vicinity*. Waverly, NY: Waverly Sun, 1943.

Alexander, Charles C. *John McGraw*. New York: Viking Penguin, 1988.

-------. *Turbulent Seasons: Baseball in 1890-1891*. Dalas: Southern Methodist University Press, 2011.

Algeo, Matthew. *Pedestrianism: When Watching People Walk Was America's Favorite Spectator Sport*. Chicago: Chicago Review Press, 2014.

Appel, Marty, "Retroactive Rewards," *Memories and Dreams, the Official Magazine of the Hall of Fame* 38, no. 5 (Fall 2016). Also available via: http://www.appelpr.com/?page_id=3320

Aswad, Ed and Meredith, Suzanne M., *Images of America: Endicott-Johnson*. Charleston, SC: Arcadia, 2003.

Bernstein, Peter L. *Wedding of the Waters: The Erie Canal and the Making of a Great Nation.* New York: Norton, 2005.

Bevis, Charlie. *Jimmy Collins: A Baseball Biography.* Jefferson, NC: McFarland, 2012.

Blatz, Perry K. *Democratic Miners.* Albany, New York: SUNY Press, 1994.

Blight, David W., *Frederick Douglass.* New York: Simon & Schuster, 2018.

Brands, H.W. *The Reckless Decade: America in te 1890s.* Chicago: University of Chicago Press, 1995.

Brewster, William H. *The Workingman's Game: Waverly, NY, the Twin Tiers, and the Making of Modern Baseball, 1887-1898.* Eugene, OR: Luminare Press, 2019.

Brock, Darryl. *Two in the Field.* New York: Plume, 2002.

Browne, Paul. *The Coal Barons Played Cuban Giants.* Jefferson, NC: McFarland, 2013.

Browning, Reed. *Cy Young: A Baseball Lif.* Amherst, MA: University of Massachusetts Press, 2000.

Burk, Robert F. *Never Just a Game: Players, Owners, and American Baseball to 1920.* Chapel Hill, NC: University of North Carolina Press, 1994.

Burt, Silas W. *New York and the War with Spain: History of the Empire State Regiments.* New York: Argus Company, 1903.

Casway, Jerrold, "Bacteria Beat the Phillies," *SABR Baseball-Research Journal*, Volume 1, Number 45 (Spring 2016): 116-122.

Cook, William A. *August "Garry" Herrmann: A Baseball Biography.* Jefferson, NC: McFarland, 2008.

Creamer, Robert W. *Babe: The Legend Comes to Life.* New York: Simon and Schuster, 1974.

Deford, Frank. *The Old Ball Game.* New York: Atlantic Monthly Press, 2005.

DeMarco, Michael. *Dugout Days: Untold Tales & Leadership Lessons From the Extraordinary Career of Billy Martin.* New York: American Management Association, 2001.

DeMotte, Charles. *Bat, Ball & Bible: Baseball and Sunday Observance in New York*. Washington, DC: Potomac, 2013.

Deutch, Jordan A., Richard M, Cohen, Roland T. Johnson and David S. eft. *The Scrapbook History of Baseball*. New York: Bobbs-Merrill, 1975.

Douglass, Frederick. *Two Speeches of Frederick Douglass; one of West India Emancipation, Delivered at Canandaigua, Aug. 4th, and the Other on the Dred Scott Decision, Delivered in New York on the occasion of the Anniversary of the American Abolition Society, May 1857*. Rochester, NY: C. P. Dewey, 1857.

Dubofsky, Melvyn. *Industrialism and the American Worker 1865-1920*. Arlington Heights, IL: Harlan Davidson, 1975.

Endicott Johnson Corporation. *Labor and Capital Honor Themselves*. Endicott, NY: Endicott Johnson Corporation (undated pamphlet).

Factory Inspectors of the State of New York. *Second Annual Report*. Troy, NY: Troy Press, 1888.

Falk, Candace, editor. *Emma Goldman: Made for America, 1890-1901*. Champaign, IL: University of Illinois Press, 2008.

Friedlander, Brett and Robert Reising. *Chasing Moonlight: The True Story of Field of Dreams' Doc Graham*. Winston-Salem, NC: John F. lair, 2009.

Frick, Ford C. *Games, Asterisks and People*. New York: Crown, 1973.

Gagnon, Cappy. *Notre Dame Baseball Greats: From Anson to Yaz*. Charleston, SC: Arcadia, 2004.

Gay, W.B. *Historical Gazetteer of Tioga Couny, New York, 1785-1888*. Interlaken, NY: Heart of the Lakes Publishing, 1985.

Gibb, George Sweet. *The Whitesmiths of Taunton: A History of Reed & Barton, 1824-1943*. Cambridge, MA: Harvard University Press, 1943.

Goldman, Steven. *Forging Genius: The Making of Casey Stengel*. Washington, DC: Potomac, 2005.

Golenbock, Peter. *Dynasty: The New York Yankees 1949-1964.* Englewood Cliffs, NJ: Prentice-Hall, 1975.

Goodrich, Thomas. *Bloody Dawn: The Story of the Lawrence Massacre.* Kent, OH: Kent State University Press, 1991.

Goodwin, Doris Kearns. *The Bully Pulpit.* New York: Simon & Shuster, 2013.

Gordon, John Steele. *An Empire of Wealth.* New York: Harper Collins, 2004.

Green, Guy W. *The Nebraska Indians and Fun and Froic with an Indian Ball Team.* Edited by Jeff P. Beck. Jefferson, NC: McFarland, 2010.

Hair, William Ivy. *Carnival of Fury: Robert Charles and the New Orleans Race Riot of 1900.* Baton Rouge: LSU Press, 1976.

Hardy, James D. *The New York Giants Base Ball Club.* Jefferson, NC: McFarland, 2006.

Helyar, John. *Lords of the Realm.* New York: Ballantine Books, 1994.

Hogan, Lawrence D. *Shades of Glory.* Washington, DC: National Geographic Socety, 2006.

Honig, Donald. *The American League: An Illustrated History.* New York: Crown, 1983.

Horigan, Michael. *Elmira – Death Camp of the North.* Mechanicsburg, Pennsylvania: Stackpole Books, 2002.

Howells, William Dean. *A Hazard of New Fortunes.* New York: Harper and Brothers, 1890.

Jobs, Sebastian. *Welcome Home Boys: Military Victory Parades in New York City, 1899-1945.* New York: Campus Verlag, 2013.

Jones, Mary Harris. *Autobiography of Mother Jones.* Chicago, Illinois: Charles H. Kerr and Company, 1925.

Kashatus, William C. *Diamonds in the Coalfields.* Jefferson, NC: McFarland, 202.

Kazin, Michael. *A Godly Hero: The Life of William Jennings Bryan.* New York: Alfred A. Knopf, 2006.

Kingman, Leroy W. *Our County and Its People.* Elmira, NY: W.A. Fergusson and Company, 1900.

Kirsch, George B. *Baseball in Blue & Gray: The National Pastime during the Civil War*. Princeton, NJ: Princeton University Press, 2003.

Kissel, Tony and Scott Fiesthumel. *The Legend of Wild Bill Setley*. Kearney, NE: Morris Publishing, 2002.

Krist, Gary. *Empire of Sin*. New York: Crown, 2014.

Kurkjian, Tim. *America's Game*. New York: Crown, 2000.

Lamster, Mark. *Spalding's World Tour*. New York: Public Affairs, 2006.

Layden, Tim, "Tinker to Evers to Chance . . . to Me," *Sports Illustrated*, December 3, 2012.

Lang, Louis J., ed. *The Autobiography of Thomas Collier Platt*. New York: B.W. Dodge, 1910.

Leavengood, Ted. *Clark Griffith: The Old Fox of Washington Baseball*. Jefferson, NC: McFarland, 2011.

Lardner, Ring. *Selected Stories*. New York: Penguin, 1997.

Linker, Andrew. *One Patch of Grass*. Harrisburg, PA: Andrew Linker, 2012.

-------. *Clippings*. Harrisburg, PA: Andrew Linker, 2012.

Lomax, Michael E. *Black Baseball Entrepreneurs, 1860-1901*. Syracuse, NY: Syracuse University Press, 2003.

Lott, Eric. *Love & Theft: Blackface Minstrelsy & the American Working Class, 20th Anniversary Edition*. New York: Oxord University Press, 2013.

Lowenfish, Lee. *The Imperfect Diamond*. Lincoln, Nebraska: Universiy of Nebraska Press, 1980.

Lowman, Seymour. *The Lowmans in Chemung County*. Elmira, NY: The Commercial Press, 1938.

Maggiore, Jim and McCann, Michael J. *Celebrating 100 Years of Baseball in Greater Binghamton: Tales from the Binghamton Baseball Shrine*. Vestal, NY: Superior Print on Demand, 2014.

Martin, Billy and Golenbock, Peter. *Number 1*. New York: Dell, 1980.

Mathewson, Christy. *Pitching in a Pinch: Baseball from the Inside*. New York: G.P. Putnam's Sons, 1912.

Mayer, Bob. "The Asylum Base Ball Club. *The Natioal Pastime: New York, New York, Baseball in the Big Apple*. Phoenix, AZ: Society for American Baseball Research, 2017.

Mayer, Ronald A. *Christy Mathewson: A Game-by-Game Profile of a Legendary Pitcher.* Jefferson, NC: McFarland, 2008.

McDonald, Brian. *Indian Summer.* New York: Rodale, 2003.

McGraw, Blanche S. *The Real McGraw.* New York: David McKay, 1953.

McGraw, John J. *My Thirty Years in Baseball.* New York: Boni and Liveright, 1923. Reprint edition: Lincoln, NE: Bison Books, 1995.

McKelvey, G. Richard. *For It's One, Two, Three, Four Strikes You're Out at the Owners' Ball Game.* Jefferson, NC: McFarland, 2001.

McNamara, Robert F. *The Diocese of Rochester in America, 1868-1993.* Rochester, NY: Diocese of Rochester, NY, 1998.

McPherson, James M. *Drawn With the Sword – Reflections on the American Civil War.* New York: Oxford University Press, 1996.

Mead, William B. and Paul Dickson. *Baseball – The President's Game.* Washington, DC: Farragut Publishing, 1993.

Melone, Harry R. *150 Year of Progress.* Auburn, NY: Finger Lakes Press, 1929.

Miller, Scott. *The President and the Assassin.* New York: Random House, 2011.

Morgan, Lewis Henry. *League of Ho-de-no-sau-nee, orIroquois.* (Two Volumes in One.) New York: Dodd, Mead and Company, 1922

Morris, Edmund. *Theodore Rex.* New York: Random House, 2001.

Morris, Peter. *Catcher: The Evolution of an American Folk Hero.* Chicago: Ivan R Dee, 2009.

Murphy, Cait. *Crazy '08.* New York: Harper Collins, 2007.

Murray, Elsie. *Teaoga – Annals of a Valley.* Athens, Pennsylvania: Tioga Point Museum, 1939.

Nack, William, with special reporting by Mike Donovan, "Collision at Home" *Sports Illustrated*, June 4, 2001.

Nash, Bruce and Zullo, Allan. *The Baseball Hall of Shame: The Best of Blooperstown*. Guilford, T: Lyons, 2012.

National Baseball Hall of Fame Almanac 2014 Edition. Durham, NC: Baseball America, Source Interlink Magazines, Inc., 2014.

Nemec, David. *The Rank and File of 19th Century Major League Baseball*. Jefferson, NC: McFarland, 2012.

------ and Saul Wisnia. *Baseball: More than 150 Years*. Lincolnwood, IL: Publicaions International, 1996.

Novak, Michael. *The Guns of Lattimer*. New York: Basic Books, 1978.

Overmye, James. *Frank Grant*. Baseball History 4.

Palmer, Richard. *The Coming of the Railroad to Sayre*. Sayre, PA: Sayre Historical Society, 2017.

Paterson, Tomas G., Clifford, J. Garry and Hagan, Kenneth J. *American Foreign Policy: A History/to 1914*. Lexington, Massachusetts: D.C. Heath and Company, 1983.

Pellechia, Thomas. *Over a Barrel – The Rise and Fall of New York's Taylor Wine Company*. Albany, NY: State University of New York Press, 2015.

Pennington, Bill. *Billy Martin: Baseball's Flawed Genius*. New York: Houghton Mifflin Harcourt, 2015.

Perry, Bliss. *The Plated City*. New York: Charles Scribner's Sons, 1895.

Peterson, Robert. *Only the Ball Was White*. New York: Oxford Unversity Press, 1970.

Publishing Society of New York. *Republicans of New York*. 1902

Quest, Richard. *Tioga County, New York*. Charleston, SC: Arcadia, 1999

Rice, Edward Le Roy. *Monarchs of Minstrelsy, from "Daddy" Rice to Date*. New York: Kenny Publishing Company, 1911.

Riess, Steven A. *Sport in Industrial America 1850-1920*. Arlington Heights, IL: Harlan Davidson, 1995.

Ritter, Lawrence S. *The Glory of Their Times*. New York: Macmillan and Company, 1966.

Roberts, Randy & Carson Cunningham, eds. *Before the Curse: The Chicago Cubs' Glory Years, 1870-1945*. Champaign, IL: University of Illinois Press, 2012.

Rosenberg, Howard W. *Cap Anson 3: Mugsy McGraw and the Tricksters: Baseballs' Fun Age of Rule-Bending*. Arlington, Virginia: Tile Books, 2005.

Ross, Robert B. *The Great Baseball Revolt*. Lincoln, NE: University of Nebraska Press, 2016

Schiff, Andrew J. *The Father of Baseball: A Biography of Henry Chadwick*. Jefferson, NC: McFarland, 2008.

Schultz, Duane. *Quantrill's War: The Life and Times of William Clarke Quantrill*. New York: St. Martins Press, 1996.

Seymour, Harold. *Baseball: The Early Years*. New York: Oxford University Press, 1960.

Shipton, Alyn. *A New History of Jazz*. New York: Continuum, 2001.

Smiles, Jack. *"Ee-Yah": The Life and Times of Hughie Jennings, Baseball Hall of Famer*. Jefferson, NC: McFarland, 2005.

Snyder, Brad. *A Well-Paid Slave: Curt Flood's Fight for Free Agency in Professional Sports*. New York: Penguin, 2006.

Solomon, Burt. *Where They Ain't*. New York: Free Press, 1999.

Somers, Dale A. *The Rise of Sports in New Orleans*. New Orleans: Pelican Publishing, 1972

Stacy, Bonnie. *Athens, Sayre and Waverly*. Dover, NH: Arcadia, 1996.

Standiford, Les. *Meet You in Hell*. New York: Three Rivers Press, 2005.

Stump, Al. *Cobb – A Biography*. Chapel Hill, NC: Algonquin, 1996.

Swanon, Krister. *Baseball's Power Shift: How the Players Union, the Fans and the Media Changed American Sports Culture*. Lincoln, NE: University of Nebraska Press, 2016.

Terry, James L. *Long Before the Dodgers: Baseball in Brooklyn, 1855-1884*. Jefferson, NC: McFarland, 2002.

Thompson, E.P. *The Making of the English Working Class*. New York: Vintage Books, 1966.

Thorn, John, ed. *The National Pastime*. New York: Warner Books, 1987.

-------. *Baseball in the Garden of Eden*. New York: Simon & Schuster, 2011.

Tiemann, Robert L. and Rucker, Mark, eds. *Nineteenth Century Stars, 2012 Edition*. Phoenix, Arizona: Society for American Baseball Research, 2012.

Tye, Larry. *Satchel: The Life and Times of an American Legend*. New York: Random House, 2009.

Wageheim, Kal. *Babe Ruth: His Life and Legend*. Washington, DC: Waterfront Press, 1990.

Ward, Geoffrey, et al. *Mark Twain: An Illustrated Biography*. New York: Alfred A. Knopf, 2001.

Welch, Lewis Sheldon ad Camp, Walter. *Yale, Her Campus, and Athletics*. Boston: L.C. Page and Company, 1899.

Wendel, Tim. *High Heat: The Secret History of the Fastball*. Cambridge, MA: DaCapo Press, 2010.

White, Sol. *Sol White's History of Colored Base Ball*. Lincoln, NE: University of Nebraska Press, 1995.

Wilbert, Warren N. *A Cunning Kind of Play: the Cubs-Giants Rivalry, 1876-1932*. Jefferson, NC: McFarland, 2002.

-------. *The Arrival of the American League*. Jefferson NC: McFarland, 2007.

Wood, Allan. *Babe Ruth and the 1918 Red Sox*. New York: Writer's Club Press, 2000.

Zoss, Joel and John Bowman. *Diamonds in the Rough: The Untold History of Baseball*. New York: Macmillan, 1989.

Index

A

Abbaticchio, Ed 93, 167
Accorsini, Leo 93
Accorsini, Victor A. "Vic" 74, 75, 76, 92, 93, 94, 96, 99, 100, 102, 111, 118, 119, 121, 123, 166, 167, 179, 182, 183, 184, 200, 201, 203, 204, 213, 215, 218, 219, 222, 255, 288, 290
Addison (NY) 260, 262, 274
Akron (OH) 116
Albany (NY) 72, 105, 117, 140, 172, 174, 191, 200, 203, 204, 211, 212, 213, 215, 216, 217, 222, 227, 234, 244, 253, 263, 289, 300, 301
Alger, Horatio 193
All Cubans 22
Allegany College (NY) 8, 23
Allen, Lee 168
Allentown (PA) 72, 89
Altoona (PA) 20
Altrock, Nick 77
Ambridge (PA) 197, 198
American Bridge Company 194, 284
American Federation of Labor 51, 194
American Protective Association 135
American Sabbath Union 80
Ames Iron Works (Oswego) 175
Amsterdam (NY) 245, 249
Anderson, Charles W. 205, 206
Anderson, (Unknown) 111
Anson, Cap 6

Arnot (PA) 49
Athens (PA) 2, 7, 33, 67, 85, 87, 88, 89, 99, 100, 101, 102, 103, 104, 116, 166, 194, 259, 284, 286, 296, 297, 298
Atlanta (GA) 69, 93
Atlantic City (NJ) 21
Atlantic League 7, 72, 84, 89, 92, 96, 102, 255
Auburn (NY) 36, 95, 138, 152, 153, 154, 174, 186, 198, 228, 229, 230, 231, 239, 240, 248
Augusta (GA) 275
Avoca (NY) 116
Avon (NY) 145

B

Bailey, George 167, 168
Baker Bowl (Philadelphia) 268
Baker, Charles 203, 215, 217
Baker, Frank "Home Run" 267
Baldwin, Hugh 179, 185
Baltimore (MD) 5, 7, 8, 26, 36, 40, 42, 159, 168, 169, 170, 171, 179, 235, 264, 267, 279, 280
Bancroft, Dave 53, 54, 270, 271
Baraca Club 284
Barnett, John F. "Jack" 33, 92, 93, 94, 97, 99, 100, 101, 103, 104, 106, 113, 114, 115, 118, 121, 122, 123, 134, 135, 166, 179, 181, 182, 183, 185, 187, 224, 243, 274, 290
Barnie, Billy 78
Barrett, James M. 150
Barrow, Ed 274, 280
Bath (NY) 101, 106, 137, 145, 189, 297, 298
Battle Creek (MI) 273
Beardsley, Edward 66, 68
Beecher, Thomas K. 134
Bellefonte (PA) 6, 20, 40
Bemidji (MN) 69
Bergen, Marty 37, 38, 39, 40, 42, 45, 46, 47, 48

Bernard, Curt 213
Binghamton (NY) 6, 17, 28, 72, 74, 75, 76, 80, 92, 93, 95, 98, 99, 102, 103, 109, 117, 118, 119, 138, 150, 172, 175, 180, 181, 182, 187, 200, 202, 205, 207, 208, 209, 210, 211, 213, 219, 220, 222, 227, 241, 244, 247, 252, 255, 256, 274, 289, 295, 296, 298, 299, 300, 301
Birmingham, Joseph "Dode" 262
Blue Hill (NE) 116
Boggs, Charles 90, 179
Boston (MA) 14, 15, 17, 25, 32, 36, 37, 38, 39, 40, 41, 43, 44, 45, 46, 47, 48, 77, 78, 90, 159, 160, 168, 170, 196, 234, 248, 257, 258, 267, 278, 279, 280, 281
Bottenus, Billy 82, 90, 92, 93, 103, 117
Brady, Tom 25, 26
Brandt, Willie 78
Bridgeport (CT) 34, 35
Bright, John 19, 20, 91, 187, 191
Bristol (CT) 35, 181, 292
Brockport (NY) 137
Brockton (MA) 16, 27, 219, 223, 224, 242, 274
Broderick, Matt 174, 200, 257
Brooklyn (NY) 8, 13, 36, 40, 41, 44, 45, 54, 67, 69, 73, 76, 79, 124, 161, 171, 179, 248, 253, 257, 268, 269, 274
Brooks, Charles "Chief" 65, 67
Brooks, E.A.U. 205
Brotherhood of Professional Baseball Players 6, 156
Brown, Mordecai "Three Finger" 257, 258
Brownson Athletic Club (Wilmington, DE) 187, 299
Brush, John 162
Bryan (Unknown) 290
Bryan, William Jennings 63, 83, 126, 130, 131, 132, 133, 135, 136, 137, 138, 140, 141, 146, 147, 197, 198
Buckheart, Jacob 110, 112, 114, 115, 116, 294
Bucknell University (PA) 21, 29, 31
Buffalo (NY) 8, 13, 32, 37, 73, 105, 110, 123, 135, 136, 137,

138, 140, 145, 151, 159, 160, 163, 174, 176, 183, 184, 188, 189, 213, 219, 220, 222, 223, 224, 225, 226, 229, 233, 234, 236, 254, 281
Burgess, Earl 228, 229
Burk, Robert 197
Burns, Daniel 135, 144
Burns, Felix 144, 145
Burns, George 270
Butler, Nicholas Murray 130

C

Callahan, "Reddy" 87, 290
Cambridge (MA) 16, 18
Camden (NJ) 42, 138
Campau, Charles C. "Count" 175, 181, 207, 208, 289, 294
Canandaigua (NY) 35, 101, 145, 174, 204
Canisteo (NY) 95, 96, 297
Canton (OH) 130
Carew, Rod 272
Cargo, Chick 213
Carlisle Indian School (PA) 110
Carmody House (Waverly) 68
Carnegie, Andrew 193
Carrigan, Bill 279, 280
Carriveau, Frank 103
Carter, Charles "Kid" 20
Cascade (NY) 153
Castleman, Frank R. 101
Causey, Red 270
Chaffee, (Unknown) 71
Chapman, John C. "Jack" 34, 78, 79, 281
Chase, Percy 64
Chautauqua Lake (NY) 154
Chesbro, Jack 171, 267, 282
Chester (PA) 21, 28, 120, 187, 280, 299

Chicago (IL) 19, 20, 40, 41, 77, 82, 102, 110, 116, 120, 124, 159, 168, 169, 174, 176, 181, 189, 195, 227, 234, 248, 251, 254, 258, 260, 277
Churchville (NY) 154
Cincinnati (OH) 39, 79, 82, 126, 169, 171, 175, 248, 257, 264, 268
Claire, Davey 273
Clapp, John 6, 34, 62, 90, 290
Clarke, Bill "Boileryard" 5, 39, 42, 48, 50, 124, 162
Clemens, Samuel "Mark Twain" 134, 238
Cleveland, Grover 63
Cleveland (OH) 8, 35, 55, 83, 159, 162, 179, 195, 213, 262
Clifton Springs (NY) 111, 190
Clines, Patrick 152
Coaldale (PA) 132, 133
Cobb, Ty 267, 275, 276, 277, 282
Cochecton (NY) 97
Coffey, Jerry 253, 303
Cohoes (NY) 42
Coleman Field (Sayre, PA) 273
Collins, Jimmy 5, 7, 37, 86, 160, 168, 170, 260, 282
Collopy, Jim 75, 181
Columbia Giants (Chicago) 102, 110, 120, 169, 265
Columbia Hotel (Elmira) 135
Columbia University (NY) 6, 23, 265
Comiskey, Charles 165, 169
Concord Hymn 254
Concord (NH) 255
Connecticut State League 30, 32, 34, 255
Connelly, Tim 87, 290
Connolly, Joe 270
Connor, Roger 34, 35
Coogan, Dan 174, 200
Coogan's Bluff (NYC) 272
Cooper, George 200, 289

Corbett, Jim (boxer) 95, 96, 290
Corbett, Jim (Nebraska Indians) 112, 114, 116
Cornell University (NY) 6, 8, 23, 51, 73, 148, 161, 162, 168, 169, 170, 171, 180, 194, 236, 241, 262, 267
Corning (NY) 88, 116, 137, 142, 145, 168, 184, 187, 200, 274, 284, 295, 296, 297, 299
Corona Typewriter (Groton, NY) 284
Cortland (NY) 72, 82, 92, 102, 117, 118, 140, 143, 172, 174, 183, 191, 194, 199, 200, 201, 210, 216, 219, 220, 222, 234, 235, 243, 257, 301
Coulter, Cy 175, 289
Coyle, George 66
Crabill, Ernest 103, 118, 208
Creighton, Jim 78
Cristall, Bill 213, 214, 215, 217, 254
Croft, Hary 75, 181, 252
Crothers, Doug 203
Cuban Giants 12, 19, 20, 22, 23, 63, 91, 102, 120, 187, 200, 281, 296, 298, 299
Cuban X Giants 19, 20, 21, 22, 119, 120, 121, 122, 188, 189, 298
Cunningham, Bill 270
Curtiss Aeroplane and Motor Company (Hammondsport, NY) 284
Czolgosz, Leon 195, 196, 224, 225, 226, 229, 230, 231, 232, 233

D

Daley, Edward 175
Darrow, Frank 148, 150, 151
Dartmouth College (NH) 265
Davenport, Henry 78
Davis, George 42, 44, 240
Day, Eddie 189, 190
Dean, Jimmy 82, 92, 93, 174, 200, 220, 288, 290
Decatur (IL) 69

Delaware River Shipbuilding League 280
Delehanty, Ed 171
DeMontreville, Lee 183
Derby, J. L. 101
Detroit (MI) 83, 159, 168, 175, 225, 248, 256, 264, 267, 268, 273, 274, 275
Dewey, George 40, 41, 63
Dewey, (Unknown) 290
Dineen, (Unknown) 179, 180
Doheny, Ed 42
Donahue, Elizabeth "Lizzie" 70, 151
Donovan, Bill "Wild Bill" 171, 267, 274, 275, 276, 277, 279, 282, 290
Doran, John F. 7, 33, 34, 35, 37, 38, 63, 79, 168, 259, 260, 264, 286, 294
Douglas, Phil 269
Douglass, Frederick 139, 204
Doyle, Jack "Dirty Jack" 42, 162
Drinkwater, Vianello 29
Duffy, Hugh 37, 47, 168
Duffy, John 213
Duffy, (Unknown) 106
Dunham, Owen 68, 85, 87, 90, 96, 100, 150, 258, 290
Dunkirk (NY) 145
Dunkle, Edward "Davy" 77, 290
Dwyer, Tom 87, 96, 98, 99, 100, 111, 113, 119, 122, 123, 166, 179, 184, 201, 202, 213, 215, 218, 249, 288, 291

E

Earl, Howard 174, 228
Eason, Mal 74, 92, 117
Eastern League 13, 28, 36, 73, 76, 183, 184, 187, 191, 219, 223, 236, 242, 247, 249, 277, 278
Eby, John G. 40, 42, 45
Egnor, Clarence 231

Ehret, Philip "Red" 83
Elmira (NY) 6, 7, 32, 33, 34, 36, 49, 51, 63, 64, 72, 74, 75, 76,
    80, 81, 82, 85, 89, 90, 92, 93, 94, 101, 102, 103, 104, 106,
    109, 117, 118, 119, 123, 134, 135, 137, 139, 140, 141, 142,
    144, 145, 149, 166, 168, 172, 175, 181, 194, 198, 205, 206,
    211, 219, 233, 242, 247, 253, 258, 260, 262, 274, 284, 295,
    297, 298, 299
Emancipation Day 204
Emerson, Ralph Waldo 254
Endicott-Johnson (E-J) 193, 194
Endicott (NY) 193
Erie Railroad 62, 64, 66, 208
Evans, A. J. 239, 240
Evers, Johnny "Crab" 249, 251, 258

F

Faatz, W. G. 101
Factoryville (PA) 20, 23, 31
Falconer (NY) 154
Farrell, John 173, 174, 201, 219, 228, 242, 243, 244, 245, 248, 282
Farr, Jim 286
Fassett, Jacob S. 142, 143, 144
Fishel, Leo 36
Fitchburg (MA) 16, 18
Fitzsimmons, Bob 96
Fleming, Tom 42
Flint (MI) 259
Flood, Curt 285
Flood, Frank 81
Flood, Tim 257
Fonda, Johnstown, and Gloversville Railroad 245
Fort Lauderdale (FL) 273
Foster, (Unknown) 101
Fowler, Bud 237
Frank and Dugan Company (Waverly) 283

Friend, Danny 77
Friendship (NY) 182
Frisch, Frankie 270
Fry, H. L. 191, 200, 201, 211, 217, 220, 246
Fullerton, Hugh 57

G

Gamble, E. 100
Gannon, Bill 200
Ganther (Krist), Josephine 62, 64
Garcia, John 189
Garey, (Unknown) 88, 291
Garfield, James 111, 131
Gaston, Alex 270
Genung, George, D. 185, 206
Ging, William J. "Bill" 33, 34, 35, 36, 40, 41, 42, 43, 44, 45, 76, 77, 78, 87, 88, 89, 90, 91, 99, 100, 101, 103, 105, 108, 111, 112, 118, 119, 122, 123, 134, 135, 138, 166, 179, 180, 182, 187, 190, 201, 202, 203, 204, 207, 208, 209, 210, 211, 212, 213, 215, 216, 217, 221, 222, 243, 249, 251, 252, 253, 286, 288, 291
Gleason, William J. "Kid" 5, 42, 43, 44, 168, 277
Glezen, Oscar B. 148, 150
Gloversville (NY) 245, 249, 253
Goldman, Emma 195, 196, 197, 198, 225, 228, 231
Gompers, Samuel 51, 126, 194, 197, 198
Gonzalez, Mike 269, 270
Goodwin, Doris Kearns 132
Gordon, Wallace 189
Gore, Charles 67
Gorton, Joe (Gorton's Minstrels) 182
Graham, Archibald "Moonlight" 254
Grand Rapids (MI) 40, 159
Grant, Charlie 169
Grant, Frank 12, 13, 20, 79, 102, 120, 188, 189, 190, 191, 237,

281, 282, 283, 294
Grant, George W. 11, 12, 13, 14, 15, 16, 17, 18, 19, 23, 24, 25, 26, 27, 28, 29, 30, 32, 74, 75, 76, 82, 92, 94, 96, 97, 100, 106, 117, 181, 291
Green, Guy Wilder 109, 110, 112, 113, 116, 294
Green, Joe 102, 189, 190
Greenleaf, J.T. 150
Greenwich Village (NY) 281
Griffin, Sandy 245
Griffith, Clark 50, 124, 157, 158, 165, 168
Grillo, J. Ed. 126
Grinspan, Jon 131
Groh, Lew 260
Groton Bridge Company 194
Groton (NY) 194, 197, 284
Grove, James 82
Guidry, Ron 3

H

Haggerty, Peter 82, 93
Haley, I. F. 291
Haley, (Unknown) 111, 114
Hall and Lyon (Waverly) 61, 228, 284
Halsey Valley (NY) 6, 90, 236
Hamburg, Charlie 35, 36, 79, 83, 102, 103, 117, 175, 201, 220, 245, 251, 267, 275, 289, 294
Hamilton, Billy 16
Hamilton, (Unknown) 87, 291
Hammondsport (NY) 97, 101, 104, 106, 116, 168, 177, 189, 284, 297, 298
Hanlon, Edward H. "Ned" 8, 36, 45, 73, 124, 161, 257, 274
Hanna, Mark 128, 138, 237
Hanna, Tim 99, 104, 105, 111, 119, 123, 288, 291
Hardenburgh, John 228
Harnden, Rufus 68, 143, 150, 185

Harrisburg (PA) 13, 37, 38, 89, 121, 188, 189
Harris, Daniel 51
Harris, (Unknown) 291
Harrison, George 208
Hartford (CT) 183, 224, 274
Hart, Jim 162
Hastings (NE) 116
Hatfield, Gil 36
Havana (Cuba) 120
Haverhill (NH) 12
Hawkes, Frederick E. 148, 258
Hayes, Tom 101
Hearne, Hughie 208, 289
Hedges, Job E. 143
Heine, William Charles "Bill" 7, 33, 35, 36, 37, 85, 86, 87, 89, 91, 94, 96, 98, 99, 100, 102, 103, 104, 111, 112, 113, 115, 118, 119, 123, 134, 135, 140, 166, 179, 180, 181, 183, 185, 190, 200, 201, 202, 204, 208, 210, 211, 212, 213, 215, 218, 219, 220, 223, 224, 260, 262, 263, 265, 271, 274, 281, 288, 291
Heine, William Henry "Bud" 119, 263, 264, 265, 268, 269, 270, 271, 272, 273, 274
Hemingway, Orlando 197, 198
Hendrick, Thomas 186, 232, 233
Henline, Butch 270
Hess, Tom 213
Higgins, Bob 203
Hill, Eddie 75, 213, 214, 215, 288, 291
Hill, John 120
Hoadley House (Waverly) 140
Holls, Frederick W. 130
Honesdale (PA) 20, 21, 23
Hooper, Harry 279, 280
Hornellsville (NY) 145, 168
Horseheads (NY) 194

Hosmer Band (Athens, PA) 166
Howard Street Grounds (Waverly) 84, 87, 89, 90, 91, 95, 100,
    101, 109, 119, 121, 178, 179, 187, 190, 201, 203, 205, 207,
    222, 273, 281, 283, 284
Hoyt, Waite 279
Hughes, William "Dell" 87, 94, 96, 99, 111, 115, 119, 122, 123,
    166, 179, 180, 190, 201, 202, 203, 291
Hunter, Jim "Catfish" 285
Hunt, (Unknown) 88
Hutchinson, Ralph 34
Hyland, Fred (AKA Fred Krist) 63
Hyland, Katie (AKA Katie Tobin) 63

I

Ilion (NY) 172, 200, 201, 203, 217, 218, 221, 222, 227, 234,
    244, 253, 289, 299, 300, 301
Indianapolis (IN) 146, 159, 273
Ingersoll-Rand (I-R) (Athens, PA) 284
Inglewood (CA) 116
International League 237, 276
Irwin, Arthur 78
Ithaca (NY) 6, 61, 62, 65, 73, 90, 140, 150, 152, 153, 180, 194,
    198, 205, 207, 233, 239, 240, 241, 264, 284, 299

J

Jackson, Andy 20, 120, 122
Jackson, Joe "Shoeless Joe" 255
Jackson, Reggie 3
Jamestown (NY) 145, 185, 189, 299
Jennings, Hughie 5, 7, 8, 13, 23, 35, 48, 50, 51, 52, 55, 63, 73,
    79, 83, 89, 124, 126, 136, 157, 161, 162, 163, 168, 169,
    170, 171, 180, 234, 264, 265, 267, 268, 270, 273, 274, 276,
    281, 282, 286
Jersey City (NJ) 72, 87, 89, 276
Johnson, Byron Bancroft "Ban" 53, 54, 57, 88, 124, 125, 126,

155, 159, 160, 164, 165, 169, 171, 173, 235, 264
Johnson, C. M. 207
Johnson, George F. 17, 101, 193, 194
Johnson, George W. 101, 108
Johnson, Walter 282
Johnson, William E. 139, 140
Johnston, Bill 82
Johnson City (NY) 193, 194
Johnstown (NY) 245, 249, 251
Jones, James 213, 289
Jones, John W. 134
Jones, Marry Harris "Mother" 132, 133
Jordan, Dutch 182
Jordan, Robert 120, 122

K

Kain, E. M. 101
Kansas City (MO) 159, 263
Keeler, Willie 5, 7, 8, 49, 73, 86, 124, 162, 181, 260, 267, 274, 282
Kelley, Joe 124, 274
Kelley, William 189, 190
Kellogg's 273
Kelly, George "High Pockets" 269
Kelly, John 289
Kelly, J. W. E. 239, 240
Kennedy, Edward A. "Kick" 291
Kennedy, Frank P. 291
Kennedy, John 220, 288, 291
Kennedy, J. S. 142
Kennedy, Sherman "Snapper" 36
Kenney, Albert "Bert" 7, 265
Kerin, John 26
Ketchum, Fred 82
Keyser Valley Shops (Scranton) 284

Kimble, John 75
King, J. W. 16, 17, 23, 25, 26, 27, 189, 294
Klem, Bill 252
Konetchy, Ed 270
Krist, Fred 61, 62, 63, 64, 65, 66, 67, 68, 69, 96, 105, 147, 148, 149, 150, 151, 152, 153, 154, 186, 196, 228, 229, 230, 231, 232, 233, 239, 240, 241
Kuntzsch, George N. 242, 243, 245, 246

L

Lackawanna Railroad 176
Lajoie, Napoleon "Nap" 5, 86, 160, 168, 169, 170, 260, 262, 282
Lamar, E.B. 19, 20
Lancaster (PA) 263, 267
Landis, Kenesaw Mountain 193
Lang, Percy Lyford 90, 292
Lattimer (PA) 132, 174, 195
Lawlor, Jack 174
Lawrence (MA) 18, 33, 37
Lawson, Alfred "Al" 22
Leach, Tommy 171
LeBaron, Frank 87, 98, 99, 100, 107, 292
Lee, Cliff 270
Lee, Eddie 292
Lee, George "Knotty" 103, 117, 255, 292
Lee, Jack 200, 201, 203, 207, 208, 211, 220, 221, 222, 288, 292
Lee, Sam 182
Lehigh Valley Railroad (LVRR) 84, 97, 98, 152, 220, 241, 259, 273, 284
Lenares, Abel 22
Lestershire (NY) 17, 97, 101, 107, 108, 109, 116, 118, 168, 193, 200, 201, 297, 298, 299
Lewis, Edward 47
Lewis House (Binghamton) 208, 209, 210, 211
Lewiston (ME) 12

Lexington (KY) 182
Liddy, Martin 69
Lincoln, Abraham 206
Lincoln (NE) 116
Lincoln Street Field (Waverly) 284, 285
Little Rock (AR) 255
Livingstone, Jake 36
Livonia (NY) 116, 137, 145
Lock Haven (PA) 40, 123, 262
Louisville (KY) 7, 35, 82, 181
Lowe, Bobby 41
Lowell (MA) 12, 18
Lumley, Harry 101, 108, 201, 289, 294
Lynchburg (VA) 74, 123, 256
Lynch, Henry 183
Lynch, Mike 36

M

Mack, Billy 260, 262
Mack, Connie 165, 169, 170
Mack, Mary 67
Mains, Willard 201
Malone (NY) 189
Malone, William 20
Manchester (NH) 16, 18, 23, 24, 25, 26, 27, 29, 30, 31
Manning, Jack 101
Manning, Tommy 78
Manoil Manufacturing Company (Waverly) 283
Mansfield (PA) 122
Mantle, Mickey 3
Maris, Roger 3
Maroney, Stephen 166, 179, 180, 183, 184, 190, 201, 202, 213, 222, 288, 292
Martin, Billy 4, 272, 281, 282, 286
Martin, Frank 42

Martin, John 231
Marymount College (NY) 241
Mathewson, Christy 21, 23, 24, 25, 26, 27, 28, 29, 30, 31, 32, 42, 169, 171, 181, 264, 282
Mattice, Burr J. 151, 152
Maxcy, (Unknown) 33
McAdoo (PA) 132
McCarthy, Joe 236
McCormick, James Ambrose "Jim" 174, 200, 201, 213, 215, 220, 249, 288, 292
McDougald, Gil 272
McDougal, John Auchanbolt "Sandy" 13, 14, 15, 16, 17, 18, 19, 23, 25, 26, 27, 29, 30, 31, 32, 74, 75, 76, 82, 89, 93, 94, 97, 99, 100, 102, 103, 106, 107, 111, 112, 113, 114, 115, 119, 123, 166, 184, 185, 190, 201, 202, 207, 208, 218, 220, 221, 222, 249, 251, 252, 254, 258, 288, 292
McDuffee, George 67
McFadden, Barney 174, 257
McGinnity, Joseph J. "Iron Man" 257, 264, 274
McGlynn, U.S. Grant "Stoney" 89, 292
McGraw, John Joseph 5, 7, 8, 22, 23, 35, 40, 42, 43, 86, 89, 96, 124, 165, 168, 169, 170, 171, 213, 236, 260, 262, 264, 265, 266, 267, 268, 269, 270, 271, 272, 273, 274, 281, 282, 286
McGuffie's Orchestra (Waverly) 166, 243
McGuire, Jim 245
McKenna, Brian 38
McKinley, William 63, 83, 126, 127, 128, 129, 130, 131, 132, 133, 137, 138, 145, 147, 223, 224, 225, 226, 227, 228, 229, 231
McLellan, Dan 120
Mead, Howard J. 59, 258
Mead, J. Warren 232, 233, 240
Meadows, Lee 270
Memphis (TN) 238, 255
Meriden (CT) 34

Merrill, H. G. 172, 181, 201
Messersmith, Andy 285
Meusel, Emil F. "Irish" 270
Mexican Baseball League 262
Middletown (NY) 138
Miller Brothers 110
Miller, Dakin E. "Dusty" 161
Miller, Howard 66
Miller, Joseph "Cannonball" 189
Miller, Scott 229
Millerick, Pat 213
Milltown (Sayre, PA) 286
Milwaukee (WI) 124, 159, 168, 174, 235
Miner, Garfield 111, 112, 114, 115
Minneapolis (MN) 83, 124, 159
Molesworth, Carlton 75, 92, 93, 174, 183, 200
Monroe, John 270
Montreal (QC) 36, 183, 286
Moravia (NY) 98, 106, 107, 116, 153, 297, 298
Morgan, James Pierpont "J. P." 133, 194, 197
Morrissey, Frank 26, 27
Mullin, Michael J. "Mickey" 174, 200, 202, 207, 208, 209, 210, 211, 222, 256, 288, 292
Murnane, Tim 15, 16, 23, 39, 47
Murphy, Frank 36
Murphy, J. J. 69
Murphy, Thomas "Tom" 27, 92
Murray Hills Nine (NY) 221
Murray, John J. "Red" 260, 261, 262, 263, 264
Murray, John R. 87

N

Nack, William 38
Nadeau, Phil 117, 174, 183, 200, 201, 202, 213, 214, 215, 219, 220, 222, 255, 288, 289, 292

Nashville (TN) 93, 255
National Association of Professional Baseball Leagues
    (NAPBL) 227, 228, 234, 247, 248
National Youth Administration 241
Nation, Carrie Amelia Moore 141, 146, 192, 226, 227
Nelson, John 120, 122
Newark (NJ) 72, 89, 278
Newark Valley (NY) 107, 298
New Bedford (MA) 25, 34
New England League 12, 13, 14, 15, 16, 17, 23, 30, 74, 94, 97,
    117, 181, 255
New Haven (CT) 7, 63, 277
New London (CT) 32, 34, 36, 44, 54, 77
New Milford (PA) 83
New Orleans (LA) 175, 255
New Rochelle (NY) 281
New York State League (NYSL) 4, 17, 35, 36, 72, 74, 78, 83, 92,
    95, 102, 117, 118, 167, 172, 173, 174, 180, 181, 183, 191,
    199, 200, 201, 203, 208, 211, 213, 216, 217, 218, 219, 221,
    222, 227, 228, 234, 235, 242, 243, 245, 246, 249, 251, 252,
    254, 262, 287, 288, 289, 295
Newport (RI) 12, 15, 16, 18, 27, 30, 31
Niagara Falls (NY) 137, 176, 256
Nichols, Charles "Kid" 37, 39
Nieman, see Czolgosz, Leon 195, 225
Ninhan, Albert 112, 114
Noblit, George 28, 29
Norfolk (VA) 31
North Brookfield (MA) 37, 39
Norwich (CT) 34, 78
Notre Dame University (IN) 262

O

Odell, Benjamin B. 128, 147, 186, 240
Ogdensburg (NY) 189

O'Hara, Thomas Francis "Snibs" 118, 263, 292
Oil City (PA) 161
Olean (NY) 7, 145, 274
O'Loughlin, Francis "Silk" 224
Omaha (NE) 257
O'Neil, James 94, 95, 96, 99, 100, 111, 112, 113, 119, 121, 123, 166, 179, 180, 184, 201, 213, 288, 292
Orioles (Baltimore) 5, 7, 8, 40, 43, 48, 73, 96, 124, 161, 236, 264, 279, 281
O'Rourke, Jim 34, 35
Osborne, (Unknown) 111
Osceola (NY) 107
O'Shaughnessy, Bill 60
Oswego (NY) 35, 36, 62, 72, 78, 82, 83, 92, 102, 138, 172, 175, 183
Ott, Mel 262
Owego (NY) 6, 59, 63, 69, 70, 96, 107, 108, 127, 129, 134, 135, 146, 147, 149, 150, 152, 168, 186, 187, 190, 258, 259, 295, 298, 299
Oyster Bay (NY) 146

P

Pacific Coast League 255
Packer Band, R. A. (Sayre, PA) 139, 166, 243
Packer Hospital, R. A. (Sayre, PA) 185
Page Fence Giants 19
Pan-American Exposition (Buffalo) 176, 177, 193, 223, 233
Pawtucket (RI) 15, 16, 17, 27
Payn, Louis F. "Lou" 128
Pearce, Harvey "Doc" 292
Pearce, Richard J. "Dickey" 281
Penn State University (PA) 23, 286
Penn Yan (NY) 186, 189
Peters, John 270
Philadelphia (PA) 6, 21, 40, 54, 72, 105, 120, 122, 129, 159,

160, 168, 169, 170, 171, 181, 189, 196, 234, 248, 256, 258, 260, 268, 270, 276, 277, 285
Pickett, David 15, 16, 17, 19, 32, 74, 75, 76, 97, 101, 289, 293
Piedmont League 273
Pierce-Arrow 263
Pierce, George W. 101
Piniella, Lou 4
Pittsburgh (PA) 110, 124, 138, 171, 197, 234
Pittston (PA) 7
Platt, Thomas Collier 127, 128, 129, 130, 134, 146, 147, 226
Players' League 6, 45, 53, 156, 161
Players' Protective Association (PPA) 1, 9, 50, 53, 55, 57, 77, 124, 155, 156, 157, 159, 160, 161, 162, 163, 164, 165, 171, 196, 234, 236
Polathec Club 284
Polhamus, (Unknown) 88, 293
Polyhymnia Club 65, 71
Port Jervis (NY) 138
Portland (ME) 16, 17, 18, 27, 28, 29, 31
Portland (OR) 255
Potsdam (NY) 189
Pottsville (PA) 20
Powers, Maurice 83
Preston, Frank W. 184, 185, 186, 200, 258
Princeton University (NJ) 34, 48
Providence (RI) 28, 60, 77, 78, 84, 87, 111, 180, 183, 187, 276, 279

Q

Quinlan, Larry 78
Quinn, Jack 101

R

Rader, Don 270
Raines, George 186

Rapp, Goldie 270
Rawlings, Johnny 270
Reading (PA) 72, 89, 94, 95, 189, 297
Reed and Barton (Taunton, MA) 11, 12
Renssalaer (NY) 212
Richardson, Danny 51
Richmond (VA) 274
Richter, Francis C. 163
Riley, Daniel 117
Ring, Jimmy 270
Roach, Mary 61
Robert, Henry Martyn 134
Robinson, Jackie 23, 237, 253
Robinson, James 120, 122
Robinson, Wilbert 5, 73, 168, 170
Robison Field (St. Louis) 268
Robison, Frank and Stanley 8
Roche, J. D. 117
Rochester (NY) 35, 72, 104, 105, 142, 183, 186, 218, 240, 260, 284
Rockefeller, John D. 134
Rodman, E. W. 152
Rogers, John Ignatius 196
Rome (NY) 72, 74, 117, 118, 119, 172, 174, 175, 181, 183, 200, 201, 203, 217, 220, 227, 242, 243, 244, 245, 275, 289, 298, 299, 300
Roosevelt, Theodore "Teddy" 63, 126, 127, 128, 129, 130, 131, 132, 133, 135, 138, 139, 140, 141, 142, 143, 144, 145, 146, 147, 165, 186, 197, 226, 237, 238
Rosenbach, Albert J. 93
Roth, Andy 35, 36, 82, 83, 254, 275, 276
Rudderham, Frank 119
Ruth, George Herman "Babe" 267, 272, 276, 278, 279, 280, 281, 282
Ryan, Dennis 36, 293

Ryan, Jack 83
Rynone Industries (Waverly) 284

S

Sacandaga Park (NY) 245
St. Bonaventure University (NY) 8, 89, 184, 185, 253, 264
St. Joseph (MO) 257
St. Joseph, Sisters of 239
St. Louis (MO) 8, 37, 42, 69, 82, 175, 234, 235, 254, 263, 268, 285
Salene, Danny "The Terrible Swede" 112, 116, 294
Sampson, Clarence "Clem" 20, 189
Saratoga (NY) 228
Sayre (PA) 2, 84, 87, 97, 116, 166, 185, 227, 259, 260, 262, 273, 284, 285, 286, 295, 296, 297
Schacht, Al 77
Schenectady (NY) 72, 80, 92, 117, 118, 138, 172, 174, 183, 200, 203, 212, 218, 219, 221, 222, 227, 228, 244, 252, 289, 300, 301
Schreckengost, Ossee 167
Schrieber, Hank 270
Schulte, Frank "Wildfire" 97, 101, 105, 249, 250, 251, 254, 258, 293
Scott, Everett 35, 82, 229, 278
Scranton (PA) 20, 72, 89, 218, 228, 254, 267, 284
Scudder, D. and W. 101
Seattle (WA) 255
Seldon, Bill 20
Selee, Frank 37, 38, 42
Setley, William W. "Wild Bill" 35, 101, 294
Seybold, Ralph O. "Socks" 168, 169, 267
Seymour, Harold 182, 236
Shaw, Albert 130
Shinnick, Time 83, 289, 294
Sickler, Layton 87

Siegle, Johnny 174
Siever, Ed 276
Simms, Charles 152
Simon, Hank 174, 203, 204, 213, 215, 216, 289, 294
Sioux City (IA) 159
Smith, Clarence 293
Smith, George (Churchville) 154
Smith, George (Elmira) 82
Smith, Harry C. 92, 93
Smith, John D. 112, 114
Smith, Johnny 293
Smith, John "Phenomenal" 28, 29, 31
Smith, J. Pollywog 50, 55
Smith, Tom 25
Smith, William T. "Big Bill" 120, 121, 122, 294
Smyth, S. W. 152
Sockalexis, Louis 167
Soden, Arthur H. 47, 159, 162, 196
Somerset (MA) 11
Sousa Band, John Philip 41
Southern League 255
Southern Michigan League 259
Southern Tier League 260, 262, 274
Spalding, Albert Goodwill "Al" 6, 288
Stahl, Chick 16, 44, 168
Stanchfield, John B. 134, 135, 141, 142, 143, 145, 147, 258
Steffens, Lincoln 128
Stengel, Charles D. "Casey" 268, 269, 270, 272, 277, 281, 282, 286
Stevens, J. W. 209
Stratton, Scott 35, 82, 83
Sullivan, Billy 40, 42
Sullivan-Clinton Campaign 228
Sullivan, John L. 96, 122
Susquehanna (PA) 106, 116, 295, 298, 303

Swanson, Krister 156
Swarthmore College (PA) 265
Symington-Anderson Company (Rochester) 284
Syracuse (NY) 72, 76, 77, 78, 87, 94, 100, 123, 138, 166, 168, 178, 183, 184, 187, 192, 193, 203, 205, 218, 223, 228, 242, 243, 244, 245, 246, 249, 251, 252, 298, 299

T

Taft, William H. 128
Talada, Fred (see also Tucker, Fred) 7, 38, 58, 59, 139, 285, 293
Talada, Guy 58
Tamsett, Jimmy 213
Tankard, Squire 154
Tannehill, Jess 51
Taunton (MA) 9, 11, 12, 13, 16, 17, 18, 23, 24, 25, 26, 27, 28, 29, 30, 31, 54, 74, 181, 264
Taylor, Harry L. 1, 6, 7, 8, 23, 35, 48, 51, 55, 56, 57, 73, 79, 83, 90, 104, 106, 124, 130, 148, 155, 156, 157, 159, 160, 161, 162, 163, 164, 165, 170, 171, 174, 234, 236, 260, 267, 285, 286, 293
Terpko, Jeff 285, 286
Thomas-Morse Aircraft (Ithaca) 284
Thompson, Andy 75
Thomson, Bobby 254
Thurston, Abe 152, 153, 154
Tissot, Jacques Joseph "James" 65
Titus, John 254
Tobin, James 61, 240
Tobin, Katie 61, 62, 63, 65, 69, 72, 84, 85, 96, 105, 151, 185, 186, 240
Tobin, Mary 61, 62, 240
Tokohama, Charlie 169
Toledo (OH) 159
Tonawanda (NY) 116
Topeka (KS) 69

Toronto (ON) 13, 183, 224, 262
Townsend, Cy 200
Townsend (MA) 26
Tracy, Benjamin F. 134
Troy (NY) 72, 80, 95, 117, 172, 175, 200, 204, 207, 208, 211, 217, 222, 227, 228, 244, 249, 251, 289, 300, 301
Troy (PA) 295, 296
Truck, John 154
Truxton (NY) 7, 22, 265
Tucker, Fred (See also Talada, Fred) 7, 58, 59, 60, 61, 62, 63, 68, 72, 84, 85, 86, 87, 88, 89, 90, 91, 92, 95, 96, 97, 98, 100, 102, 103, 104, 105, 106, 107, 108, 111, 113, 115, 118, 119, 122, 139, 150, 166, 167, 168, 178, 179, 181, 182, 184, 185, 186, 187, 190, 191, 200, 202, 204, 217, 218, 258, 259, 293

U

Union Carbide 256
Unions, Chicago 19, 20, 120
United Mine Workers of America 133
University of Nebraska 109
University of Pennsylvania 31, 196
U.S. Steel 194, 197
Utica (NY) 35, 72, 80, 117, 118, 172, 174, 200, 202, 203, 212, 220, 221, 227, 244, 252, 289, 299, 300

V

Van Halteren, George "Rip" 42
VanNorstrand, Ed 67
Van Zant, Ike (AKA Van Zandt) 34
Vardaman, James K. 238
Viau, Lee 103, 175, 222, 289, 294
Villanova University (PA) 174
Virgil (NY) 154
Von der Horst, Harry 8

Vought, William 16, 17, 18, 19, 23, 25, 26, 27, 28, 30, 74, 78, 181, 183, 293

W

Wagenheim, Kal 279
Wagner, Charles G. 150
Wagner, Charles "Heinie" 221, 222, 278, 279, 280, 281, 288, 293
Wagner, Honus 5, 7, 86, 171, 260, 280, 282
Wagner, Johnny 293
Waller, John "Bud" 63, 69, 94, 220, 258, 293
Waltham (MA) 37
Ward, John Montgomery 6, 7, 23, 53, 55, 156, 161
Warford House (Waverly) 64, 65, 66, 67, 90, 179
Warner, Jack 42, 350
Washington, Booker T. 206, 237, 238
Washington (DC) 39, 77, 83, 159, 175, 179, 223, 248, 274, 285
Washington Square (NY) 40
Waterbury (CT) 34, 274
Watertown (NY) 138, 228
Watkins [Glen] (NY) 49, 205, 295
Watkins, John "Pop" 20, 189, 294
Weaver, Farmer 83
Weedsport (NY) 100, 297
Weiss, George 277, 282
Wellsboro (PA) 122
Wells Fargo Express Wagon 88
Wellsville (NY) 22
Wennerholm, Frank 154
Western League 53, 159, 161, 257
West New York (NJ) 21
Wheeler, George 119, 175, 245, 289
Wheeling (WV) 36
Wheelock, Bobby 36
White, King Solomon "Sol" 3, 19, 43, 102, 110, 111, 120, 237, 238, 248, 268, 277, 281, 282, 284, 294

Wilhelm, Irvin "Kaiser" 268
Wilkes-Barre (PA) 63, 69, 72, 82, 89, 201, 218, 296
William and Mary College (VA) 286
Williams, Clarence 20, 120, 121, 122, 294
Williams, Cy 270
Williams, Joseph "Smokey Joe" 281
Williamsport (PA) 142, 263, 285
Willis, Vic 37, 38, 39, 282
Willys-Morrow (Elmira) 284
Wilmington (DE) 187, 299
Wilson, Ed 189, 190
Wilson, Ray 120, 121, 122
Wolfe, Maurice 182
Women's Christian Temperance Union 192
Woodruff, Pete 36, 42, 181, 182
Woods, Walt 183
Woodward (PA) 40
Worcester (MA) 77, 183
Wrightstone, Russ 270
Wye, John C. 207
Wyoming Seminary (PA) 182, 299

Y

Yale University (CT) 90
Young, Denton True "Cy" 69, 139, 168, 170, 171, 285
Young People's Society of Christian Endeavor 139
Youngs, Ross 270

Z

Zimmer, Charles "Chief" 50, 124, 157, 159, 160, 162, 163, 165, 171

www.ingramcontent.com/pod-product-compliance
Lightning Source LLC
LaVergne TN
LVHW011757060526
838200LV00053B/3616